Ex Libris

Merchant Taylors'
School for Girls

CONCORDIA PARVÆ RES CRESCUNT

THE LIFE AND TIMES
of
DAVID LLOYD GEORGE

Edited by Judith Loades

HEADSTART HISTORY

Published by   HEADSTART HISTORY
               PO Box 41, Bangor, Gwynedd, LL57 1SB

Set by   THE WORDSMITH GROUP
               The Manor House, Tarvin, Chester

Printed by   THE IPSWICH BOOK COMPANY LTD
               The Drift, Nacton Road,
               Ipswich, Suffolk IP3 3QR

ISBN   1 873041 05 5
A CIP catalogue record for this book is available from the British Library

---

Acknowledgements

The portrait on the cover and the photographs of Lloyd George and of Megan Lloyd George are re-produced by kind permission of the National Library of Wales. The portrait of Dr. W. R. P. George was provided by W. R. P. George himself. I record my thanks to him and to the National Library for their help in this respect.

Acknowledgements are due to the Trustees of the Beaverbrook Foundation and the Clerk of the Records, House of Lords, for permission to cite the Lloyd George and Bonar Law papers; and to the British Library for permission to cite the Balfour papers.

It is a particular pleasure to thank Roderick Boyd of The IPSWICH BOOK COMPANY who not only printed this volume but designed the cover.

CONTENTS

Preface

Foreword: W. R. P. George

ESSAYS

ILLUSTRATIONS

Front Cover   : portrait of David Lloyd George

   Inside   : Lloyd George 1908
                (South Wales Daily News)

             : Informal photo in the garden

             : Megan Lloyd George.

             : W. R. P. George.

PREFACE

In September 1990 HEADSTART HISTORY celebrated the centenary of the election of David Lloyd George for Caernarfon Boroughs. For three days there was a mingling of scholars, church and state.

The focus of the first evening was an address by Kenneth Morgan and this was attended by the Minister of State at the Welsh Office, Sir Wyn Roberts, the Archdeacon of Merioneth, Dr. Barry Morgan, the Mayors of Bangor, Caernarfon and Conway: many Town Clerks and Community Clerks: scholars from numerous academic institutions: and it was a particular pleasure to welcome Dr. William George and his wife. The second evening HEADSTART HISTORY organised a party in Caernarfon Castle and drank a toast to Lloyd George who had once been Constable.

The discussions which took place were both valuable and fruitful and resulted in the essays presented in this volume. David Lloyd George was clearly a man of ability, energy and charm. He was also a man of controversy and made many enemies but he never lost the support of the masses. After Lloyd George's death, Winston Churchill declared, "When the English history of the first quarter century is written it will be seen that the greatest part of our future in peace and war was shaped by this one man." At the time of the HEADSTART celebrations parliament had just been re-called to debate the growing crisis in the Gulf and readers will note that Professor Morgan has shown Lloyd George's involvement there. There is no doubt that the earlier part of the twentieth century was the Age of Lloyd George, but the world continues to be affected by his decisions and we continue to be fascinated by the charisma of this great Welshman.

Judith Loades,
St. David's Day, 1991.

FOREWORD

by

W. R. P. George

On December 14, 1990 at Llanystumdwy, Gwynedd, Lord Callaghan formally opened a new Museum dedicated to the memory of David Lloyd George, his life and times. This new and extended building has cost in all about £250,000, the money having been raised in response to the Lloyd George Centenary Parliamentary Appeal, in the promotion of which the Gwynedd County Council had played a leading role. Several people asked me why Lord Callaghan had been invited to open the new Museum. I explained that to date he is the only other person representing a Welsh constituency who had been Prime Minister, an explanation which was readily accepted. Others asked why the Rt. Hon. Michael Heseltine, M.P. had not been invited to the function; I was told afterwards that he was a great admirer of D. Ll. G. and was known to display a photograph of D. Ll. G. in his study. When the invitation list was compiled this fact was not, so far as I am aware, known to those responsible for drawing it up and he had not then emerged as the principal toppler of Mrs. Margaret Thatcher from the premiership. It was nevertheless an unfortunate omission.

Hardly a week goes by without D. Ll. G's name featuring in the national press. The publication and contents of this book are in themselves testimony to his importance as a major political figure of this century. His historical reputation has shed his earldom; I remember calling with my father in Christmas week 1944 to see my uncle at Ty Newydd, Llanystumdwy. Uncle David was greatly agitated, not knowing whether to accept or refuse the offer which his friend Winston Churchill had sent to him by special messenger. Diplomatic enquiries had been made whether or not he would be opposed at the forthcoming general election, and it was clear that he could not expect to be returned unopposed to represent the Caernarfon Boroughs. He wanted to make a major speech on the 'Peace', and in view of this he decided to accept the earldom, the House of Lords being the only parliamentary venue to fulfil this expectation. My father told him that he would have liked to have seen him following the example of Gladstone and going down in history as a great Commoner. The members of his family knew then that he was terminally ill, but neither my father nor any one else had the heart to tell him that he would never make it to the House of Lords. I am glad to think that it is as a great Commoner he will always be remembered. He would not have wished otherwise, and I am sure the museum at Llanystumdwy will prove to be an important venue for an appreciation of his career.

The Museum was opened just within the centenary year of D. Ll. G's election to Parliament by the narrow margin of 18 votes, following a recount on April 11, 1890. Those who have read an account of the election and circumstances leading up to it will, no doubt, agree with Richard Lloyd's diary entry: **'ALMOST A MIRACLE'**. It was a characteristic of my uncle during his lifetime to polarise personal feelings towards him, and according to a diary entry made by my father William George in April 1890, shortly before polling day, this became evident at the commencement of his career:

'We are in the thick of the fight. Personal rather than party feeling runs high. The Tories began by ridiculing D.'s candidature; they have now changed their tune . . . The struggle is not so much a struggle of Tory v. Liberal or Radical even; the main issue is between country squire and the upstart democrat.'

Richard Lloyd's dominant influence upon D. Ll. G. during his formative years has rightly been acknowledged; this influence was not restricted to the essential task of inculcating into his nephews a lifelong respect for an austere regime of hard work and self-help, but also in awakening in them a sensitive social conscience combined with a practical regard for the welfare of their fellows. I was, for instance, struck by Richard Lloyd's diary entry dated July 4, 1883, when D. Ll. G. was 20:

'Beginning to build the Cei (Quay) at Criccieth today. It's pitiful to see the crowd searching for work at a miserably low wage and for a short time at that.'

D. Ll. G's social conscience was aroused not only by comments such as this by Richard Lloyd but also stimulated by his own professional experience as a young and struggling solicitor. He qualified in 1885. A significant amount of the work consisted in collecting debts due to impoverished local tradesmen. The terms of remuneration generally were that the solicitor was allowed a commission of 10% on the amount of debts collected, and when a tradesman had become bankrupt the Official Receiver would sometimes sell to the solicitor the total of the book-debts due to the bankrupt tradesman. The 1880's in Britain were years of depression in trade and industry; this was brought home to D. Ll. G. by experiencing at first hand the problems and hardships of social deprivation. When attending funerals he would have seen the mourners placing coins on the coffin for the benefit of an impoverished family before the funeral cortège started from the deceased's house. These early experiences implanted in him an ambition, in his own words to 'promote myself by honest endeavour to benefit others'.

The extent of the successful pursuit of his endeavour to benefit others will be under consideration by the authors who have contributed to this volume. A cable which my father William George received on January 17, 1963 from the late President John F Kennedy provides further testimony of this; the occasion was a children's tea-party held at the Memorial Hall, Criccieth on the occasion of the centenary of D. Ll. G's birth:

I am pleased to send warmest greetings to you, the members of your family and the children of Criccieth. The people of the free world will be forever indebted to your distinguished brother for his unflagging dedication to the Liberal principles of justice and freedom for all and for his many years of inspiring leadership, particularly during the First World War and during the years of Peace negotiation which followed.

No brief summary of D. Ll. G's formative years would be complete without a reference to his religious views. There are, as it happens, many entries in D. Ll. G's early diaries revealing how irksome he found the chapel services, redeemed only by the eloquence and passion of Richard Lloyd's sermons. For instance, the two following entries from his 1881 diary:

Sun. 8 May.	Been to chapel - Enforced sanctity - Farce of breaking bread - I believe in the God of Nature.
Sun. 21 August	Richard Lloyd preaching 6 o'clock service. It is a pity that his genius should waste its fragrance on the desert air of Capel Ucha auditors.

He wrote the above entries when he was 18 and in my view they should be regarded as the instinctive reaction of an ebullient youth against religion being imposed upon him. The use of Capel Ucha as the Baptist Chapel for Criccieth and district was discontinued in 1886 following the erection of Berea which continues to be the meeting place for the Criccieth Baptists. D. Ll. G. continued to be a member of Berea, and was a regular attender at our services whenever he visited Criccieth. On Sunday evenings during the summer in the 1930's the Berea deacons would still occasionally hold services in Capel Ucha, and I remember D. Ll. G. attending one such service when my father gave the address. The presiding deacon then asked my uncle to say a few words. He would then have been in his early seventies and in full possession of his oratorical gifts. In his beautifully modulated voice he said a few words in Welsh on the importance of keeping the lamp of faith alight, before he was overcome with emotion and unable to carry on. I do not think there was a dry eye in the congregation as he resumed his seat. There was, however, something deeper to these diary entries protesting against his enforced religious observance than youthful impatience or boredom. He realised that he had to free himself both mentally and socially from the strict Puritan way of life in which he had been nurtured. He clearly wished to influence his younger brother William to become similarly emancipated, otherwise why should he have bought and given him a copy of Carlyle's SARTOR RESARTUS on William's sixteenth birthday? Sartor Resartus was written by Thomas Carlyle in 1836 and describes his loss of Christian belief.

Neither D. Ll. G. nor my father would have been able to 'promote themselves' by honest endeavour but for the fact that, following the death of their father, the itinerant schoolmaster William George, who died in the summer of 1864 at his tenanted Pembrokeshire smallholding, his extensive and varied collection of books had been transported to Highgate, the home of Richard Lloyd in Llanystumdwy. One of the main reasons for my writing the book THE MAKING OF LLOYD GEORGE (Faber & Faber 1976) was to give prominence to the key role of the deceased father through his books in the educational advancement of his children, Mary, David and William. William George gave up his work as schoolmaster on account of his deteriorating health, and took the tenancy of a smallholding in Bullford, South Pembrokeshire in a desperate attempt to stave off the tuberculosis to which he realised he had succumbed in Manchester where he noticed the telltale traces of blood on his handkerchiefs. I listed some of these books and sought to explain their significance; (pp 66-68, The Making of Lloyd George).

When I was asked to write some verses for the opening ceremony of the Museum, it was this Manchester-Pembrokeshire-Llanystumdwy theme which I decided to develop, relating how D. Ll. G., the crying and unknown infant was born one January in a time of hardship in Manchester (Manceinion); his parents under the tight claws of ill-health had but one thought - to find a health-bestowing haven in Pembrokeshire; but woe! At harvest-time the hidden scythe of death struck down the ailing father; the stricken family returned to Eifionydd with the uncle, the shoemaker craftsman; there, reading and reading in the daytime the books of their lost father and their endless evening discussions laid the foundations of future progress during summers fading into autumns, and in the teeth of winter gales, a sturdy lad, like a meadow oak matured, into his future.

The verses were written in the form of ENGLYNION and were sung by Bethan Haf Price to the tune Rhos y Nant set by D. G. Jones (Selyf). The harpist was Tudur Jones. The singing of *penillion* to harp accompaniment always appealed to my uncle, a great Eisteddfodwr; Viscount Tenby, one of his grandsons, said to me after the meeting - 'I wonder if *Taid* heard your englynion? He would have enjoyed them'.

D. Ll. G.
(Yn ôl yn Llanystumdwy)

Ym Manceinion mewn cyni, ryw Ionawr,
Ceir hanes ei eni:
Baban dinod a thlodi
Uwch ei grud a'i fynych gri.

Tan fachau tyn afiechyd, - rhieni
Gyda'r un meddylfryd,
I gael hoen ym Mhenfro glyd
A'u hafan yno hefyd.

Ond gwae! Adeg gynhaeaf - i dyddyn
Tad eiddil daeth anaf
Yr angau cudd, hirddydd haf,
I'w deulu'r ergyd olaf.

I fwynaf dir Eirionydd, - yn yr ha'
Gyda'r ewythr celfydd,
Adref daeth teulu llwydrudd
O dir craith i weithdy'r crydd.

Darllen a darllen bob dydd, - trwy'r nosau
Trin hanesion gwledydd;
Llyfrau'r coll dad, llafur cudd
Yn gynnar sail i gynnydd.

Drwy hafau'n troi'n hydrefol, ac anterth
Y gwyntoedd gaeafol,
Bachgen praff fel derwen dôl
Aeddfedodd i'w ddyfodol.

W. R. P. George

D. Ll. G.
(back in Llanystumdwy)

One Manchester January
how inauspiciously was the babe born,
with poverty giving a cutting edge
to every cry from his cradle.

His innercitylocked parents,
struggling and ailing,
had but one thought, -
O! For a haven in Pembrokeshire.

But Woe! At harvest time
a sudden sweep of the scythe
struck down the stricken father,
a swathe of early mown hay.

To the fairest land of Eifionydd,
basking in the June sun,
the shattered family returned
sheltered by the shoemaker uncle.

Nightlong political discussions,
reading, reading every day
their lost father's books
dug foundations of advancement.

Throughout autumns transformed from summers,
and in the teeth of winter gales
a sturdy lad, like a meadow oak,
matured to face his future.

W. R. P. George

LLOYD GEORGE AND WELSH LIBERALISM

KENNETH O. MORGAN

No political figure more comprehensively justifies a conference being devoted to studying his career and outlook than does David Lloyd George. As Churchill rightly declared to the Commons at the time of his old ally's death in March, 1945,[1] Lloyd George was the central personality in early twentieth-century British history, and indeed one of the great mass leaders of the modern age. Hitherto he has inspired over a hundred biographical works, along with thousands of other monographs and studies. This is, indeed, the second volume devoted uniquely to a series of Lloyd George studies: the first, edited by Mr. A. J. P. Taylor (to which the present writer also contributed) was published in 1971.[2] And yet the mystery of his career, the controversies and enigmas of his outlook, style and personality remain. Historians are not that much nearer 'painting the chameleon' or 'tethering the broomstick' than when Keynes first wrote his brilliant, if highly misleading, 'essay in biography' shortly after the Treaty of Versailles in 1919.[3]

This article will concentrate on at least one feature of Lloyd George which is generally acknowledged even if the interpretations of it vary enormously - namely the centrality to his career of this association with Wales. He was, without question, the most important and influential Welsh politician who has ever lived. He is, at the time of writing (the autumn of 1990) the only Welshman who has been prime minister. As a party politician in time of peace and of war, as Chancellor, Minister of Munitions and supremely as Prime Minister, his impact on domestic politics and on social policy was immense. For a time, perhaps between the summer of 1919 and the late autumn of 1921, he was the most important politician in the world. In the Soviet Union, in Ireland, in India, in the founding of Palestine, in the Middle East, his legacy is still direct and powerful. The crisis surrounding Iraq's occupation of Kuwait in the summer of 1990 was yet another political consequence of Lloyd George, since it flowed from his original definition of the boundaries of Mesopotamia, made up of the *vilayets* of Basra, Baghdad and Mosul, in 1921. His mighty shadow looms over Saddam Hussein.

Yet, throughout all these great events, he was transcendently associated with Wales. He created, single-handed, much of its national rhetoric and sense of identity. More than anyone else in Welsh life between the 1860s and 1914, he symbolized the revolutionary impact of democracy, national and local. He came to transcend normal partisan and class differences since his admirers ranged from the Communist preacher/agitator/bard, the Revd. Thomas Nicholas, Glais, to the serpentine Bishop A. G. Edwards, first Archbishop of Wales.

He was closely identified with the political advance of Wales in highly personal terms. Long before the outbreak of war in 1914, there was a veritable cult of Lloyd George, almost resembling the cult of Hawarden in Gladstone's later years. There was the annual triumphal visitation to the Eisteddfod on 'Lloyd George's Day'; the family association with Castle Street

---

1   *Parl. Deb.*, 5th series, vol. 409, col 1335.
2   A. J. P. Taylor (ed.), *Lloyd George: Twelve Essays* (London, Hamish Hamilton, 1971).
3   J. M. Keynes, *Essays in Biography* (London, Mercury Books edition, 1961), pp. 32-3.

Baptist church; fond boyhood tales of climbing, swimming in the Dwyfor, and (implicitly) poaching. There was indeed a good deal of romanticism in the way the Lloyd George legend was projected by early biographers such as J. Hugh Edwards or Beriah Gwynfe Evans.[4] Before 1914, his very identification with Wales, indeed, was a source of strength, the personification of grassroots populism, in the saga of the 'cottage-bred boy' who trod the primrose path from Llanystumdwy to Downing Street. He took on the 'unholy Trinity' of the bishops, the brewers, and the squires (afforced by the backwoodsmen of the House of Lords) and laid them low as that earlier David had slain the Philistines.

Yet after the World War I, Lloyd George's identification with Wales became increasingly a source of weakness. His methods as Prime Minister, his un-English disregard for institutional propriety, his contempt for the honours system, made him increasingly suspect.[5] After all, Taffy was supreme among thieves, while T. H. W. Crosland (not to mention Caradoc Evans) currently expounded the theme of the 'unspeakable Celt'. Lloyd George's very virtues as a Welsh outsider, now came to be widely seen as defects. With his unorthodox private life as well, he was made a personal scapegoat for the wider decline of Welsh and British Liberalism, perhaps the decline of Britain itself since 1918. This theme became fashionable even amongst his fellow Welsh Liberals. In 1937 there appeared *Wales Drops the Pilots* by the literary critic, W. Hughes Jones, 'Elidir Sais'. He dwelt lovingly on the nationalist crusade waged by Tom Ellis and the young Lloyd George back in the 1890s. But the book was really an implicit attack on Lloyd George himself for neglecting the ideals of his own youth, the ideals of *Cymru Fydd* and the Wales that was to be.[6] Even more was it an attack on the Welsh of their generation for failure to respond to their youthful champions.

In his emergence as a politician, Lloyd George was intimately caught up in that immense Welsh political resurgence that took place between the general election of 1868 and that of 1906, which saw the land of Wales left with no Tory member at all, and only Keir Hardie in Merthyr interrupting the solid mass of Liberals. Lloyd George was deeply caught up in this Liberal ascendancy. Far from being 'rooted in nothing' as Keynes falsely claimed,[7] he was rooted in a political culture far removed from the acquaintance of 'the Apostles' and a fellow of King's. Lloyd George was certainly far more intimately enmeshed with Welsh politics and society in the later nineteenth century than was Tom Ellis, who went to New College, Oxford, and served as the adviser of Liberal politicians in London.[8] The comparison applied all the more strongly to the

4   J. Hugh Edwards, *From Village Green to Downing Street: the Life of the Rt. Hon. D. Lloyd George* (London, Newnes, 1908); Beriah Gwynfe Evans, *The Life Romance of Lloyd George* (London: n.d., Everyman, [1916]).

5   See especially G. R. Searle, *Corruption in British Politics, 1895-1930*, (Oxford, Clarendon Press, 1987), pp. 350ff.

6   W. Hughes Jones, *Wales Drops the Pilots* (London, Foyle's, Welsh Co., 1937), especially pp. 88-90.

7   Keynes, op. cit., p. 36.

8   See Kenneth O. Morgan, 'Tom Ellis versus Lloyd George: The Fractured Consciousness of *fin-de-siècle* Wales'. in Geraint H. Jenkins and J. Beverly Smith (eds.), *Politics and Society in Wales*(Cardiff, University of Wales Press, 1988), pp. 91ff.

leader of the Welsh Liberals at the time of Lloyd George's first election to parliament in April 1890, Stuart Rendel, an Englishman, and Anglican and, amazingly, an arms manufacturer.[9]

Lloyd George was a politician from the age of five. His first memory was of the great Liberal victory in Caernarfonshire in 1868, when he was carried on Uncle Lloyd's shoulder to election meetings. He referred to this at the time of the fight for the 'People's Budget' in 1910.[10] As a young schoolboy at Llanystumdwy National School he came into conflict with the Anglican authorities, not least in organizing a kind of strike amongst the pupils as a protest against reciting the Creed - in effect against clerical and squirearchical control. He became articled as a solicitor in Portmadoc, an admirable base for a career in late nineteenth-century politics, and was later active in political protest movements like the anti-tithe campaign in southern Lleyn. He participated in local journalism and briefly founded a new radical newspaper, *Udgorn Rhyddid,* the 'Trumpet of Freedom', with his friend, D. R. Daniel.[11] He entered local government as the 'boy alderman' on the first Caernarfonshire county council in 1889. In the North Wales Liberal Federation, he represented a kind of militant tendency, denouncing his own party's leadership for failing to devote sufficient attention and priority to disestablishment and the other demands of Wales.[12] He was elected to parliament in the famous by-election at Caernarfon Boroughs in April 1890 on a strongly nationalistic programme, including Church disestablishment, and land, temperance, and education reform.[13] He appeared to be, therefore the most typical product of Welsh Liberalism at its most buoyant and determined.

Yet it is crucial to the understanding of Lloyd George as a Welsh Liberal to see that, even in these very early years (and, after all, he was only 27 when he entered parliament for all his earlier frenetic activity) he was a maverick and an outsider, even in Wales.

In the first place, he was an outsider even in the world of Welsh nonconformity. He was, after all, a Campbellite Baptist, a minority within a minority, a fringe sect of strongly radical persuasion. Further he viewed with scorn the social pretensions and petty jealousies of chapel life - the 'glorified grocers' and 'beatified drapers' of the big seat.[14] He complained to his young wife of 'being cramped up in a suffocating, malodorous chapel listening to some superstitions I had

9   Kenneth O. Morgan, 'The Member for Wales: Stuart Rendel (1834-1913)', *Trans. Hon. Soc. Cymmrodorion,* (1984), pp. 105ff.

10   Speech at Queen's Hall, 23 March 1910, quoted in *Better Times* (London, Hodder & Stoughton, (1910)) 'It woke the spirit of the mountains, the genius of freedom that fought the might of the Normans .... The political power of landlordism in Wales was shattered as effectively as the power of the Druids.'

11   Lloyd George to D. R. Daniel, 12 December 1887 (National Library of Wales, Aberystwyth, Daniel Papers, 2744); Emyr Price, 'Newyddiadur Cyntaf David Lloyd George', *Journal of the Welsh Bibliographical Society,* XI (1975), 207ff.

12   North Wales Liberal Fenderation minute-book, 1887-92 (N.L.W.).

13   See Emyr Price, 'Lloyd George and the Caernarvon Boroughs Election of 1890', *Trans, Caernarvonshire Hist. Soc.,* XXXVI (1975).

14   D. Lloyd George to Mrs. Lloyd George, 10 June 1890 (N.L.W. Lloyd George Papers, 20,406, f.98), for 'beatified drapers'. For 'glorified grocers', see Lucy Masterman, *C.F.G. Masterman,* repr. (London, Cass, 1968), . 200: Lloyd George told Balfour in 1911, 'I know that our glorified grocers will be more hostile to social reform than your Backwoodsmen'.

heard thousands of time before'.[15] He had some tension with his father-in-law, his wife, and his brother, William, on this point. Truly Lloyd George was no puritan. His daughter, Lady Olwen, was to observe much later that her father really only went through the motions as far as religious observance was concerned.[16] He was a free-thinker in religion, as in finance.

Secondly, although the leader of a rural radicalism, a kind of British version of American Mid-West or southern Populism, David Lloyd George was never truly an agrarian figure. He knew little directly of farming - another point of tension with his father-in-law. Only in his old age did he go in for market gardening and small-scale horticultural production in Churt. Far from being a typically rural figure, on the model of Tom Ellis, he represented rather the aspirations and ambitions of the small-town bourgeoisie.

Again, he had only a scant interest in the cultural or literary aspects of the Welsh nationalism of his youth. He was very different in spirit from Tom Ellis or Llewelyn Williams, both of them of scholarly inclination and deeply versed in Welsh antiquities, history, and poetry. Lloyd George had relatively scant concern with Welsh literary or musical culture, other than the lusty singing of Welsh hymns. Nor did he have any particular involvement with moves to protect the Welsh language - although it should be said that Lloyd George in this respect was typical of virtually every Liberal of his time since there was not the same anxiety about 'the fate of the language' of the kind that emerged in the inter-war period.[17] Lloyd George's approach to Welsh culture was genuine enough, but it was the result of knowledge gained by upbringing, personal contact and conversation. It was instinctive and intuitive, rather than intellectual. At times, it was plain sentimental.

And finally, be was a maverick even in the world of Welsh politics. From his earliest rebellious entry into parliament, he was a member of what used to be called in the army 'the awkward squad'. When Rosebery's government appeared slow in taking up the cause of disestablishment, he briefly resigned the party whip, along with Herbert Lewis, Frank Edwards, and D. A. Thomas, in April 1894.[18] He failed to support his party in key divisions on the Welsh disestablishment bill committee stage in June 1895 - when the Liberals had a majority in the house of only two![19] He was always liable to engage in covert negotiations with Bishop A. G. Edwards or other clerical enemies, as in 1895 or in 1903.[20] Like his hero, Theodore Roosevelt, [21] he was not at all a 'party regular'.

---

15   David Lloyd George to Mrs. Lloyd George, 13 Aug. 1890 (N.L.W., Lloyd George Papers, 20,407C, f. 126).

16   Lady Olwen Carey-Evans, *Lloyd George was my Father* (Llandyssul, Gomer Press, 1985).

17   There was a useful pressure-group. *Cymdeithas yr Iaith Gymraeg*, 'The Society for the Utilization of the Welsh Language', with Beriah Gwynfe Evans as secretary, but it was a body of scholars and educationalists in the main.

18   Kenneth O. Morgan, *Wales in British Politics, 1868-1922*, 3rd. edn., (Cardiff, University of Wales Press, 1980), pp. 144-5.

19   Ibid., pp. 152-3.

20   Eluned. E. Owen, *The Life of Bishop Owen* (Llandyssul, Gomer Press, 1961), pp. 179-81; J. Arthur   Price to Tom Ellis, 21 Jan. 1895 (N.L.W. Ellis Papers, 1701).

21   See D. Lloyd George, *The Truth about the Peace Treaties, II* (London, Gollancz, 1938), p. 232. This added to

From the time of his entry into parliament in 1890, he promoted all the main national themes, and took up all the main points on the Welsh Liberal agenda. But he did so in a manner distinctly his own. On most of the key issues of the time, he supplied his own nuances and twists. More than almost any other key Liberal of the time, he related the major issues on the Welsh national programme to aspects of social class, the maldistribution of property, and of political and economic power. Thus he placed his own stamp on a succession of key issues.

On the central issue of Welsh land, he took a distinctly different view from fellow Liberals such as Tom Ellis, Llewelyn Williams, or Ellis Griffith. They focused on tenurial aspects, on landlord-tenant relations within a relatively static rural class structure. Lloyd George was rather anxious for the disestablishment of the landlords, no less than of the Church. He followed with enthusiasm the campaign of the Revd. E. Pan Jones of Mostyn for land nationalization in the columns of *Y Celt*.[22] It was the agrarian socialism, as much as the Irish nationalism of Michael Davitt, with whom he shared a famous platform at Ffestiniog in February 1886, that appealed to him.[23] In his 'People's budget' in 1909 he took up the theme of land taxation, and attempted, though in vain, to tax the 'unearned increment' acquired by landlords as a result of general urban development. In his even more remarkable budget of 1914, one deflected by procedural and other problems in the House, he tried for the first time to make land taxation an integral feature of the fiscal system,[24] mainly through the taxing of site value. For modern readers, it might be added that one option which he totally rejected as impracticable and socially regressive was that of a poll-tax, even if disguised under the soubriquet of 'community charge'.[25]

Another theme in which he took his own course was that of education. He largely stood outside the great inter-party movement for secondary and higher education, which absorbed so many Welsh Liberals at the time - Rendel, Ellis, Herbert Lewis, Arthur Humphreys-Owen to name but a few. It was a movement which yielded great results - the 1889 Intermediate Education Act, which created the famous 'county schools', the Central Welsh Board, the Welsh university colleges at Aberystwyth and later at Bangor and Cardiff, the national and federal university of Wales in 1893. Although a schoolmaster's son, Lloyd George saw education more as a political weapon, and kept aloof from these educational campaigns. Humphreys-Owen was to complain during the county councils 'revolt' against the Balfour Education Act of 1902: 'Having no literary education himself he is unable to realize the needs of the education system'.[26] Not until around 1914, when Haldane worked on him and persuaded him to create the basis of the University Grants Committee, did Lloyd George involve himself more fully in public education for its own

---

22   See Peris Jones Evans, 'Evan Pan Jones - Land Reformer', *Welsh History Review*, vol. 4, 2   (Dec. 1968), pp. 143ff.
23   W. R. P. George, *The Making of Lloyd George*, (London, Faber, 1976), pp. 129-30.
24   Budget speech of 4 May 1914.
25   See Bruce K. Murray, 'Lloyd George, the Navy Estimates and the Inclusion of Rating Relief in the 1914 Budget'. *Welsh History Review*, vol. 15, 1 (June 1990).
26   A. C. Humphreys-Owen to Stuart, Lord Rendel, 18 June 1905 (N.L.W., Rendel Papers, xiv. 704a).

sake.[27] Even then, his earlier background continued to assert itself. During the discussions on economies in educational and other public expenditure on the Geddes committee in 1921, when he was prime minister, Lloyd George was still cavalier about such matters as the school entry age and the size of classes.[28] 'He was sure that the brighter children would learn just as quickly and readily in a class of seventy as they would in a much smaller class.' He would continue to uphold the common-sense of the self-taught common man, rather than arid learning, or scholarship - though that did not prevent his winning the devotion of great scholars such as the historian Herbert Fisher and the philosopher, Sir Henry Jones.

Much of the same applied to another shibboleth of many Welsh Liberals - local government. An idealist like Tom Ellis saw the county councils created in 1889 as the instruments of populism. He compared them to small autonomous communities like the Tyrol, the Swiss cantons - or the Boer republics. Other Liberals like Herbert Lewis or Arthur Humphreys-Owen had detailed and expert first-hand knowledge of how local government really worked and its potentialities.[29] Lloyd George did not. He played little part in the Caernarfonshire county council to which he was elected an alderman in 1899, and was only indirectly involved with the expansion of the Welsh local government, rural or urban, in the 1890s. Then, in the rebellion against the 1902 Balfour Education Act, in the period 1903-5, he emerged as the leader of the Welsh county councils, all of them with a Liberal majority from February 1904.[30] But this was because of their political potential in undermining the Tory government and frustrating its educational reforms. Again, he developed his interests more fully in mid-career. His 'People's Budget' of 1909 was in part designed to relieve the pressing burdens of local government finance, with the enormous pressures impinging on local authorities as their welfare and other responsibilities expanded.[31] But here again was a key issue in the Welsh Liberal agenda where Lloyd George followed his own line.

Again, on the dominant issue of Welsh home rule, Lloyd George's vision of *Cymru Fydd* in the 1890s was again distinctive. It had none of Tom Ellis's cultural/imperial overtones, with its adoration of the mystical nationalism of Giuseppe Mazzini or Thomas Davis.[32] The Irishman that most impressed Lloyd George was the agrarian radical Michael Davitt, not the

27   Eric Ashby and Mary Anderson, *Portrait of Haldane at Work on Education*, (London, Macmillan, 1974), pp. 114-18. Lloyd George and Haldane had earlier clashed on educational policy: 'Land not education was the next great subject to be taken up by the government'. (ibid., 115).

28   *Report, Proceedings and Memoranda of the Cabinet Committee ...on Public Expenditure*, 22 Jan. 1922 (Public Record Office, CAB 27/165).

29   See K. Idwal Jones (gol.) *Syr Herbert Lewis, 1858-1933* (Caerdydd, Gwasg Prifysgol Cymru, 1959), tt. 79ff., and, for Humphreys-Owen, the Glansevern Papers, N.L.W., *passim.*

30   Morgan, *Wales in British Politics*, pp. 187-98; Gareth Elwyn Jones, 'The Welsh Revolt Revisited: Merioneth and Montgomeryshire in Default', *Welsh History Review*, vol., 14, 3 (June 1989), 417ff.

31   See Bruce K. Murray, 'Lloyd George and the Land' in J. A. Beynon *et al.* (eds.), *Studies in Local History* (Oxford University Press, 1976), pp. 37 ff.

32   See Neville Masterman, *The Forerunner*, (Llandybie, Christopher Davies, 1971), esp. pp. 17-18.

philosopher, Thomas Davis. To him, *Cymru Fydd* was far from being the embodiment of a cultural or quasi-mystical ideal. Rather was it a totally realistic method of putting pressure on the Liberal Party machine and on Liberal headquarters in London on behalf of the various Welsh national causes. Lloyd George saw the 'revolt' of 1894-6, the attempt to merge the Liberal Federations of North and South Wales within a 'Welsh National Federation' in strictly political terms. It was thus a narrowly-conceived movement - and hence its downfall, in much acrimony. It collapsed after the ignominious South Wales Liberal Federation meeting at Newport in January 1896 when Lloyd George was howled down by the anglicized mercantile Liberals of the South Wales ports.[33] But the causes lay in wider factors than merely the regional rift between North and South Wales. Rather was there a fatal ambiguity, implicit in Lloyd George's vision of *Cymru Fydd,* between liberalism and nationalism. It emerged that Welsh Liberalism was, in general, far from separatist. As a result, separatism, in however modest form, was not a major force in Welsh politics for the next seventy years, not until the devolution measures for Scotland and Wales put forward by the Callaghan government in the later 1970s. Lloyd George's version of Welsh self-government had dissolved. On the other hand, so had that of everybody else. Perhaps what Lloyd George's abortive *Cymru Fydd* campaign really achieved was to show that pressure for self-government in Wales was limited and largely sentimental. The defeat of devolution in 1979 was to confirm the point. *Cymru Fydd's* collapse thus demonstrated vividly to the world that Wales was not Ireland.

A final area where Lloyd George took his own course is perhaps more unfamiliar - the theme of Empire. Contrary to what legend has sometimes maintained, the Welsh Liberals were in the main highly attracted to the appeal of empire.[34] In the 1890s they saw the expansion of the British empire as intimately linked with the progress of Wales out of poverty and neglect. This especially applied to 'imperial south Wales' where trade, industry and urban growth boomed in the wake of the transatlantic and imperial economy.[35] But it applied to much of Liberalism in North and Mid-Wales, also. Most Welsh Liberals emphatically supported the war against the Boer republics, the Orange Free State and the Transvaal, in 1899; men like Ellis Griffith or David Brynmor Jones were as imperialist as were Asquith or Rosebery. Lloyd George took quite the reverse view. He had been prepared to defend the expansion of British interests in Africa in the 1890s, though reluctant to oppose France in the Fashoda in the Sudan in 1898.[36] He was no 'little Englander' and indeed later in his career was the close associate of imperialist evangelists such as Philip Kerr or Lord Milner. He regarded the Boer War, though, as unjustified and unjust, the

33   South Wales Daily News, 17 Jan. 1896.

34   On this theme, see Kenneth O. Morgan, 'Wales and the Boer War - a Reply', *Welsh History Review,* vol. 4, 4 (Dec. 1969), pp. 367ff.

35   For a brilliant discussion, see Gwyn A. Williams, *When was Wales?* (London, Black Raven Press, 1985), pp. 221ff.

36   Harold Spender, *The Fire of Life,* (London, Hodder and Stoughton, n.d. [1920]), p. 53 but cf. John Grigg, *The Young Lloyd George,* (London, Eyre Methuen, 1973), p. 223 for a different view.

product of incompetent diplomacy, corrupt finance, and vainglorious jingoism. He withstood with passion and courage the hostility and violence of imperialist mobs, not only in Chamberlain's Birmingham but even in his own constituency. In the cathedral city of Bangor he had to flee from the frenzy of a jingo mob. He wrote to Herbert Lewis of how 'the mob were seized of a drunken madness and the police were helpless'.[37] It was indeed a distinctly minority position to be a 'pro-Boer' in Liberal Wales in 1900. By the end of the war in May 1902, the sympathy aroused by the Boer 'guerrillas' and the distaste resulting from the death of women and children in Kitchener's concentration camps, the tide of opinion was turning in Lloyd George's favour. But at the time of Mafeking, in the face of the overwhelming imperialist passion of the Welsh press and politicians, it required courage indeed to stand up against the storm. It is truly amongst the most glorious passages in Lloyd George's career.

Lloyd George's heyday in Wales was the Edwardian period, if we may extend the period to continue down to 1914. It was for the Welsh nation a unique time of prosperity, influence, self-awareness and national pride.[38] Welsh industry reached new heights of productive growth, symbolized by the domination of Welsh steam coal in the world's export trade, and the colossal expansion of the ports of Cardiff and Barry in particular. Cardiff became a new metropolis, the bastion of 'King Coal'.[39] In Welsh cultural life, it was a period of extraordinary literary renaissance, of poets like T. Gwynn Jones and the young Parry-Williams, of scholars like Sir John Morris-Jones and Sir John Lloyd, of popular evangelists for the Welsh language like Sir Owen M. Edwards. In religion, Welsh nonconformity reached its high noon, with the 'big guns' of the pulpit blazing away, and chapel membership inflated to unprecedented levels by the 1904-5 religious revival.

In politics, this national resurgence was perhaps the most dramatic of all, with Liberals virtually sweeping the board at the 1906 general election, and Welshmen prominent in the Liberal government. Lloyd George, President of the Board of Trade from December 1905, Chancellor of the Exchequer from April, 1908, the most dynamic and charismatic politician of the day, symbolised all of this and more. In the later words of one excited Welsh journalist, he was 'the greatest Welshman yet born'.[40] With Old Age Pensions, the People's Budget, the Parliament Act, then National Health Insurance, triumph followed upon triumph.

Lloyd George's role, indeed, indicates that profound difference between England and Wales as political cultures in the early twentieth century. In Edwardian England, he was a deeply controversial and divisive figure. His onslaughts on the peers, land, and vested interests generally drew upon him the virulent opposition of Conservatives in general, from up-country squires to

---

37   Lloyd George to Herbert Lewis, 13 April 1900 (N.L.W., Penucha MSS.)

38   See, generally, Kenneth O. Morgan, *Rebirth of a Nation Wales, 1880-1980* (Oxford University Press and University of Wales Press, Cardiff, 1981), ch.5

39   M. J. Daunton, *Coal Metropolis: Cardiff 1870-1914*, (Leicester University Press, 1977).

40   See generally *Wales*, 1911-14 edited by Lloyd George's biographer, J. Hugh Edwards, MP.

King GeorgeV. A *Punch* cartoon depicted him in the guise of John Knox, denouncing 'motorists, golfers and all those miserable sinners who happen to own anything'.[41] During the Marconi affair of 1912-13, when it emerged that the Chancellor had bought (and sold at a loss) some shares from the Marconi company, which was shortly to be contracted to the British government, his opponents came close to driving Lloyd George out of public life for ever.[42]

By contrast, in his own Wales, Lloyd George was increasingly a unifying force, a reflection in part of the almost blanket domination of Welsh political and cultural life by the Liberal party. His prestige was far from being confined to Gwynedd or to the rural areas; on the contrary, while President of the Board of Trade, he was approached about the Liberal candidacy for the metropolis and seaport of Cardiff.[43] His nationwide leadership in the promotion of social reform added to his supra-party appeal, as the Welsh belatedly took an interest in the New Liberalism that had long been exciting journalists and politicians in London.[44] No episode illustrated how transcendent Lloyd George had become within Wales, even amongst Conservative/Anglican opponents, than his role in orchestrating (and, indeed part inventing) the ceremonial and ritual that attended the investiture of the young Edward as Prince of Wales at Caenarfon Castle in 1911. Lloyd George's ally in this enterprise was his old sparring partner, Alfred George Edwards, Bishop of St. Asaph.[45] In return, Lloyd George rewarded his nation with much assistance from the public purse. As Chancellor he was able to approve grants of £1,500 to the National Museum, £2,500 to the National Library at Aberystwyth, £15,000 to the Welsh University Colleges in the course of an eventful twenty-four hours in February 1909. As he gaily told Herbert Lewis, 'What's the use of being a Welsh Chancellor of the Exchequer if one can do nothing for Wales?'[46] Even the triumphs of the Welsh rugby football team in that golden era were adroitly turned to advantage by a man who had once condemned the unresponsive colliers of the South Wales coalfield for their morbid 'footballism'.[47]

Yet there were signs, even before August 1914, that his position in Wales, like that of Liberalism in general, was becoming less secure. There were clear indications that the man who in 1910 proposed a cross-party coalition to grapple with the mighty themes of social welfare and national defence[48] was becoming impatient, if not positively bored with the old Welsh causes. Welsh land reforms receded as the volumes of the 1896 Royal Commission of Welsh land mouldered away on library shelves, unread except by ardent history research students.

41   *Punch*, 26 Oct. 1910.
42   Frances Donaldson, *The Marconi Case* (London, Hart-Davis, 1962.
43   Lloyd George to Mrs. Lloyd George, 31 July 1907, Kenneth O. Morgan (ed.), *Lloyd George: Family Letters, c. 1885-1936* (Oxford University Press and Cardiff, University of Wales Press, 193), p. 147.
44   Kenneth O. Morgan, 'The Liberalism and the Challenge of Labour: the Welsh Experience, 1885-1929' in K. D. Brown (ed.), *Essays in Anti-Labour History*, (London, Macmillan, 1974), pp. 159ff.
45   Archbishop A. G. Edwards, *Memories*, (London, John Murray, 1927), pp. 141ff.
46   John Grigg, *Lloyd George and Wales*, (Aberystwyth, National Library of Wales, 1988), p. 9.
47   Lloyd George to Mrs. Lloyd George, 19 Nov. 1895 (*Family Letters*, p. 91).
48   John D. Fair, *British Interparty Conferences*, (Oxford, Clarendon Press), pp. 91ff.

Temperance had stalled, while the Chancellor took little interest in the worthy efforts by E. T. John, Liberal member for East Denbighshire, to promote the cause of Welsh devolution, perhaps on the basis of 'home rule all round'.[49] As regards the transcendent issues of Welsh disestablishment, while Lloyd George made aggressive speeches during the Commons debate in 1912-13 (Lord Hugh Cecil's family was accused of having 'hands dripping with the fat of sacrilege'),[50] behind the scenes the Chancellor was anxious to bury the issues. Back in 1906 he had told Randall Davidson, the Archbishop of Canterbury, that he hoped that appointing a royal commission on the Welsh churches would lead to 'a moderate bill' being framed, with concessions on disendowment to speed on the rapid passage of a measure that would resolve a century-old and increasingly irrelevant question for ever.[51] Compared with health, housing, and child malnutrition, the Welsh Church hardly loomed in the forefront of the public agenda.

Apart from Lloyd George's own inclinations, there were signs, too, that Wales in general was beginning to drift away from him and the old Liberal inheritance. This was most emphatically true in the mining valley of South Wales. By 1914, there were five Labour MPs there, a myriad of Labour-controlled councils and an increasingly powerful socialist movement mostly focused on the spread of the Independent Labour Party. More ominous still were the new quasi-revolutionary currents surging through the South Wales Miners' Federation.[52] Although 'Lib-Labbism' in the mould of 'Mabon' and William Brace remained powerful throughout the coalfield down to 1914, the new movements associated with the Unofficial Reform Committee and the Plebs League, the Marxist tutorial classes of the Central Labour College and quasi-syndicalist *Miners' Next Step* published at Tonypandy, heralded a quite new era of industrial politics. Industrial South Wales, which had thrilled to the oratory of Lloyd George in the immediate past, seemed now almost the cockpit of the class war. Welsh Liberalism truly had many mansions. But it was quite unable, socially or ideologically, to accommodate the labour movement, not only fringe radicals like Noah Ablett or Will Hay but even more mainstream miners' agents like James Winstone, Enoch Morrell, and Vernon Hartshorn.

Lloyd George's decline from political eminence after 1918 is, of course, part of the wider decline of Liberalism in Britain as a whole in the post-war period. It had deep-seated socio-economic causes - the erosion of nonconformity, the weakening of the rural communities and of agrarian radicalism, the collapse of the old free-trade staple industries of coal, shipping and textiles, all of them important adjuncts of the Liberal Party across the land. But, in Lloyd George's case there were more specifically Welsh and personal causes as well. Of course, he remained down to the World War II a politician of immense national and international authority,

49   J. Graham Jones, 'E. T. John and Welsh Home Rule, 1910-1914'. *Welsh History Review*, vol. 13, 4 (Dec. 1987), pp. 453ff.

50   *Parl. Deb.*, 5th series, vol. 37, cols. 1278, 25 April 1912.

51   G. K. A. Bell, *The Life of Archbishop Davidson*, (London, Oxford University Press, 1935), p. 504.

52   See Hywel Francis and Dai Smith, *The Fed*, (London, Lawrence & Wishart, 1980), ch. I.

the only one of the three 'peacemakers' at Versailles to survive as a significant force into the thirties. He was a fount of new economic ideas in the late twenties, the first major politician to see the political implications of the ideas of Maynard Keynes. He generated new discussion of both domestic and international issues in the thirties, and his Council of Action for Peace and Reconstruction in 1935 made a notable impact, with even some suggestion that Lloyd George might join the National government under his old adversaries MacDonald and Baldwin.[53] In May 1940, at the age of 77, he was still an effective force in helping to remove Neville Chamberlain from Downing Street, and was subsequently offered a government office by Churchill.[54]

For all that, the later phase of Lloyd George's career is clearly one of waning influence, and, amidst all the other factors bearing on the question, there are some important features relating to Liberalism in Wales. In particular, it can be argued that he failed adequately to engage with newer currents of thought in Welsh life. This applies especially to the three major themes of socialism, nationalism, and militarism.

As regards socialism, there was no obvious social reason why Lloyd George should not have become a socialist or at least joined the Labour Party. After all, the Labour government included some far more improbable figures who did, upper-class figures like Attlee, Dalton or Cripps. Quite apart from his astonishing achievements as a social reformer, Lloyd George was well-known for his special relationship with the labour movement before 1914, and for his rare skill in settling contentious issues with trade union leaders. He showed this facility during the settlement of a threatened national railway strike in the autumn of 1907 and, even more dramatically, in ending the national miners' strike on behalf of a minimum wage in 1912.[55] In the Treasury Agreement concluded with the TUC in March 1915 to prevent wartime strikes he showed himself yet again a patron and an ally of organized labour, and one deeply sympathetic to the needs of the ordinary working man.

Yet he was, by background and understanding, remote from the sense of class identity and the roots of social conflict that characterized the British industrial working class. As Keir Hardie had rightly observed in the *Labour Leader* in 1905, Lloyd George, a man with whom radical socialists could collaborate over anti-imperialism, the rights of women or world peace, 'had no settled opinions on social questions'.[56] Lloyd George's imagination could cope with local issues like the three-year strike of the Bethesda quarrymen in 1900-3, which partly concerned his own constituents. He was forthright in condemning the autocratic role of Lord Penrhyn, his refusal to acknowledge trade unions in his quarries, and his wanton calling out of the militia to

53   Keith Middlemas and John Barnes, *Baldwin*, (London, Weidenfeld & Nicolson, 1969), 808 - 10.
54   See David M. Roberts, 'Clement Davies and the Fall of Neville Chamberlain, 1939-40', *Welsh History Review*, vol. 8, 2 (Dec. 1976), pp. 208-11. Harold Nicholson actually records that a Lloyd George government was thought to be imminent in May 1940.
55   Lucy Masterman, op. cit., pp. 233-5.
56   Keir Hardie, *Labour Leader*, 22 Dec. 1905.

coerce the quarrymen back to work.[57] But Lloyd George was really out of his depth when confronting the continuing turbulence within the South Wales labour movement from the war years onwards. Even during the war, he deeply antagonised Welsh and other workers with the controls imposed by the Munitions of War Act, the enforcement of 'dilution' of skilled men and the imposition of military conscription.[58]

After the war, his 'anti-Bolshevik' rhetoric directed against the Miners' Federation, his apparent deceit of the Federation over the Sankey Commission in 1919 and again in resolving 'Black Friday' in April 1921, the widespread use of troops (and even the navy airforce) in putting down striking Welsh miners during the national stoppage in 1921, the use of emergency powers as an anti-strike strategy, the government's support for neo-fascist police chiefs like Captain Lionel Lindsay in Glamorgan[59] - all this tarnished Lloyd George's reputation amongst the Welsh working class, and fatally so. The Coalition, allegedly a government of national unity, now seemed a class formation devised to suppress labour.[60] The most influential and representative Labour Party leader of the day, Arthur Henderson, humiliated by the 'doormat' incident after his visit to Stockholm in 1917, became Lloyd George's most formidable antagonist.[61] Despite the sympathy with the TUC shown during the 1926 general strike Lloyd George lost in the twenties any credible claim to be a serious spokesman for the British workers. There was a powerful resonance in the young Nye Bevan's bitter attack on Lloyd George in the House in 1930 - reminiscent of the young Lloyd George's own onslaught on Joseph Chamberlain - 'better dearer coal than cheaper colliers'.[62]

Lloyd George retained a broad appeal for Labour spokesmen in North and Mid-Wales: witness his impact on rising young socialists like Cledwyn Hughes in Anglesey or Tom Ellis in Wrexham, both powerful supporters of the Lloyd George tradition and of the centenary appeal in 1990.[63] But for the serried ranks of working men and their wives in industrial south Wales, the Lloyd George tradition represented a world well lost.

Something of the same applied to the idea of nationalism, too. Lloyd George rose in the early 1890s as a vehement champion of the Welsh nationalism of his day: his election addresses in Caernarfon Boroughs in 1890, 1892, and 1895 were largely a rehearsal of the Welsh demands of the day. He was anxious to try to turn the disendowment provisions of the 1895 Welsh

---

57   Merfyn Jones, *The North Wales Quarrymen, 1873-1922*, (Cardiff, University of Wales Press, 1980).
58   C. J. Wrigley, *David Lloyd George and the British Labour Movement*, (Hassocks, Sussex, Harvester Press, 1976), 149ff.; Kenneth and Jane Morgan, *Portrait of a Progressive: the Political Career of Christopher Viscount Addison*, (Oxford, Clarendon Press, 1980), pp. 62-6
59   See Jane Morgan, *Conflict and Order: the Police and Labour Dispute in England and Wales, 1900-1939*, (Oxford, Clarendon Press, 1979). pp. 190ff.
60   Cf. Kenneth O. Morgan, *Consensus and Disunity: the Lloyd George Coalition Government of 1918-1922*, (Oxford, Clarendon Press, 1979).
61   See Chris Wrigley, *Arthur Henderson*, (Cardiff, University of Wales Press, 1990).
62   *Parl. Deb.*, 5th series, vol. 235, cols. 24, 62-8 (27 Feb. 1930).
63   Personal knowledge; Emyr Price, *Lord Cledwyn of Penrhos*, (Bangor, Cyhoeddiadau Mai, 1990).

Disestablishment Bill into a means of promoting Welsh self-government, by creating a national council to administer the secularised endowments such as tithe and glebe.

But his nationalism did not last. He never really managed to produce a satisfactory sequel to the *Cymru Fydd* movement after its collapse in early 1896. He was involved, from time to time, in attempts to promote Welsh administrative devolution, such as the Welsh department in the Board of Education in 1907 (the first secretary being an old political ally, Alfred T. Davies) and the Welsh Board of Health in 1919.[64] He showed some interest in the notion of a Welsh Secretary of State after 1919 and urged his fellow-countrymen to 'go for the big thing' in this regard,[65] but he seemed very distant from some of the newer nationalist currents promoted by Welsh writers in the twenties. He was detached from the nationalist ideas advocated by writers like W. J. Gruffydd and R. T. Jenkins in the *Llenor* at this time. Neither did he respond particularly to the modest devolution proposed in the monthly *Welsh Outlook,* founded by his Cabinet Secretary, Thomas Jones, and largely financed by his former assistant, Lord Davies of Llandinam.[66] Plaid Cymru emerged in the later twenties, minuscule though it was, as an updated Europe-based, intellectual nationalism to replace the tired pre-war 'radicalism' of the Eisteddfod, the Honourable Society of Cymmrodorion and the Edwardian Liberal Party.[67] The real outcome of this emerged after Lloyd George's death. The advance of Plaid Cymru after 1966 - starting with Gwynfor Evans's election triumph in Carmarthen, the former seat of Megan Lloyd George, reinforced the decline of Liberalism in rural Wales. Nor did Welsh Liberalism derive any particular bonus from its support of Welsh devolution in the later 1970's; the 1979 election saw the defeat of Emlyn Hooson in Montgomeryshire, though it is true that Rendel's old constituency later reverted to the Liberal faith in 1983.

Curiously enough, Lloyd George managed in the end to achieve a more final settlement with regard to Irish nationalism. His record in relation to Ireland has been traced by the present writer elsewhere.[68] It is full of twists and turns with a particular dark chapter in the 'troubles' of 1919-21 with the terrible policy of 'retaliation' against the IRA and the use of freelances like the Black and Tans. Yet in the end, he managed to produce a settlement with Sinn Fein, in the Treaty of December 1921. Warts and all, it brought a more peaceful period to Ireland than that unhappy island had known since 1798, a more tranquil phase which endured until the 1960s, even if Ulster was subjected to an insensitive one party rule. Lloyd George managed, after a fashion, to reconcile the demands of Irish nationalism, the refusal to coerce Protestant Ulster, and the need to

---

64   A. T. Davies, *The Lloyd George I Knew,* (London, Henry Walter, 1948), pp. 51ff.
65   *Welsh Outlook,* Jan. 1921, p. 302.
66   *Welsh Outlook,* 1917-22 *passim,* and article by Gwyn Jenkins in *National Library of Wales Journal,* XXIV, 4 (Winter 1986).
67   See Saunders Lewis in *The Welsh Nationalists,* Jan. 1932, p. 1, where he pours scorn on 'the ardent Welsh Nationalists' of pre -1914.
68   Kenneth O. Morgan, 'Lloyd George and the Irish' in *Ireland since the Union,* (Oxford University Press for the (British and Irish Academies, 1989), pp. 83ff.

keep open new channels of communication between London and Dublin. He cannot be reasonably blamed for the intransigence of the Ulster Protestant ascendancy or the centuries-old gulf between the rival cultures or Ireland, both dating from the Plantations of James I's reign if not earlier. In Ireland there was, for a time, a settlement of a kind. But the more indirect, more subtle, claims of Welsh nationalism remained unfulfilled.

Finally, from August, 1914 there was the challenge of militarism. The war, of course, turned Lloyd George's career in radically new directions. He moved on to become Minister of Munitions, Secretary for War and in December 1916 Prime Minister of Great Britain. His commitment to conscription caused a breach with Asquith and other old Liberal comrades, and impelled him towards an unexpected alliance with leading Unionist, including imperialist zealots like Milner. He used the language of 'no surrender' and of 'the knock-out blow'.[69] In Wales itself, he used shamelessly sentimental rhetoric about the warlike tradition of the Welsh; the Welsh bowmen at Crècy and Agincourt were dragged out of history or folklore, and a Welsh Division created, which saw ferocious action later on at Mametz Wood.[70] A 'Welsh Mafia' emerged in Downing Street, from December 1916, both in the Cabinet secretariat and the Garden Suburb, featuring Thomas Jones, J. T. Davies, David Davies, Sir Joseph Davies and many others. Other pillars of Welsh Liberalism went even further than Lloyd George in producing nationalist 'anti-Hun' propaganda. Even detached writers and intellectuals like Sir John Morris-Jones and Sir Owen M. Edwards lent their talents to the cause,[71] while another prominent Liberal, the Revd. John Williams of Brynsiencyn, Anglesey, caused something of a sensation by preaching in the pulpit in full military uniform. Prominent Welsh academics like Sir Henry Jones and Sir Wynn Wheldon took part in recruiting campaigns to boost the trenches on the Western front, while the eminent German scholar, Hermann Ethé, was hounded out of Aberystwyth after a disreputable campaign in the town.

Yet a reaction against this mood was discernible in Wales even during the war years. As we have noted, in the south Wales mining valleys, the socialist movement, fanned by the 1917 revolution in Russia, was vocal in denouncing a long and bloody war. Even in rural north and mid-Wales there were important voices of dissent like the poets, Thomas Gwynn Jones and Thomas Parry-Williams, and the two remarkable journals produced at the University College of Wales, Aberystwyth, *Y Wawr* and *Y Deyrnas*.[72] After the war, it became clear that significant elements in the Welsh intelligentsia, appalled by the juggernaut of war-mania, were turning

69   See particularly the interview with Roy Howard printed in *The Times*, 29 Nov. 1916.
70   For Lloyd George's 'Welsh Army', see Colin Hughes, *Mametz*, (Gerrards Cross, Orion Press, 1985).
71   See, for instance, Sir John Morris-Jones in *Y Beirniad*, Hydref 1914, tt. 217-24, and Sir Owen M. Edwards, ('Cwymp yr Almaen', in *Cymru*, Chwefror 1915, along with Hazel Davies, *O. M. Edwards* (Cardiff, University (of Wales Press, 1988).
72   Kenneth O. Morgan, 'Peace Movements in Wales, 1899-1945', *Welsh History Review*, 10, no. 3 (June 1981), pp. 409-13. The authorities at Aberystwyth closed down Y Wawr in 1917 and there was controversy in 1919 when one of its leading writers, the eminent poet, Thomas Parry-Williams, was appointed to a chair of Welsh.

against their Liberal background. A sign of the times was the astonishing victory in the 1923 general election by the Christian pacifist, George Maitland Lloyd Davies.[73] Radical sentiment turned to Labour, perhaps to inter-party movement such as the League of Nations Union.[74] Some, like Lloyd George's long term friend, D. R. Daniel, left political activity entirely.[75]

The irony was that after 1918 Lloyd George himself emerged as a foremost 'peacemonger' and a prophet of reconciliation.[76] He called for genuine attempts to bring the pariah nations of Weimar Germany and Soviet Russia into the comity of nations, culminating in the abortive Conference at Genoa in April-May 1922. He called for a radical modification of the provisions of war reparations, a moratorium on war debts, for naval disarmament, and (in the thirties) for international action to promote peace through the effective use of collective security. In the best sense he was the first appeaser. In 1939-40, the ageing Lloyd George was identified with a putative 'peace party' and was compared by Churchill with the venerable Marshal Pétain for his pains.[77] But it was all too late. Lloyd George's highly personal identification with the full rigour which many of his radical countrymen regarded as a bloody betrayal of Liberal values was damaging, even fatal. Welsh Liberalism in many ways died at Passchendale. Like truth, it was another casualty of total war, as young Welshmen said 'good-bye to all that'.

Lloyd George is obviously a key figure in the making of modern Wales. Throughout his career he was an innovative, radical figure, for all the 'centrist' tags often imposed on him. His quest for party 'fusion' in 1919-20 is often misunderstood. As far as Wales was concerned, though a master negotiator who 'could charm a bird off a bough', he was not really a consensus man. He focused on schisms, tensions, class conflicts endemic in the Wales of his time, and sought to find political solution for them. He thus played an essential part in defining the Welsh political identity. In many ways he was unfairly attacked, not only over his domestic life, but also over the friends he was liable to attract. To claim that 'he had no friends and did not deserve any' is hard to reconcile with the devotion of men like Sir Herbert Lewis or the preacher-poet Elfed Lewis, or indeed of equally respectable men like H. A. L. Fisher and C. P. Scott of the *Manchester Guardian* in England.

His volatility and flexibility, as a Welsh outsider, was a major key to his triumphs down to 1914, or perhaps, December 1916. Thereafter, they became a factor in his downfall, by giving an image of untrustworthiness, as novelists such as Arnold Bennett or Joyce Cary were to portray.[78] In the end, the great symbol of modernity and of restless, perpetual change had become a survival from the past. The great Welsh democrat had become another Cromwell, the model of autocracy, perhaps of reaction. For many years past he had been removed from Welsh life, with

---

73   Morgan, ibid., p. 417, citing the Davies Papers in N. L. W., Aberystwyth.
74   See Goronwy Jones, *Wales and the Quest for Peace*, (Cardiff, University of Wales Press, 1969), pp. 125ff.
75   K. W. Jones-Roberts, ' D. R. Daniel', *Journal Merioneth Hist. and Record Society*, V (1965), 58-78.
76   For this see Morgan, *Consensus and Disunity*; Richard H. Ullmann, *The Anglo-Soviet Accord*, (Oxford, Clarendon Press, 1973).
77   After Lloyd George's last major Commons speech, 7 May 1941.
78   Lloyd George appears, thinly disguised, as Andy Clyth in Bennett's Lord Raingo, (1926) and as Chester

his life with Frances Stevenson at Churt looming ever larger, and not many close advisers to "mind the shop" as brother William had once done in his constituency. Indeed the kind of men with whom Lloyd George associated in the thirties, ranging from Lord Lothian to Liddell Hart were almost totally removed from the humdrum processes of normal party politics. Never in his entire career had he been a machine politician or an organization man. In the end, on New Year's day 1945, the Welsh Great Commoner, member for Caernarfon Boroughs for almost 45 momentous years, became an earl. At the very last, the Establishment had captured him. After his death, his constituency was won by the Tories, and then was merged into a Labour seat. His son, Gwilym Lloyd-George, retained the Hyphen and became a Conservative MP and Cabinet minister. His daughter Megan, hyphenless, went the other way, as had been long predicted, and was elected Labour MP for Carmarthen in 1957.[79] His other child, Lady Olwen Carey-Evans, alone remained on in Criccieth as a custodian of the old values and lived on, bright and stimulating to the last, to reach the age of 97. The age of Lloyd George, and of the Welsh Liberal ascendancy which he symbolized, was truly over. The new Wales of post-1945, the Wales of Jim Griffiths and Nye Bevan, of the Welsh Language Society and the Welsh Office, was the product of different, and perhaps more appropriate, hands.

---

79   See the present writer's entries on both Gwilym and Lady Megan Lloyd George in *The Dictionary of National Biography*, supplement for 1961-70 (Oxford University Press, 1981). A biography of Lady Megan by Mervyn Jones is shortly to appear in 1991.

LEFT IN THE CENTRE? LLOYD GEORGE AND THE CENTRIST TRADITION IN BRITISH POLITICS

MARTIN PUGH

There is good reason to regard any attempt to reduce the complicated politics of David Lloyd George to a definite creed as doomed to failure; Keynes's much-quoted chameleon seems more than equal to the broad brush of historical synthesis. Yet during the last twenty years historians have re-established Lloyd George as the greatest constructive statesman of the twentieth century, and such scholars as Kenneth Morgan, John Grigg, R. J. Scally, Chris Wrigley, Michael Fry and John Campbell have, admittedly from different perspectives, drawn attention to the elements of continuity and consistency in his career.[1] However, one has the impression that scholars and students, not to mention the reading public, continue to see him largely in terms of mere rootless opportunism. It is undoubtedly easier to deal with Lloyd George's long and tempestuous career by taking him simply as a bundle of talents and ambitions largely unhindered by attachment to party, principle, programme or ideology. The high politics approach to modern history has, perhaps, strengthened this tendency. Yet the fact is that any meticulous examination of decision-making or legislation based on source material tends to give an exaggerated impression of the ad hoc, opportunistic element in the work of politicians; certainly Lloyd George, with his distinctly chaotic, hand-to-mouth methods, is vulnerable to this treatment. The other contributory factor is our British intolerance towards those politicians who fail to remain loyal to a single political party, a prejudice which claims Lloyd George as a natural victim. This has always seemed odd to me, since it is apparent that the best opportunists have often been those who stuck to their party regardless of their opinions; history is littered with examples all the way from Sir William Harcourt in the 1880's to Mr Roy Hattersley in the 1980's. But as Baldwin put it, a dynamic force is a terrible thing; and no political party has thought its own interests likely to be served by claiming men like Lloyd George or Joseph Chamberlain as its heroes. Even in the Tory ranks there is no obvious Churchillian brand of Conservatism, just a great patriotic poster and the dubious link with 'Winston' to which Margaret Thatcher periodically laid claim.

In the face of established wisdom one should not be too ambitious. There should be no attempt to deny the extraordinary features of Lloyd George, nor to ignore the flexibility and opportunism in his method. Clearly it is difficult to categorise satisfactorily any politician whose career spanned sixteen long years as a backbencher, followed by seventeen in office and finally twenty-two in opposition. A figure who could just conceivably have become the leader of any of the three main parties, and perhaps of a Welsh Nationalist Party too, must present an unusual challenge. Yet the cynical view of Lloyd George does seem doubly inadequate. It does little justice to his constructive achievements. His marked penchant for solving specific problems surely distinguishes him from the empty opportunists in politics. Also, when he is seen in a broad context it seems clear that he actually shared a good deal

---

1   K. O. Morgan, *Lloyd George*, (London, 1974); John Grigg, *The Young Lloyd George*, (London, 1973); R. J. Scally, *The Origins of the Lloyd George Coalition: the politics of social imperialism 1900-18*, (Princeton, 1975); C. J. Wrigley, *David Lloyd George and the British Labour Movement*, (Hassocks, 1976); M. G. Fry, *Lloyd George and Foreign Policy 1890-1916*, (Montreal, 1977); John Campbell, *Lloyd George: the goat in the wilderness*, (London, 1977).

with certain other politicians; there was, in short, a consistent thread of ideas and attitudes running through his career. Although a great individual he was also part of a tradition in politics. But what exactly was, or is, the tradition?

We have it on the authority of the distinguished French political scientist, Duverger, that the centre in politics is something of a geographical expression. For him the two-party system corresponded to the nature of things, for every policy implied a choice between two solutions. Consequently: the centre does not exist in politics: there may well be a Centre party but there is no centre tendency, no centre doctrine.[2]

Similarly some recent British political scientists have used the term 'centre' as a convenient label to cover several groups outside the Labour and Conservative Parties. For historians the grey area between the main parties has appeared a field of considerable interest. It is characterised by the regular ebb and flow of groups and individuals breaking away from their original party allegiance. Though some aspire to become an independent party, they invariably end in absorption by a larger one, or simply hang on for a few years before giving up the struggle. As the then Mr Roy Jenkins put it as long ago as 1956, 'centre parties have never had a happy or successful existence in England ... their lives have been difficult and depressing.'[3]

Depressing or not they have recurred persistently throughout the nineteenth and twentieth century; and, moreover, they have often had a crucial formative effect on the pattern of politics. One thinks of the Peelites in the 1840's and the 1850's, the Adullamites in the 1860's and the Liberal Unionists in the 1880's. Around the turn of the century there emerged two groups, the Liberal Imperialists and the Tory Free Traders, neither of whom broke decisively with their parent parties, though there were some notable exceptions who took the plunge. In spite of the tightening grip of party organisation in the twentieth century politics has continued to be punctuated by similar breakaways including the Coalition Liberals after the First World War, and their Conservative counterparts who remained semi-detached from their party for several years. The political and economic crisis of 1930-31 generated the New Party under Sir Oswald Mosley, the National Labour split which persisted until 1945, and the National Liberals who were not finally absorbed into the Conservative Party until 1964. After 1945 when the two-party system reached its peak in terms of the popular support commanded by Labour and the Conservatives, the impetus for centrist breakaways dwindled; there appeared to be no room for any third force, and little need for one. However, by the 1960's symptoms of discontent, including recruitment from both major parties into the Liberal ranks, heralded a return to the traditional pattern. The most conspicuous manifestation of this came in 1972 in the shape of the new Democratic Socialist Party under Dick Taverne. Subsequently the 1970's saw a wave of defections from Labour comparable to the departure of the Whigs from Gladstonian Liberalism, including Reg Prentice, Richard Marsh and George Brown to mention only some prominent examples. The climax came in 1981 with the establishment of the Social Democratic Party which, for a short time boasted the support of twenty-six former Labour MP's and one Conservative.

---

2   Maurice Duverger, *Political Parties*, (London, 1964 edition) 215.
3   Roy Jenkins, 'A Genius for Compromise?', Encounter, March, 1956, 11.

Why, in spite of the strength of feeling behind them, have these breakaways either not lasted as independent parties, or not even aspired to such a status? To this there are broadly two answers. The first is that they tend to grow out of splits at the parliamentary level; as a result they are over-endowed with senior, ministerial figures, some might say prima donnas, but find it difficult to develop an organisation in the country capable of matching their pretensions and sustaining their ambitions. The dismal fate of the Coalition Liberals in the 1920's is, perhaps, a case in point.[4] Their difficulties are, no doubt, exacerbated by the operation of the single-member, first-past-the-post electoral system. Success and even survival have been crucially dependent upon an electoral deal with one of the major parties as the fortunes of the Liberal Unionists and National Liberals suggest. But there is a further explanation, namely that the breakaways cannot put down strong enough roots because they lack the firm ground of a distinctive and coherent political position. The assumption here is that they are essentially bland or moderate versions of one or other of the main parties, and, therefore, they seem to lack a real purpose beyond that of serving to prolong the careers of their leaders for a few years. Thus, after a period of detachment centrist politicians have often accepted office under one of the main parties on the basis that in this way they would exercise a moderating influence upon them.

In Lloyd George's case the assumption that he was perpetually scheming for a return to office was commonly made after 1922. Earlier generations, however, took a more relaxed view. Walter Bagehot, for example, pointedly praised those who judiciously shifted their loyalties in order to maintain some sort of balance and continuity; the result was that British politics was almost inevitably blessed with a government of the centre, in his view, even though no party bore this label.[5] Even in the twentieth century it can be argued that politicians like Baldwin, Macmillan and Wilson have regarded the control of the centre ground as their guiding strategy. Consequently some scholars have been tempted to see the influence of centrists as an all-pervading feature of British politics. Dr. Brian Harrison, in an important study of the subject, identified a wide range of centrists from the early nineteenth century onwards.[6] These included Canning, Huskisson, Melbourne, Palmerston, Aberdeen, the fifteenth Earl of Derby, Granville, Sir Stafford Northcote, Hartington, Rosebery, Bryce, Campbell-Bannerman, Haldane, Grey, Asquith, H. A. L. Fisher, Baldwin, Astor, Lord Lothian, Samuel Hoare, Lord Halifax, Dalton, Attlee, Gaitskell, Macmillan, R. A. Butler, Macleod, Maudling, Sir Edward Boyle, Anthony Crosland, Heath, Callaghan, Healey, Geoffrey Ripon, James Prior and the leaders of the Social Democratic Party.

However, one wonders whether such a comprehensive list can represent any coherent political tradition. At the most what one has here is a tendency towards *moderation*, characterised by a relaxed Whiggish sense of politics as a matter for cautious and timely concession. What surely lies behind this view of centrism is tactics rather than political ideas and attitudes. These are statesmen largely steeped in government and conscious of the

---

4   See K. O. Morgan's essay, 'Lloyd George's Stage Army', in A. J. P. Taylor, (ed.) *Lloyd George: Twelve Essays*, (London, 1971).
5   N. St. J. Stevas (ed.), W. Bagehot, *Works*, vii, (London, 1974), 198.
6   Brian Harrison, *Peaceable Kingdom*, (Oxford, 1982), 321-22.

desirability of distancing themselves from extreme or novel policies for fear of jeopardising their tenure of office. This is principled moderation or trimming for short-term advantage, according to taste.

However, some of the notable omissions from the list suggest a different perspective on the centre of politics, and a more coherent political tradition, for example, Joseph Chamberlain, Lloyd George, and Winston Churchill. Their careers were clearly characterised by a certain detachment from party, and, taken with some of the other figures in Dr. Harrison's list, they do, I suggest, constitute a distinct political tendency. The breakaways by these individuals can scarcely be described in terms of moderation; indeed they have often been seen as extremists, or perhaps as excessively enthusiastic about ideas and policies, men who lack a proper sense of proportion. Although usually closely involved in government they have invariably been deficient in some of the skills of the politician, and their enjoyment of office has, thus, been a matter of luck rather than judgement in spite of their reputation for opportunism. In Lloyd George's case no one would wish to credit him with a full-blown political philosophy. His whole approach was essentially practical, and never left room or inclination for the production of a considered statement of his creed. Yet there seems sufficient consistency in his political ideas and in his approach to the problems of politics to enable us to place him squarely within a political tradition in British life which is discernable from the time of Joseph Chamberlain onwards.

What is distinctive in this tradition is not so much the ideas as the mixture of attitudes: on the one hand a positive view of the state and a tendency towards intervention in domestic affairs, on the other hand a bold, patriotic approach to defence, foreign and imperial questions. The point is that politicians with this kind of combination can pursue their careers within the two main parties, but are not completely comfortable in either of them. Thence the recurrent breakaways, new parties and defections. It may reasonably be suggested that the proper description for this phenomenon is social imperialism, and several historians have placed Lloyd George in this context.[7] While not quarrelling with much of what they say, I hesitate to use this concept largely because social imperialism seems to arise in a rather narrower context. It is seen as a strategy by the governing classes for attaining working-class acquiescence in the status quo and the maintenance of the empire by means of certain concessions on social welfare, if you like a Bismarckian view which finds its closest echo in the young Churchill or Lord Milner. Also social imperialism is a typical product of late-nineteenth century fears about the vulnerability of the British Empire, whereas I am suggesting a wider and more continuous tradition. Modern centrism is not limited to social reform but extends to the wider role of the state in economic affairs; nor is it something that dies when Britain's colonies gain their independence. In the second half of the twentieth century such issues as Britain's role in Europe and her claim to be an independent nuclear power have been central for the group of politicians under discussion. Finally, there is also a matter of temperament and style to be taken into account. The centrists manifest a single-minded

---

7   Bernard Semmel, *Imperialism and Social Reform*, (London, 1960); R. J. Scally, *The Origins of the Lloyd George Coalition*.

enthusiasm for solutions and a corresponding disregard for orthodoxy and caution, which results in what might well be described as a *managerialist* approach to government.

For Lloyd George it is significant that from quite early in his political apprenticeship he had before him a prominent alternative to party orthodoxy in the shape of Joseph Chamberlain whose career reflects the classic dilemmas of centrist politicians in Britain. Although successful up to a point in winning the Liberals to his domestic radicalism and interventionism, he was checked by the prevailing Gladstonian approach to Ireland, empire and foreign affairs even among many domestic radicals. Nor was his position wholly satisfactory after 1895 when he joined Lord Salisbury's Conservative government. The new situation was the reverse of that in the Liberal Party; now he could work with the grain in external affairs, but could not risk pursuing his domestic ideas very far. His most imaginative attempt to break out of his position by recreating the Tory Party in a centrist mould came with the tariff reform campaign from 1903, which brought together the themes of internal reconstruction and patriotism in a most satisfying way. Yet, again, Chamberlain found that, as with the Liberals he could lead them only so far in the desired direction.[8]

The point is that for Lloyd George Chamberlain exercised a considerable fascination whether originally as a hero or subsequently as a renegade and rival. By 1885 when his growing ambition should have made him into a sound Gladstonian he had come to feel the attraction of Chamberlain's ideas, and regarded him as the future of Liberalism. So much so that several acquaintances picked up the notion that in May 1886 he was on the verge of aligning himself publicly with him over the Irish Home Rule controversy.[9] It is impossible to know how close he came, but in the event he wisely avoided joining the Liberal Unionists; yet he continued to exhibit the symptoms of dissatisfaction with Liberal orthodoxy that had provoked their revolt.

This, of course, was obscured from many of his contemporaries by his devotion to questions of concern to his constituency, Wales and the Nonconformist Churches, as well as to his prominent role as a critic of Chamberlain during the Boer War. However, it is generally agreed now that Lloyd George was neither a pacifist nor a Little Englander. During the 1890's issues such as the extension of British control in Uganda and the near-clash with the French at Fashoda found Lloyd George sympathising with expansionist imperial policies; he was consequently detached from many of the radicals who in other ways were natural allies, and looked to the man upon whom, their criticisms focussed, Lord Rosebery. Lloyd George's direct knowledge of the empire was limited to a short visit to Canada which impressed him for the scope it offered to enterprising British citizens. His perspective does not seem to have been clouded by any interest in or concern for the non-European peoples in South Africa, or, later in his career, in India; rather he viewed the empire from the point of view of its material value to Britain. That British influence in South Africa should be extended, perhaps along the lines of a confederation of states as had been achieved in Canada,

---

8   This emerges strongly from Alan Sykes, *Tariff Reform in British Politics 1903-13*, (Oxford, 1979).
9   John Grigg, *The Young Lloyd George*, 51; J. Hugh Edwards. *The Life of David Lloyd George*, II, (London, 1913), 143; E. H. Spender, *The Prime Minister*, (London, 1920), 46.

was perfectly legitimate and desirable; he simply considered Chamberlain's use of war to attain this objective as unnecessary and reckless.

The significance of Lloyd George's attitude is underlined by the manner in which he handled the party politics of the South African controversy. He was conspicuously reluctant to do the obvious thing, namely to capitalise on his reputation as a pro-Boer by moving closer to the party leader, Campbell-Bannerman. Instead he went out of his way to praise Rosebery who, by 1901 had begun to pose what looked like a very serious challenge for the leadership of the party. Even Lloyd George's famous meeting at Birmingham in December 1901, in which he was the victim of the Chamberlainite mob, was conducted under the chairmanship of a Liberal Imperialist and was designed to carry the message that Rosebery's bold initiative in his Chesterfield speech should be followed up, and that he was indispensable to the Liberal Party.[10]   In fact this made good sense in the context of Lloyd George's fundamental approach. Rosebery now stood out as a more attractive and exciting leader than Campbell-Bannerman who appeared to remain trapped in the tired faddism of the National Liberal Federation. Lloyd George appreciated the Liberal Imperialists' brisk attitude to the Irish problem in terms of Home Rule All Round; this would have the advantage of cutting the Irish Question down to size, helping to resolve Welsh demands, and yet retaining a strong and coherent British state. Moreover, Rosebery appeared to be more in touch with social and urban problems than the more orthodox Liberals, and his combination of patriotism and national efficiency seemed to offer the best means of enabling the party to regain its former popularity in the country.

Lloyd George found himself in much the same awkward position when the next major controversy arose over Balfour's 1902 Education Act. Reasons of party tactics pointed to energetic opposition to the measure. But his reaction to the government's proposals was rather like that of Liberal Imperialists like Haldane: it was a constructive and very necessary measure of interventionism by the state in social policy.[11]   Clearly what attracted Lloyd George in the politics of Rosebery and the Liberal Imperialists was essentially what had appealed in Chamberlain's earlier campaigns. In the event Rosebery's personal inadequacy as an alternative leader, and the failure of the Liberal Imperialists to develop their alternative programme, in favour of some amateurish manoeuvring for office, left something of a gap. Consequently, as Lloyd George recognised, the Liberals soon became vulnerable to an outflanking movement in the shape of Chamberlain's post-1903 campaign. Indeed, his greatest service to his party was his capacity to respond to this challenge. He came close to acknowledging that they were competitors in the same race in 1910, when he delivered what was virtually a public tribute to Chamberlain for his recent campaign, which, he said, had:

10   H. Du Parcq, *Life of David Lloyd George*, II, (London, 1913), 301-3; Marquess of Crewe, *Lord Rosebery*, II, (London, 1931), 589-91.
11   D. Lloyd George to Margaret Lloyd George, 24 March, 1902, K. O. Morgan, (ed.) *Lloyd George: family letters 1885-1936*, (Cardiff, 1973), 131-2.

... rendered one outstanding service to the cause of the masses. It has helped to call attention to a number of real crying evils festering amongst us, the existence of which the governing classes in this country are ignorant of or had overlooked.[12]

And he went on to recite the chief propositions in Chamberlain's case culminating in the recognition that 'the time has come for seeking a remedy, not in voluntary effort, but in bold and comprehensive action on the part of the state'.

The second phase of Lloyd George's career as a minister under Campbell-Bannerman and Asquith provides a good example of a period in which it proved possible for a centrist to work successfully within the framework of a major party, the other outstanding one being the 1945-51 Attlee administration. Essentially Lloyd George was able to follow his own political instincts in the shape of a series of major interventionist measures on the domestic front combined with the development of a coherent policy in national defence and foreign relations. While his work as Chancellor is well-known it is worth emphasising here the significance ideologically of his initial experience as President of the Board of Trade from 1905 to 1908. There he performed his immediate political task by providing a spirited, if ritual, defence of free trade. But his detailed policy-making, somewhat to the general surprise, involved him in a number of measures for the regulation and stimulation of private business. One should not exaggerate the significance of this. Lloyd George had not become a protectionist as some contemporaries like to suggest. But he showed both that as a free trader he would stand up for the British interests when other states infringed them, and also that he regarded the state as, at the least, a necessary complement to individual enterprise.

Also telling is the stance Lloyd George adopted on wider matters that fell outside his own remit during the Edwardian period. For example, he continued to downgrade the Irish problem, treating it in a distinctly matter-of-fact way as it began to return to the centre of the stage. Speaking in Belfast in 1907 he declared the separation of Ireland from the empire as 'unthinkable'; in 1910 he returned to his earlier preference for a federal solution; and by 1912 he had reached the conclusion that the matter could only be resolved on the basis of the exclusion of Ulster from any Irish Parliament.[13] Of much greater importance was the steady evolution of Lloyd George's position in defence and foreign policy. Although he seemed to be throwing his weight sometimes for and sometimes against the Grey-Haldane policy based on the idea of the continental commitment, his attitude was, in fact, much more consistent. His increasingly threadbare reputation as a natural opponent of war rested on little more than some well-publicised remarks about the need to retain the friendship of Germany, and on his battles in cabinet to restrict the naval estimates proposed by McKenna and Churchill. It is difficult to escape the conclusion that much of this was shadow-boxing. Even when, as in 1911, there was a good case for adopting a more relaxed view of the naval threat on account

12   Speech, 17 October 1910, John Grigg, *Lloyd George: the People's Champion 1902-11*, (London, 1978), 269-70.

13   K. O. Morgan, 'Lloyd George and the Irish', Lord Blake (ed.) *Ireland After the Union*, (Oxford, 1989), 88-89.

of the exaggeration of Germany's actual rate of building, he failed to win substantial reductions. Essentially, in spite of some face-saving deals, he provided the money required for the Dreadnought programme. Hence Lord Esher's comment: 'Lloyd George in his heart does not care a bit for economy', he wrote, 'he is plucky and an imperialist at heart if he is anything'.[14]

What was less clear at the time was Lloyd George's growing familiarity with the strategic ideas of the experts on the Committee of Imperial Defence, though his growing alarm at German belligerence was, of course, well-publicised. His famous Mansion House speech in 1911 expressed in less conventional language the central assumption of Sir Edward Grey's policy, namely that it was in Britain's national interest to ensure that France was maintained in her position as a great power. And it is interesting that in the 1913 he seems to have played a similar role during the Balkan War. This time it was a matter of using the Mansion House speech to issue a warning to Austria against undue provocation of Russia. As a result Lloyd George appears to have been intellectually committed to British participation in a continental war well before 1914. He had already begun to prepare his erstwhile supporters for the shock, noting on one occasion that he had been engaged in 'an endeavour to inculcate a little common sense and patriotism into the head of (C.P.) Scott'.[15] In the crisis of July 1914 he showed Scott the results of his involvement with official policy by explaining the process by which a major war would break out, and the military dilemma that Britain's Expeditionary Force was designed to tackle. This was before Austria had attacked Serbia. Nor was there any indication, as might have been expected in a conversation with a Liberal like Scott, that the violation of Belgian territory was of any more than incidental importance for British participation in the conflict; the B.E.F. must be thrown into the struggle primarily to redress the crucial strategic weakness of the Dual Alliance powers. Thus, as Frances Stevenson crisply summed up the position:

> L. G.'s mind was really made up from the first, that he knew we would
> have to go in, and that the invasion of Belgium was, to be cynical, a heaven-
> sent excuse for supporting a declaration of war.[16]

The one really striking indication of dissatisfaction with the party straightjacket on Lloyd George's part came in 1910 in the form of his proposals for a coalition government with the Conservatives as a way out of the constitutional deadlock. Since several historians have explored this initiative thoroughly there is no need here to go over the ground in detail.[17] What seems worth emphasising is what the episode reveals about the strengths and weaknesses of Lloyd George's centrism. First, the whole initiative was characteristic in so far as it was

---

14   Esher's diary, 12 February 1909, Viscount Esher, *Journals and Letters*, vol. II, (London, 1934), 370.

15   A. C. Murray's diary, 22 July 1911, T. Wislon, (ed.) *The Political Diaries of C. P. Scott 1911-1928*, (London, 1970), 46.

16   Frances Stevenson, *The Years That Are Past*, (London, 1967), 73-4.

17   G. R. Searle, *The Quest for National Efficiency*, (Oxford, 1971); J. D. Fair, *British Inter-Party Conferences*, (Oxford, 1980); R. J. Scally, *Origins of the Lloyd George Coalition*.

provoked by sheer frustration at being checked by the opposition to his schemes for National Insurance; as in the past he began to cast around for a neat, decisive means of unblocking his path. Secondly, however, it does remind us how unrealistic Lloyd George could be when he allowed himself to become absorbed by the search for immediate solutions to his problems. There was, after all, little chance of the leaders of either party accepting his scheme, and, had they done so, the effect on Liberal morale, in particular, would have been highly damaging, as was the case in May 1915 when a coalition was sprung upon the party. Thirdly, the proposals met with a warm response only from those like Churchill and F. E. Smith who shared something of Lloyd George's own detachment from the conventional parties. At this stage they lacked the influence to breathe life into the scheme; but the ground had been laid for effective cross-party collaboration in more favourable circumstances.

The Great War was not only the third and climactic phase of Lloyd George's career, it also proved to be the most satisfying period from the perspective of centrist politics. For the war concentrated in office many of the individuals who most closely reflected Lloyd George's own approach to government, and at the same time it went some way to discrediting the more orthodox party alternatives. The bold managerial approach to the problems of government manifested itself during the first two years of war in Lloyd George's work in connection with munitions, his abortive but characteristic efforts to subject the brewing industry to state control, and in his support for conscription. But it was when he attained the premiership in December 1916 that he began to enjoy real scope for implementing his ideas. All that can be done here is to draw attention to three main features of this period.

In the first place the war offered Lloyd George a fine opportunity to indulge in a good deal of hasty, ad hoc innovation involving interventionism in economic and social life including the experiments with manpower planning, regulation of prices, rationing of food, and the management of several major industries. In the second place the crisis inevitably brought to the fore Lloyd George's simmering antagonism towards the Gladstonians in the Liberal and Labour Parties in foreign affairs. In the long run this breach was probably of fundamental importance in preventing Lloyd George from recapturing the support of the Liberal Party even in the later 1920's when he was offering them an attractive and potentially life-saving domestic programme. The peace settlement brought him up against one of the more self-righteous of Gladstonians in the person of President Woodrow Wilson. However, he largely succeeded in defending what he understood to be British national interests; thus the German navy was safely disposed of, the threat from nationalism in the empire was held off, and Britain actually attained her peak as a colonial power by means of the mandated territories acquired from Germany. Lloyd George also seems to have shared Clemenceau's sceptical view of the new approach to diplomacy and the idea of the League of Nations; it was worth going along with the establishment of the League as a sop to Woodrow Wilson provided one was reasonably sure that the organisation would lack the power to threaten British interests. His own post-war diplomacy, though obviously resented by the traditionalists of the foreign office, was nonetheless very much in the old style.

Thirdly the crisis of war allowed Lloyd George to undertake some characteristic innovations in the methods and personnel of government. In many ways this meant putting into practice the ideas of the Edwardian National Efficiency enthusiasts. In particular he attempted to cut through the web of the existing bureaucracy both by establishing new departments and ministries to tackle specific problems, and also by using his own personal secretariat to provide an alternative source of information and advice. Significantly a number of the posts were filled with the 'men of push and go', the experts and businessmen with whom Lloyd George had become familiar at the Board of Trade and the Ministry of Munitions. In several cases they had little or no party political connection, but owed their appointment to the relevant knowledge or talents they could bring to a job. Perhaps the classic example was Sir Eric Geddes, a skilled railway manager and nominal Conservative. Although he had little or no interest in a long-term political career, Geddes's enthusiasm for pragmatic interventionism made him susceptible to Lloyd George's appeals to continue in office until 1922.[18] Rapid and efficient decision-making was also the ostensible object behind the new five-man War Cabinet and its supporting secretariat. Although it seemed advisable at this level to conciliate the political parties by the inclusion of Bonar Law and Arthur Henderson, there is surely a deeper significance in Lloyd George's decision to include Lord Milner in the war cabinet. In some ways it seems an odd decision given that there had been very little previous contact between the two men and that they had been on opposite sides in the Boer War. Yet Lloyd George told Lord Riddell, 'Milner and I stand for the same things.' Milner, too, had distanced himself from his early Liberalism, moved towards Chamberlainism, and become a rather pronounced advocate of imperial development. But he combined this with advocacy of state-financed social welfare and a keen appreciation of the patriotism and loyalty of the working classes. For Milner Lloyd George was a natural leader by reason of his capacity to harness this potential support, and thereby outflank both the old and, in his view, discredited parties. For Lloyd George the Milnerite vision, though not immediately practical, did suggest one way out of the confusion of wartime politics and a possible solution to the centrist dilemma.

———

The end of the war raised in acute form the question of Lloyd George's future in politics; and because the war had had a disturbing effect on each of the existing parties, though some more than others, it offered the opportunity to make a fresh start with a new national or centre party. the building bricks for such an enterprise would have included some of Lloyd George's Coalition Liberals, patriotic Labour allies like John Hodge, detached figures like Churchill and Geddes, recruits from the Milnerite ranks, and a number of the more independently minded Conservatives such as F. E. Smith, Lord Beaverbrook and Nancy Astor. The common factor was that all of these were uncomfortably placed in the existing party framework, and might have rallied around Lloyd George's blend of domestic and external policies.

In the event expectations about the birth of the new centre party, proved optimistic, and by 1920 the whole idea was losing credibility. Yet the enterprise does not seem to have

———

18   Keith Grieves, *Sir Eric Geddes: business and government in war and peace*, (Manchester, 1989), p.70, 102.

been inherently doomed, but rather to have been checked by poor decision-making and inconvenient conditions. Above all, Lloyd George allowed himself to be trapped by the huge electoral victory he had won in 1918. Though unwieldy the Coalition's very size seemed to promise a full term of office; it was difficult to resist making the most of that especially as Lloyd George's enemies on the left were longing to see him fall. Yet in effect he was leader of a government which, from the long-term perspective, should have been broken up. In this position the strictly conditional loyalty given to him by Bonar Law and Austen Chamberlain represented a major problem. Willing to keep him in office they would not seriously contemplate helping him to dismember the Tory Party in order to establish a new force in politics. As a Result of this and of his own tendency to become immersed in a series of international and domestic issues, Lloyd George failed to take the initiative. In retrospect 1918 would probably have been the best moment even though it would have meant going into opposition for a time. Subsequently he might well have made a stand over an issue such as Addison's housing programme and challenged the progressive Tories to take the risk of backing him. But he allowed himself instead to be pushed by pressure from the right, and inevitably lost many of the allies necessary for a centrist party as a result. The whole enterprise would have been easier to launch from a position in opposition, but by the time he got there he was no longer the political asset he had been four years earlier.

The failure to establish a party that would be a better fit for his own views condemned Lloyd George to wander the political system during the 1920's and 1930's widely condemned as an adventurer but still faithful to his centrist creed. For example if one looks at his position on Ireland and the empire it is noticeable how the effect of the war had been to accentuate but not change the evolution of his views. War helped to heighten his belief in the value of Britain's overseas possessions; and his four-year dependence on his Conservative allies had made him even more impatient with the Irish demand for self-government. For a time he hoped to avoid having to deal with Ireland again, and contented himself with a crude policy of physical suppression of the nationalist forces. Only when driven by the failure of this desperate approach did he bring his skills to bear in order to reach a settlement based on the exclusion of Ulster.

During the 1920's he displayed a similar impatience with other nationalist movements. In 1921 for example he took Lord Curzon's side in arguing against conceding a measure of self-determination to the Egyptians, basically because he felt this would undermine imperial strategy and communications. Over India, as is well-known, he declined to support his Liberal Secretary of State, Edwin Montagu, when he faced attack over his condemnation of General Dyer for his part in the Amritsar Massacre. This was no doubt partly because of fear of alienating the Conservatives, but he was himself unsympathetic towards the Indian National Congress and the influence it was winning under Gandhi's leadership. Nor did he appear to modify this view. In 1929 when Lord Irwin sought the backing of the party leaders for his proposal to offer Congress a promise of Dominion Status, Lloyd George followed the advice of Lord Reading, an ex-Viceroy, in declining the request. It was left to Baldwin and MacDonald to accede to Irwin's request. He justified this on the grounds that Indians were too diverse and too backward politically to be capable of governing themselves. In view of the progress already made towards Indian participation in both regional government and in the

Indian Civil Service this was a distinctly reactionary position, the more so when contrasted with the relatively liberal attitude of the Labour and Conservative leaders.

Finally the mid-1920's saw Lloyd George taking up once again the threads of his social and economic interventionism in the shape of the remarkable series of enquiries which he instituted culminating in the Liberal Industrial Enquiry and the publication of *Britain's Industrial Future* in 1928. Although now fortified by the ideas of J. M. Keynes, Walter Layton, William Beveridge and other authorities, his reconstruction strategy can be seen as essentially an extension and elaboration of the simple and undeveloped public works proposals embodied in his 1909 budget. Given the depth and persistence of the economic depression at least in several regions throughout the 1930's it is not surprising that the theme of state-engineered reconstruction continued to occupy him during the remainder of his career. It requires no further comment here except, perhaps, for the light it throws on another feature of Lloyd George in the 1930's, namely his sympathetic view of the Nazi regime in Germany especially after his visit to Hitler in 1936.[19] I think it might be possible to account for his attitude in several ways. He took a lenient view of several of the initiatives of German foreign policy, doubtless out of a sense that he had failed to get things right at Versailles. He also displayed throughout his life some prejudice against the Jews which was, of course, by no means unusual at this time. But I would also suggest that he found himself captivated by the notion of a Hitler boldly reconstructing his country - a role which, after all, he himself had hoped to play in Britain. One can see something of this admiration for firm constructive government in several similar inter-war politicians, for example, in Mosley's view of the fascist states, and in Hugh Dalton's enthusiasm for the interventionism of Mussolini's Italy as well as Stalin's Russia.[20] Common to all three politicians was an attraction for ideas and an enthusiasm for the bold managerial style of government. It hardly needs to be said that the other side of the coin was a certain blindness to the wider political context in which the ideas were applied.

What has happened to the centrist tradition in the period since 1931 when Lloyd George was pushed towards the periphery of politics? One can argue that a number of politicians have faced the same kind of dilemmas as he did. Mosley provides the most extreme example of, if you will, centrism plus electrification. It has been much easier to see this as a result of Robert Skidelsky's study which showed that Mosley espoused a considered and coherent range of policies, not merely the anti-semitism with which he eventually became associated, and that he had in full measure the penchant for diagnosing fundamental problems that is so typical of centrists.[21] With his experience in both the major parties Mosley knew how uncomfortable a fit each of them was. The combination of his wartime service and his six years in the Labour Party left him with a strongly interventionist streak in his approach to

---

19   A. J. Sylvester, *The Real Lloyd George*, (London, 1947), 202.
20   Ben Pimlott, *Hugh Dalton*, (London, 1985), 211-16.
21   Robert Skidelsky, *Oswald Mosley*, (London, 1975), 302-15.

social welfare, central regulation of investment, the direction of resources and Keynesian methods of stimulating the economy. This complemented his bold, not to say foolhardy, desire to use the markets and resources of the British Empire to safeguard British jobs. The protectionist-imperial element in his programme marks out Mosley's politics as the point where Milnerite Conservatism meets a certain sort of British socialism. Mosley's views were readily intelligible and even attractive to politicians in both parties if not wholly acceptable in either.

On the Conservative side Winston Churchill stands out as a figure who shows a similar erratic pattern to that of Lloyd George and Mosley in terms both of his mixture of views, his enthusiasm for specific solutions, and his inept handling of the party political regulars. Admittedly one has the impression that the domestic interventionist side of his politics dwindled during the later decades of his long career, though this is to some extent simply the result of his excessive absorption in external policy; also the recent reassessment of his post-1951 administration by Anthony Seldon suggests more continuity with the constructive Edwardian Churchill than one might have supposed.[22] After Churchill it is the figure of Harold Macmillan that demands some consideration on the grounds of the views he expressed during the barren years under the National Governments, and the propensity for interventionism in economic and social affairs which characterised his governments after 1956. With Macmillan one enters the post-imperial world, but it can be argued that as a centrist Macmillan tried hard to maintain Britain's role and status as a great power. Hence the importance attached to the independent nuclear deterrent during his premiership. Also significant is the readiness with which he adopted the cause of British entry into the European Economic Community; for over and above its potential economic advantages Europe was regarded as a means of restoring the influence in the world that Britain had enjoyed as the head of a great empire.

This approach was reflected in the succeeding generation of Conservatives by men like Reginald Maudling and Edward Heath. It has, it is true, become fashionable recently to regard Heath as an unsuccessful precursor of Mrs Thatcher and her brand of Conservatism on the basis of the policy revision undertaken prior to his electoral victory in 1970. Against this, however, it has been pointed out that his attempted innovations in terms of anti-union legislation, reshaping of state welfare and avoidance of excessive state support for industry were in fact both peripheral and short-lived. He retained the managerial-interventionist view of government, which he probably acquired, like many other Tories who had seen wartime service, from a conviction that the state owed a duty towards its less fortunate citizens. His attachment to Europe similarly springs from his experience of appeasement in the late 1930's and the Second World War.[23] The marked absence of the same kind of broad experience in Mrs Thatcher's shorter political life helps to account for the basic divide between them in both domestic and external affairs. Finally one notes that for politicians of both the Macmillan and Heath generations it proved possible to pursue centrist politics within the existing party framework, though at the cost of some lengthy periods out of office and on the periphery of the party. Amongst the many rebels within the post-1979 Conservative Party the one whose

22   See Peter Henessy and Anthony Seldon, *Ruling Performance*, (Oxford, 1987), 64-6.
23   Hugo Young, *One of Us*, (London, 1984), 53-8.

approach appears most nearly to reflect that of the earlier centrists is Mr Michael Heseltine. Widely seen as opportunist, plausible and ambitious, he has deliberately emphasised both his strong stand on defence and his readiness to intervene in economic and social problems.[24] His political hero, apparently, is Lloyd George. In 1990 his dilemma was not unlike that of Joseph Chamberlain a century earlier, waiting for the retirement of the G.O.M.

Turning, finally, to the Labour side of politics one sees some conspicuous exponents of centrism amongst some of the early Fabians. The stance of, for example, the Webbs over the Boer War and the First World War, combined with their detailed grasp of the idea of the benevolent state made them natural allies of Tory and Liberal advocates of National Efficiency at the turn of the century and during the Edwardian period. A more popular expression of the centrist mixture was associated with Robert Blatchford's publications including the *Clarion*, *Merrie England* (1895), and *Britain for the British* (1902). Widely credited with having made more converts to socialism than any other propagandist Blatchford criticised orthodox Labour for the same reason he criticised the Liberals, namely that he disliked their cosmopolitanism, their tendency towards pacifism, and their slowness to recognise the challenge from Germany. Also, although not formally a supporter of Chamberlain, he could see that protectionism and socialism were perfectly compatible in spite of the fondness for free trade amongst many Labour leaders. He warmed to the patriotic cause of defending British jobs by excluding the products of foreign labour from the home markets.[25]

By the 1920's the Webbs were working constructively within the Labour Party alongside former Liberal Imperialists like Richard Haldane and a number of ex-Conservatives; the latter have not, as a group, received the attention from historians that they deserve. From the centrist perspective the inter-war Labour Party was, like Edwardian Liberalism, a serviceable but imperfect vehicle; it suffered somewhat from a tendency to be weak and woolly in defence and foreign affairs. However, between the wars Labour's official position gradually shifted via advocacy of collective security towards limited rearmament, and this left the idealistic Liberals like Arthur Ponsonby and the pacifist-socialists like George Lansbury increasingly marginalised. In the process one sees the emergence of several classic Labour centrists such as Hugh Dalton and Ernest Bevin. Dalton in particular was a rather extreme, or perhaps arrogant, centrist, combining a highly patriotic, even chauvinistic, view of the world and Britain's role in it, with bold support for the state as an economic manager.[26] Nor can one read his diary without being impressed by his detached, even contemptuous, attitude towards his own party, and his preference for ideas and the individuals who shared his interest in them. That there was no centrist revolt by this generation of Labour politicians is an indication that under both the wartime coalition and under post-1951 Attlee governments they enjoyed considerable scope for pursuing their approach to politics. With its right-wing stance in defence and foreign affairs and its unequalled record of constructive domestic legislation Attlee's cabinet occupied much the same territory as the pre-1914 Asquith administration had done. In these circumstances the conditions for a breakaway by Labour centrists did not arise.

---

24   Julian Critchley, *Heseltine*, (London, 1987), 26, 36, 49-52, 75-8.

25   B. Semmel, *Imperialism and Social Reform*, 227-28.

26   Ben Pimlott, *Hugh Dalton*, 40-43, 211-16, 241-42.

In the period since the 1950's one is tempted to locate a younger generation of Labour centrists among the followers of Hugh Gaitskell, notably Roy Jenkins. His early support for British entry into the European Economic Community seems to mark him out as a member of the same political generation as Edward Heath, particularly as he regarded the political reasons for membership as of greater importance than the economic.[27] In many ways, however, it is Dr David Owen who has articulated the centrist dilemma most sharply in recent years. While his ideas lack originality, the blend of attitudes towards external and internal policy seems distinctive in a way that is true of earlier centrist politicians; drawn by the humanity and interventionism of one political party and yet also by the patriotism of the other, Owen could never fit comfortably in either of them. Nor, as he correctly saw, was the Liberal Party a much better fit.[28]

It is not only their political creed that seems to place figures like Lloyd George, Chamberlain, Churchill and Owen in the same company as centrists, but also something characteristic in their style and approach to politics. They appear to take an unusual satisfaction in policies, their interest reaching at times the level of an obsession with getting each one absolutely right - a characteristic most politicians would regard as self-indulgence. Throughout his career Lloyd George was apt to assume that if each discrete problem were diagnosed and the right solution applied, then the wider problems of party management would also be resolved. This penchant for realistic and bold solutions manifested itself in his attitude towards the Balfour Education Act, his legislation at the Board of Trade, his coalition proposals in 1910, his restructuring of the cabinet in wartime, in his exhausting post-war diplomacy, his economic plans of the 1920's and in his fruitless negotiations with Ramsay MacDonald during 1929-31. The flaw lay in a reluctance to recognise clearly the party implications of policy innovation, and to appreciate how insignificant the detail was for most of his political opponents. In a similar fashion Chamberlain had miscalculated over his party by his rash decision in 1886, and, in a sense, in 1903 too. Churchill committed a series of errors in his relations with both Liberal and Conservative Parties, although, as his career was eventually rescued triumphantly, this has seemed less obvious than it is. Mosley, too, made a colossal, and unforced blunder in 1930; had he remained in the Labour Party for another year after placing his economic proposals before the cabinet and the party conference, he would subsequently have enjoyed a very strong position as one who had, in a sense, been right. During the 1980's the rapid rise and fall of Dr Owen has been the result of a similar intransigence over policy on defence, and of a stubbornly negative attitude towards merger after the 1987 general election which saw him completely outmanoeuvred; as a result he eventually lost most of his own supporters rather as Chamberlain did in 1886. Consequently history will perhaps record of Chamberlain, Lloyd George and Owen not only that they suffered the misfortune of splitting one political party, but that they showed sheer carelessness in splitting two.

---

27   John Campbell, *Roy Jenkins*, (London, 1983), 37-9, 59-60.
28   David Owen, *A Future That Works*, (London, 1984), 146-47; P. F. Clarke, 'Liberals and Social Democrats in Historical Perspective', V. Bogdanor, (ed.) *Liberal Party Politics*, (Oxford, 1983), 27-42.

LLOYD GEORGE AND NONCONFORMITY

G. I. T. MACHIN

Among the multitude of studies which have begun to explore the fascinating enigma which was David Lloyd George, comparatively little has been said on the theme of Lloyd George and Nonconformity. This is somewhat surprising in view of the great reciprocal influence which the two forces had on each other. This paper will briefly examine the different strands of the theme and make a few suggestions concerning it.

The period between Lloyd George's taking up residence in Wales, aged two months, in 1863 and his entry to Parliament for Caernarvon Boroughs in 1890 encompassed a generation in which Welsh Nonconformity rose greatly in political strength and ambition. Nonconformity had over seventy-five per cent of the churchgoers in Wales at the time of the Religious Census of 1851, though this was only about half the Welsh population. The Liberation Society, a London-based organization which aimed at disestablishment throughout the United Kingdom, commenced an effective campaign in Wales in 1862. By the 1880's, Nonconformist claims had become partly representative of a growing sense of Welsh nationalism in cultural, educational, and political forms. The extension of the parliamentary franchise in the later nineteenth century (the reforms of 1884 and 1885 having a marked effect in Wales), the introduction of the secret ballot in 1872, the virtual elimination of electoral corruption from 1883, and the coming of democratically elected councils through the Local Government Act of 1888, had the collective result of practically removing landlord domination from Welsh politics. Membership of both Parliament and local councils was opened more widely to middle class persons, a great many of whom were Nonconformist and most of whom sought to realise reforming aims through the Liberal party. That party's growing radicalism was particularly evident after the secession of most Whigs in 1886. Among these aims were matters of concern to Nonconformists as such, including disestablishment, which was encouraged by its attainment in Ireland in 1869; the extension of undenominational education through the Board School system inaugurated in 1870; the abolition of tithes; and the confirmation of equal burial rights in parish churchyards which were granted by the Burial Laws Amendment Act of 1880.[1] Temperance, though less specifically related to Nonconformist politics, was of great concern to Dissenters as to many others, and reform of the land laws relied greatly on Nonconformist support. Anglican Liberal assistance was given to such aims, not least by Gladstone who committed himself to Welsh disestablishment in a speech of 1889. There was general Nonconformist consensus over these aims in Wales: interdenominational differences such as the comparative conservatism of Calvinistic Methodism vis-à-vis the radicalism of Congregationalists and Baptists were much less than they had been in previous years.[2]

An important indication of the growing strength behind these claims was a rise in the number of Nonconformists returned by Welsh constituencies from none in 1865 to twenty-two (out of the total of thirty-four M.Ps for Wales) in 1892.[3] Lloyd George grew up to ride the

1   K. Morgan, *Wales in British Politics, 1868-1922* (2nd ed., Cardiff, 1970), 1-119.
2   Ibid., 17; G.I.T. Machin, 'A Welsh Church Rate Fracas, Aberystwyth, 1832-3', *Welsh History Review*, vi.2 (1973), 462-8.
3   K. Morgan, op. cit., 18, 119.

crest of this tide. His return to Parliament was one of seven by-election successes for young Nonconformist Liberals in Wales from 1888 to 1890, and he went to Westminster full of radical fervour, representing the home rule demand of *Cymru Fydd* as well as the claims of temperance and disestablishment.

Lloyd George seemed to have impeccable credentials as a representative of radical Nonconformity. His father, who died when he was eighteen months old, was an orthodox or Particular Baptist; and his mother and her brother (his uncle Richard Lloyd, who acted as a father to his sister's children) were members of a small Baptist secessionist sect, the Disciples at Christ. The Disciples of Criccieth were the product of two Baptist secessions. In 1798 the Rev. J.R. Jones of Ramoth in Merioneth, searching for pure and apostolic Christianity, seceded from the main Baptist denomination (the Particular Baptists) and attached himself to the Scotch Baptists. These had been founded in Edinburgh in 1765 by Robert Carmichael and Archibald McLean. They dispensed with a trained and paid ministry, and provided for the oversight of each congregation by non-stipendiary ministers or elders. The Scotch Baptists spread not only in Scotland but also, to a small extent, in England and Wales, though they eventually died out as a separate body. Several Baptist chapels in north-west Wales followed the example of J.R. Jones, and formed a Welsh enclave of the sect.

Lloyd George's grandfather, David Lloyd, shoemaker of Llanystumdwy, was minister of one of these chapels, Capel Ucha at Pen-y-maes, Criccieth. He was later followed in both his shoemaking and his non-stipendiary ministerial capacities by his son Richard (Lloyd George's 'Uncle Lloyd'). In what they saw as the still fuller attainment of pristine Christianity, the Criccieth congregation left the Scotch Baptists in 1841 and joined the new Baptist sect of Campbellites or Disciples of Christ, founded in America by Alexander Campbell. The Disciples rejected formal creeds, took holy communion every Sunday, and held that literal interpretation of the Scriptures was the sole basis of Christian belief. Rather like the Quakers, they rejected a salaried ministry as being contrary to early Christian practice and dispensed with the title of Reverend. The chapel at Criccieth eventually became too small for its expanding congregation and was replaced by a larger one, called Berea chapel, in 1886. Six years previously Richard Lloyd, obviously a successful preacher, had given up his shoemaking business (in which he was a small proprietor, employing one or two assistants) in order to devote more time to his chapel. He had moved to Criccieth from Llanystumdwy, and was thereafter supported both by voluntary contributions from his flock and, later, by doing book-keeping work for the solicitors' firm (Lloyd George and George) established by his nephews, the brothers David Lloyd George and William George. The Disciples of Christ eventually joined the Welsh Baptist Union in the 1930s, and thus came more into the Baptist mainstream.[4] A prominent Disciple in America has been Ronald Reagan.

---

4   G. Yuille, ed., *History of the Baptists in Scotland* (Glasgow, 1926), 44-54; D.W. Bebbington, ed., *The Baptists in Scotland, a History* (Glasgow, 1988), 15-24; W.R.P. George, *The Making of Lloyd George* (London, 1976), 17-20, 26-7; J.H. Edwards, *The Life of David Lloyd George* (4 vols., London, 1913-18), ii.57-65. The name Berea was taken from that of a Grecian town visited by St. Paul: the inhabitants 'received the word with all readiness of mind, and searched the Scriptures daily' (Acts 17, 10-11); J. Hastings, ed., *Encyclopaedia of Religion and Ethics* (13 vols., Edinburgh, 1908-26), ii.519-23.

Lloyd George therefore grew up in an intensely religious environment. In his boyhood he and his family walked four miles to and from his uncle's chapel three times on Sundays and once on Wednesdays. He was a Nonconformist of the Nonconformists, separate from nearly all the rest, a member of a tiny sect which believed that it was nearer than its neighbours to original Christian practice. He became acquainted at an early age with the friction between Nonconformist denominations as well as between Nonconformists and Anglicans. Differences between Dissenting bodies contributed to the initial coolness of both his Baptist uncle and his Calvinistic Methodist future parents-in-law to his proposed marriage.[5] He associated freely with other Nonconformist children and with the Anglican ones, however, attending the Llanystumdwy village school, which was Anglican and where the religious education was consequently denominational. Here Lloyd George waged an early political battle on behalf of Nonconformity when, about 1876, he organized a refusal to repeat the Apostles' Creed on an important formal occasion. Obviously, from his point of view, the Apostles' Creed was not for Disciples. The attempt broke down and the Creed was repeated after a conciliatory lead was taken by his younger brother William (resembling the quality strikingly revealed by David in some industrial and political crises in later years). But ultimate victory in the battle of Llanystumdwy was gained by the protesting pupils: public recitations of the Creed were stopped at the school, as were the processions of the children to the parish church.[6]

The religious influences of his boyhood stayed with Lloyd George throughout his life. They moulded his political enthusiasms, so that it was natural for David as a young solicitor and budding local politician to develop his promising oratorical powers at temperance, disestablishment, and anti-tithe meetings; to act as secretary of the local branch of the United Kingdom Alliance (the main temperance organization) and of the South Caernarvonshire Anti-Tithe League; and to vindicate the Nonconformist right to parochial interment in his successful Burial Case in 1888, which made his name in North Wales and was closely followed by his selection as parliamentary candidate for Caernarvon Boroughs.[7] But already he was conscious of the need to look beyond these issues to wider social reform. In February 1890 he told a meeting of the South Wales Liberal Federation:P 'You have pledged yourselves to Disestablishment, Land Reform, Local Option and other great reforms. But, however drastic and broad they may appear to be, they after all simply touch the fringe of that vast social question which must be dealt with in the near future.'[8] Thus, even before his return to Parliament, Lloyd George was concerned with the need to alleviate the fundamental problems of society. By the time he entered Government in 1905, his broadening social concerns were superseding some of his original political enthusiasms.

Lloyd George held to Baptist beliefs, at least for large parts of his life, though he rejected the fundamentalism of the Disciples. He retained his membership of Berea chapel until he died, along with that of Castle Street Baptist Church in London. From about 1890

---

5   W.R.P. George, op. cit., 137-8; P. Rowland, *Lloyd George* (London, 1975), 46.
6   George, 75-6; P. Rowland, op. cit., 14-15.
7   Rowland, 42-3, 54-6, 60-5.
8   George, 166.

he seems to have regarded himself as an orthodox Baptist, a member of a denomination which became unified in 1891 when the Particular Baptists and the more liberal General Baptists combined. But, as was not surprising in one so independent and critical as Lloyd George, he had periods of speculation and doubt. The first of these apparently began about the age of twelve, perhaps immediately after his uncle baptized him by immersion, and is said to have lasted for several years. He was then attracted to Positivism, and expressed feelings - and sometimes behaviour such as occasional drinking and engagement in flirtations -which showed mild teenage rebellion against the twin claustrophobic domination of home and chapel. His early doubts did not last, however, and before he was twenty he was engaging in lay preaching, Sunday school teaching, and evangelical missions. An entry in his diary in 1882 referred to 'us Christians', and in a letter of 1883 he used evangelical language, saying he had 'taken an oath, before heaven and earth, to be a good soldier of Him who died for us'.[9] In September 1882 he wrote an appeal to the Churches of Wales, urging them to greater religious activity, which probably never left his hands; in January 1884 he wrote in his diary that Frederic Harrison's Positivism, though admirable, was 'taught in a far grander way and in a mode which more powerfully appeals to man's heart by Christianity'; and in a note of May 1888 he urged himself to repent of religious indifference, to 'be zealous' and to 'appreciate more fully some of the precepts the Bible lays down for our guidance in right thinking and doing'.[10] But evidently doubts recurred from time to time during his life. His son Richard said that 'my father's religious beliefs fluctuated, and there were periods in his life when he lost faith';[11] and this statement, particularly when combined with other scraps of contemporary allusion which exist on the subject, has the ring of authenticity. It would seem that Lloyd George did not, like Joseph Chamberlain, move from belief into agnosticism, but fluctuated between periods of belief and doubt, like Parnell. From Richard's statement it may be surmised that the times of belief predominated, and Lloyd George can perhaps best be described as a broad and speculative Baptist.

After Lloyd George was returned to Parliament in 1890 the political causes of Nonconformity remained prominent in his interests and activity during his fifteen years as a back-bencher. But he could do little at this time to attain such objects because Unionist Governments were in power for the whole period, except between 1892 and 1895 when Liberal ministries were in office with such a small majority that they could achieve very little. Unsuccessful efforts to pass a Welsh disestablishment bill in 1894 and 1895 were preceded by an unsuccessful attempt to defeat a Clergy Discipline Bill in 1892. Lloyd George made the latter effort on the grounds that disestablishment was preferable to control of a Church through legislation passed by a secular Parliament, even if this control took the form of desirable clerical discipline. In taking this line the young M.P. braved the wrath of Gladstone, his party

---

9   Ibid., 104ff.
10   Ibid., 110-11; W. George, *My Brother and I* (London, 1958), 75-9, 271-2.
11   Richard, Second Early Lloyd-George, *My Father* (London 1960), 20-1. Cf. F. Owen, *Tempestuous Journey: Lloyd George, his Life and Times* (London, 1954), 30-1; and Lady Olwen Carey Evans, *Lloyd George was my Father* (Llandysul, 1985), 70-1, where Lloyd George is described as a quiet believer and allegations of 'paganism' are refuted.

leader, who was anxious to have 'criminous and immoral clerks' disciplined and who rolled 'his terrible eye' at him as he was speaking in the Commons. More satisfactory was successful opposition to an education measure of the Unionist Government in 1896 which proposed to ease the financial strain on denominational schools. This had to be withdrawn and replaced by a smaller bill which was enacted the following year.[12] Even when Lloyd George's political concerns were directed at other objects in the 1890s, such as the advance of the nationalist *Cymru Fydd* movement (which collapsed in 1896), or to land law reform, or local option as a means of controlling the drink trade, or the protracted quarrel of Bethesda quarrymen with Lord Penrhyn, he was appealing largely to a Welsh Nonconformist constituency.[13] But his move to London forged important new links with English Nonconformity. His first public speech in London was at a Liberation Society meeting in Spurgeon's Baptist Tabernacle,[14] and this was followed by many other addresses to English Nonconformist gatherings. He initiated the Nonconformist Parliamentary Council in 1898; and he stimulated Nonconformist organizations to advance radical objects, as in 1894 when he persuaded the executive of the Liberation Society to oppose an Anglican Liberal parliamentary candidate who would not pledge himself to disestablishment.[15]

Lloyd George also became involved in the ritualist controversy which was prominent at the turn of the century and after. In October 1898 he told the assembly of the Congregational Union at Halifax that the 'poor atheists' who had taken part in the French Revolution 'saw Christ more clearly than the priests of Christendom with all the candles lit on their church altars'.[16] This was a reference to the growth of ritualistic practice in the Church of England, a movement which he described at a Baptist Union assembly in the same year as 'an attempt to substitute for the Protestant doctrine of justification by faith a system of salvation by haberdashery'.[17] But he was pleased to get the political support of Ritualists, based on their anti-erastian views, for his disestablishment policy.[18]

By the beginning of the twentieth century Lloyd George was clearly established as a Nonconformist champion in England as well as in Wales. Veteran Dissenting leaders saw him as a rare blast of youthful vigour in the senescent ranks of political Nonconformity. In 1901 Dr. Joseph Parker, Chairman of the Congregational Union, said that the Liberation Society needed 'copious new blood': 'a strong infusion of Lloyd Georgeism would do us a world of

---

12   W.R.P. George, *Lloyd George, Backbencher* (Llandysul,1983), 75, 118ff., 261-2; Morgan, *Wales in British Politics*, 133-58; G.I.T Machin, *Politics and the Churches in Great Britain, 1869 to 1921* (Oxford, 1987), 184-5, 208-16, 226-8.

13   W.R.P. George, *Lloyd George, Backbencher*, 188-93, 240ff.; C.J. Wrigley, *David Lloyd George and the British Labour Movement* (Hassocks, 1976), 74.

14   Rowland, 79.

15   George, *Lloyd George, Backbencher*, 128-30; D.W. Bebbington, *The Nonconformist Conscience: Chapel and Politics, 1870-1914* (London, 1982), 75.

16   H. du Parcq, *Life of David Lloyd George* (4 vols., London, 1912-13), i.193.

17   J. Grigg, *The Young Lloyd George* (London, 1973), 215.

18   Lloyd George to Margaret Lloyd George, 30 Mar. 1892; K. Morgan, ed., *Lloyd George Family Letters, 1885-1936* (Cardiff and London, 1973), 46.

good, and by Lloyd Georgeism I simply mean high spirit, hopeful courage and invincible determination'.[19]

At this time Lloyd George was a leading anti-Boer War campaigner, and this set the seal on his reputation as a foremost British radical. Nonconformists and the Liberal party were bitterly divided over the war, some Wesleyans being particularly noted for supporting the conflict.[20] But Lloyd George, though condemning the war as an unnecessary obstruction to much needed social reform, characteristically managed to conciliate Liberal Imperialists by supporting Lord Rosebery's desire for colonial self-government within the empire, rather than taking a totally anti-imperial line as did some radicals.[21] Opposition to the Education Act of 1902 helped to re-unite the Liberal party and its Nonconformist supporters. Lloyd George was the Act's most prominent opponent, but in this matter also his sympathies were divided. Despite his being a committee member of both the National Free Church Council and the Liberation Society (and vice-president of the latter), he was too independent to be simply a spokesman for Nonconformist feeling. The broad constructive administrator in him clashed with the radical Dissenting partisan. He initially liked the Education Bill on account of its proposed administrative system and the encouragement it gave to the spread of secondary education. He thought that the educational powers given to local authorities would be particularly beneficial in Wales with its Liberal councils. But his party interests soon supervened, and he opposed the bill for its intention to grant rate aid to denominational schools which were not under public control and which retained a religious test on teaching appointments. Even so, his expressed belief - characteristic of the man - that only compromise could settle the dispute was irritating to some Nonconformists.

Some Dissenters took part in a 'passive resistance' campaign against payment of rates which would help to support denominational schools, and prison sentences sometimes resulted. This protest was unsuccessful, though it did not die out until the early 1920s. In Wales and a few areas of England opposition to the Act was fiercer than elsewhere. Lloyd George advised county councils to withhold rate support from denominational schools unless they accepted full public control and dropped all religious tests on teaching appointments. When rate money was withheld by some councils, including nearly all the Welsh ones, a Default Bill was passed in 1904 in order to reduce government grants to these councils, and by the end of 1905 some councils had been penalized under this measure. This exacerbated Nonconformist anti-Government feeling in Wales, and Dissenting confidence there was boosted by Evan Roberts' evangelical revivalist movement (warmly approved by Lloyd George, who became

---

19   Quoted G.I.T. Machin, op. cit., 223.
20   D.W. Bebbington, *Nonconformist Conscience*, 106, 122-3; S. Koss, *Nonconformity in Modern British Politics* (London, 1975), 32-3.
21   M. Pugh, *Lloyd George* (London, 1988), 21-7; K. Morgan, *Lloyd George* (London, 1974), 47-52.

acquainted with Roberts). Roberts's campaign temporarily enlarged the membership of Welsh Dissenting chapels by about 82,000.[22]

The vigorous protest did not prevent the operation of the Education Act, however; and despite the encouragement of the dispute to Liberal re-union, government divisions over Tariff Reform were more important in the weakening of the Unionists and their retirement from office at the end of 1905. Nevertheless, Lloyd George's prestige was raised by the education dispute. He gained a tribute from Balfour, his chief opponent over the issue, that he was undoubtedly 'an eminent parliamentarian'. Commendation from the Unionist leader was not, of course, enough to assure him of a cabinet post in the next Liberal ministry, and it was apparently with some reluctance that Campbell-Bannerman advanced the radical tribune to this elevated position. With his hard won promotion attained, the Welsh radical graduated to imperial statesman.

When he joined the Government Lloyd George's approach to radical claims naturally changed. He had to give prior attention to the business of his ministerial post. He had the chance of realizing important social reforms, and treated more limited radical issues with caution. Although the Liberals obtained, in the general election of January 1906, an overall majority of 132 seats, their lead in the number of votes was far less impressive. The depleted Unionists took heart from this, and the Government was faced with determined resistance to several of its measures, expressed most effectively in the actions of the large Unionist majority in the House of Lords. Nonconformists had been returned in unprecedentedly large numbers - nearly 180 Nonconformists now sat as Liberal M.Ps, twenty as Labour M.Ps (and six as Unionists). But in the Government, Dissent was weaker than on the Liberal back benches: in the Cabinet formed in December 1905 only Campbell-Bannerman, Lloyd George, Bryce and Fowler were Nonconformists, though several others were ex-Nonconformists.[23]

In the attempt to satisfy its Nonconformist followers, the Government first took up reform of education policy. Welsh disestablishment, however, might have had more success in getting through the Lords on account of its position as a Welsh national question and the fact that all the M.Ps returned from Wales now supported it. The Upper House might have found it much more embarrassing to reject Welsh disestablishment than education reform, and by taking the broader issue first the Government magnified its constitutional difficulties.

Repeated efforts to reform education did not succeed, as the Lords were able to exploit (among other factors) the differences between Nonconformists and Catholics over denominational education. Resolution of the education problem in the Nonconformist interest was prevented by the insufficient strength of Dissent in England and Wales together, whereas in Wales alone Dissent was strong enough to make disestablishment practically inescapable. The Government, however, took the view that Welsh disestablishment and Irish Home Rule

---

22   Lloyd George's activities in the education dispute, and his relations with Nonconformity during it, are covered in great detail in B.B. Gilbert, *David Lloyd George, a Political Life: the Architect of Change, 1863-1912* (London, 1987), 215-66. See also Morgan, *Wales in British Politics*, 186-98; Machin, *Politics and the Churches*, 265-9; D. Cregier, *Bounder from Wales: Lloyd George's Career before the First World War* (Columbia and London, 1976), 80-5.

23   S. Koss, op. cit., 77, 228; Bebbington, *Nonconformist Conscience*, 154; Machin, 274.

could not be passed until the Lords' power to veto bills had been restricted. Over disestablishment, Lloyd George now took a conciliatory line and looked for agreement with the Church in Wales in reaching a settlement. Early in 1906 he suggested to A.G. Edwards, Bishop of St. Asaph, with whom he developed friendly relations, that 'a very mild and kindly bill' might leave the disestablished Church with all its property except tithe.[24] This proposal would almost certainly have ended the confidence of Welsh radicals in Lloyd George, if they had known about it; and Nonconformists were displeased when the Government appeared to be postponing the issue by appointing a Royal Commission in June 1906 to inquire into the work and property of all Churches in Wales.[25] Many Welsh Nonconformists believed that the immediate introduction of a government bill would have been preferable, in order to challenge the Lords on the issue. Lloyd George appeared rather too obviously as the poacher turned game-keeper at Caernarvon in January 1907 when, after saying that in order to achieve 'urgent reforms' the House of Commons needed to enforce its will against the peers, he proceeded in unfortunate military language: 'I will say this to my fellow-countrymen - if they find the Government manoeuvring its artillery into position for making an attack on the Lords, the Welshmen who worry the Government into attending to anything else until the citadel has been stormed ought to be put in the guardroom'.[26]

It seemed as though Lloyd George, having led some 'Welsh revolts' in the past, was now trying to quell an incipient one himself. There was no sign of such a revolt among the Welsh M.Ps, but more protests were made in the Principality, especially after the premier, Campbell-Bannerman, said in the Commons in June 1907 that a disestablishment bill was most unlikely to be introduced in 1908. Welsh Nonconformist meetings demanded pledges of future government action to achieve disestablishment, but government ministers stated that while the difficulty with the Lords remained no such pledges could be given.[27] Lloyd George, who was said even by the admiring Nonconformist *British Weekly* to have occasionally 'yielded to the breath of officialdom,'[28] now tried to calm the waves of opposition. He obtained nomination as a delegate to a great Nonconformist gathering at Cardiff in October, and received Campbell-Bannerman's permission to say that, while no definite promise to achieve the reform could be made, the Government wanted to carry Welsh disestablishment as soon as possible. At Cardiff he first obtained a softening of the resolutions to be put to the meeting and then delivered a rousing speech in which he defended the Government's good faith. He said that disestablishment would pass the Commons in 1909, and ended with a genuine if tear-jerking declaration: *'Duw a wyr mor anwyl yw Cymru lan i mi'* (God knows how dear to me is my Wales).[29] After that it was not surprising that he could report to Campbell-Bannerman: 'Cardiff turned out much more satisfactorily than I feared it would have. The Government will not be worried much more on the subject of Welsh disestablishment until the times comes

---

24   Rowland, 191.
25   Morgan, *Wales in British Politics*, 233-5.
26   Rowland, 192; B.B. Gilbert, op. cit., 305ff.
27   Morgan, 235-6.
28   Koss, 93.
29   Rowland, 192-3; Morgan, 237-8; Gilbert, 311-12.

to arrange the programme for 1909'.[30] The 'revolt' subsided, and Lloyd George's reputation in Wales was considerably restored: he was elected president of the Welsh Baptist Union for 1908-9.[31] In 1909 a government bill for Welsh disestablishment was brought in by Asquith, now Prime Minister. Lloyd George was preoccupied with his People's Budget, which was introduced on 29 April, a few days after the Welsh bill had received its first reading. The bill did not proceed to a second reading, but its role as a challenge to the Lords was taken over more pointedly, and with much wider application, by Lloyd George's budget. Welsh disestablishment, which the Lords might have felt compelled to grant, now helped to consolidate government support against the peers in the constitutional battle.

The crisis over the budget and the Lords' veto produced two general elections in 1910, in which the Government appealed strongly to Nonconformists among others. Lloyd George, addressing a London demonstration organized by the National Free Church Council, said that 'our very Constitution...is attributable to the effort and the sacrifice of Nonconformists'.[32] The results of the elections disappointed the Liberals, who lost their overall majority and were left depending on the Irish Home Rule party to keep them in power. The Lords' veto power was much reduced by the Parliament Act, and Irish Home Rule and Welsh disestablishment became law in 1914, though their implementation was suspended because of the outbreak of war.

Despite the restriction of the Lords' veto there was no further government attempt at educational reform in the interests of Nonconformity, largely because the ministry depended on the Home Rule party which defended Catholic interests. Moreover, the protracted passage of Welsh disestablishment through all the channels provided by the Parliament Act involved familiar arguments which were attracting declining interest. Social reform had become the main domestic concern.[33] The electorate, now largely working class, was less of a church-going body than previously and therefore less concerned with denominational political aims. The cause of disestablishment in England was much weaker than it had been. In Scotland the quest for disestablishment had recently been diverted into a search for compromise with the Established Church, and this eventually succeeded in the 1920s on the basis that a spiritually free and self-governing establishment would be maintained. The membership of Nonconformist denominations in England and Wales, having been growing less rapidly than the population for at least twenty years, went into numerical decline in the years 1905-8 with astonishing unanimity between leading denominations (though in Wales the initial decline was only from the recent increase produced by Evan Roberts). There has been no effective reversal of the decline since that time.[34] In this situation Nonconformity naturally weakened as a political force. After the passage of Welsh disestablishment Lloyd George and other leaders were not summoned by powerful Dissenting pressure to lead any further specifically

30   Rowland, 193.
31   Morgan, 238.
32   Du Parcq, iv.718.
33   Morgan, 260-74; Machin, 306-10.
34   Machin, 11-16; R. Currie, A. Gilbert and L. Horsley, eds., *Churches and Churchgoers: Patterns of Church Growth in the British Isles since 1700* (Oxford, 1977), 128-91.

Nonconformist campaigns. The popular impetus behind Nonconformist causes, on which Lloyd George's political career had been built, was disappearing - not least because some of the causes had succeeded, while others did not seem practically attainable.

The First World War hastened the decline of political Nonconformity. Lloyd George was far from intending that this should happen - and, for the rest of his life, he may well not have believed that it was happening as an irreversible process - but he was at the centre of the reasons which caused it.   Nonconformists were gratified that Lloyd George overcame opposition to secure the same terms of appointment for their chaplains in the Armed Forces as applied to the Established Churches, but many were disappointed that there was no prohibition of the drink trade. Welsh Liberal M.Ps would not be persuaded by Lloyd George to accept a bill of 1915 postponing the date of Welsh disestablishment from immediately after peace was signed until six months later, and the bill was withdrawn.[35] Nonconformists, moreover, were bitterly divided in their attitudes to war policies. Lloyd George's role in the conflict was praised by some Nonconformists and execrated by others.   Most leading Nonconformists wholeheartedly supported the war effort, and Lloyd George was regarded by some of them - especially by the Rev. Sir William Robertson Nicoll, editor of the influential *British Weekly* - as the ablest minister on the British side.   But when Lloyd George was propelled into (rather than seeking) the premiership in December 1916 - an event warmly welcomed by some Nonconformists - the ensuing split in the Liberal party shattered Nonconformist political cohesion. Most Nonconformist voters supported the Liberal party (though some had recently taken to voting Conservative or Labour), and when Lloyd George stood in alliance with the Conservatives in the general election of 1918 Liberal Nonconformists were sharply divided in allegiance between him and Asquith.[36]

Lloyd George had tried to carry Nonconformist opinion with him into the Coalition. On the suggestion of the Rev. J.H. Shakespeare, a leading Baptist whose regard for Lloyd George was shown by his statement in 1922 that he was 'one of the most indomitable, gallant, wonderful figures in the history of the world', the Prime Minister gave a breakfast to some seventy Nonconformist ministers at Downing Street in October 1917. At that gathering he tried to boost their confidence in his Government and hinted that there might be an acceptable educational reform after the war.[37] But only partially did he win Nonconformist approval, and in the 1918 election campaign he lost some of this support through his exhibitions of aggressive chauvinism and his use of the 'coupon' to eliminate Asquithian opponents at the polls. The veteran Baptist leader John Clifford moved from Lloyd George to Labour during the campaign, though the *British Weekly* and the *Baptist Times* stood by the premier.[38] Some Liberals deplored Lloyd George's continuing alliance with the Conservatives, one of them condemning 'the whilom protagonist of their faith (now) bowing the head to worship in the

---

35   Morgan, 278-9; P.M.H. Bell, *Disestablishment in Ireland and Wales* (London, 1969), 299-301.
36   Koss, 125-47.
37   Ibid., 140, 159; Sir J. Marchant, *Dr. John Clifford, C.H.: Life, Letters and Reminiscences* (London, 1924), 230-1.
38   Koss, 145-6.

heathen temple of the political Rimmon.'[39] But of the eighty-eight Nonconformists returned in the election fifty-two were Coalition Liberals, twenty were Labour, only seven were Asquith Liberals, and seven were Conservatives.[40]

Thereafter the dispersal of Nonconformist political allegiance continued, with more Dissenters turning from Liberalism to either Labour or Conservatism. The re-shaping of party politics during and after the war intensified the decay of the Nonconformist political thrust which had already begun to decline through numerical loss.

The settlement of the Welsh disestablishment controversy after the war emphasized the termination or decline of Nonconformist political causes. Supporters of the Church in Wales were anxious to revise the disendowment clauses of the 1914 Act in order to obtain a more generous settlement. A Welsh Church Temporalities Bill (or 'Amending Bill') was prepared in July 1919, after Lloyd George had returned from peace-making at Versailles. This bill postponed the date of disestablishment and granted compensation to the Church from government funds, though it was not so generous as the Church would have liked. The bill was quickly carried in both Houses and became law on 19 August. Disestablishment was to come into effect in March 1920.[41]

The Act was the kind of compromise settlement which appealed to Lloyd George, particularly now that he was leading a Coalition supported mainly by Conservatives. At the end of 1919 he extolled the settlement, in a letter to Bonar Law, almost in terms of personal ecumenical fulfilment: '[it is] an illustration of how an old controversy, which has divided a whole nationality for over fifty years, has at last been settled by common consent to the complete satisfaction of both parties without leaving a trace of bitterness'.[42]

This important turning point in the history of Wales was also important in the career of Lloyd George. After the removal of this issue he could no longer provide distinctive causes with which to lead a Nonconformist political body.

Nonconformity in Wales finished on 31 March 1920, as from that date there was no longer an Established Church in Wales. But Lloyd George's career as a Nonconformist was not over, as he was usually resident in England and he continued to appeal for support to Nonconformists in England and Scotland and ex-Nonconformists in Wales. After his fall in 1922 he made several efforts to return to power, and in doing so he was mindful of the considerable support and even reverence which he still received from many Free Churchmen. He remained assiduous in his attendance at Free Church gatherings. In 1929 he became a vice-resident of the National Free Church Council and gave £100 to its funds.[43] In July 1930 he addressed the fifth International Congregational Council, meeting at Bournemouth. At this gathering he re-affirmed his Baptist allegiance and declared:

The Churches must take the affairs of the world in hand. They must teach brotherhood once more to men of every race and clime. They must give them the wisdom

39   Quoted Machin, 315.
40   Koss, 231.
41   P.M.H. Bell, op. cit., 305-15; Morgan, 286-91; Machin, 314-16.
42   Quoted Machin, 316.
43   Koss, 181-2.

which comes from above, and then and then only would there be peace on earth and goodwill among men.[44]

In spite of unfavourable political trends Lloyd George attempted in the 1930s, when he no longer led the Liberal Party, to base a revival of his fortunes on the Nonconformist organizations with which he was so familiar. Before the general election of 1935 he planned the formation of a non-party Council of Action for Peace and Reconstruction, hoping to displace the leaders of the National Government by promising to guide the country into secure and prosperous conditions of non-socialist collectivism and international peace. Leading Nonconformists such as the Methodist Scott Lidgett and the Congregationalist Sidney Berry initially supported the projected Council. The five hundred local Free Church councils were intended to be examples and means of assistance to Councils of Action which it was hoped to form in every constituency. To provide co-ordination for the local bodies there would be nine area councils and a central National Council. The famous Lloyd George Fund would provide the necessary finance. The campaign might have had considerable success if the resources of Nonconformity, still fairly flourishing, could have been effectively marshalled behind it. But this was too difficult to achieve, as Nonconformity was now thoroughly fragmented in political allegiance. Free Church support for Lloyd George's movement was patchy. The Methodist Conference would not give its endorsement, and some leaders of other denominations had strong reservations. The National Council gave its approval to 362 candidates in the election, but only sixty-seven of these were successful. The National Government was returned to office, and although the Council of Action lasted until the outbreak of the Second World War (when it merged with the All-Party Parliamentary Action Group), Lloyd George's campaign had achieved very little.[45] Having shown realism and success in basing his political rise on Nonconformity, he was unable to find in that source effective support for a come-back. When, for example, he became an opponent of appeasement, he complained that too many Nonconformists were resisting his stand.

Lloyd George thus remained a political Nonconformist into his later life. It also seems that, for most of the time, he retained his Baptist beliefs. Several recent writers on Lloyd George have described him as being indifferent to religion or sceptical towards it. Such an interpretation is only applicable to the periods of doubt which he probably had, and underestimates the religious inclinations which he often displayed. No modern British politician, except perhaps Gladstone, has been so consistently bound up with religious issues as part of his political concerns. Apart from politics, Lloyd George attended and read sermons as enthusiastically as Gladstone, seeming to derive much satisfaction from them, and probably sang hymns with at least equal enjoyment. In many ways the antithesis of Gladstone, Lloyd George lacked his predecessor's intellectualism, his likeing for writing essays, and his appetite for lengthy correspondence. Thus, while Gladstone's religious opinions and interests are voluminously preserved for any historian to see, there is little written testimony to Lloyd George's views on religion, and this greatly inhibits an assessment of them. Lloyd George's

---

44   A. Peel, ed., *The Living Church: Proceedings of the fifth International Congregational Council, July 1st.-8th., 1930* (London, 1930), 148-50.

45   Koss, 186-217.

personality, capable of heady emotional flights but lacking in *gravitas*, perhaps gave the impression that his religion was merely superficial. Frances Stevenson, a confirmed member of the Church of England, wrote in her diary in 1917: 'What religion he has is purely emotional, and not spiritual'.[46]

But there can be little doubt that he gave considerable thought to religion. This seems to be indicated by his liking for sermons, and by his fluctuations between doubt and belief. There is also supporting evidence , if small in amount, from different stages in his career. Examples from the period before he entered Parliament have already been quoted. As Prime Minister, a message which he sent to the annual assembly of the Baptist Union in 1921 conveys a sense of genuine denominational loyalty and concern, despite the obvious political interest involved:

> I have followed with great satisfaction the raising of the Baptist United Fund. There is no object which more commands my sympathy than easing the burdens of the country Minister. The success of this effort in so short a time is sure proof of the vitality and strength of our denomination.[47]

For more convincing examples one should perhaps look to occasions when he was not appealing to a political audience of any kind. In 1904, on a Christmas holiday with Herbert Lewis, Lloyd George 'said he regretted that he had not become a preacher. The pulpit, dealing as it did with every phase of human life, offered infinite opportunities for influence and it dealt with matters of eternal consequence. Politics, after all, belong to a lower plain; they are concerned with material things.'[48] On the death of his beloved daughter Mair in 1907, he wrote to his wife that he was convinced that the blow would 'prove to be the greatest blessing that has befallen us, and through us multitudes whom God has sent me to give a helping hand out of misery a myriad worse than ours'.[49] On one of the occasions when he preached briefly in a chapel, he spoke at his own church, Berea at Criccieth, in the 1930s from a text in St. Matthew on the need to perform good works in order to glorify God. He then convinced at least one observer that he was 'deeply committed' to Christianity:

> He spoke quietly , under considerable emotional stress, for not more than ten minutes on the significance of Christians performing good works, emphasizing the importance of keeping the lamp of the chapel alight..as if he had a genuine terror of the darkness which would follow if the light of the lamp of the Christian faith were extinguished.[50]

---

46   Diary, 9 Feb. 1917; Frances, Countess Lloyd-George, *Lloyd George, a Diary* (ed. A.J.P. Taylor, London, 1917), 143.
47   Letter dated 26 Apr. 1921; *Baptist Handbook* (1922), 186.
48   Quoted T. Jones, *Lloyd George* (London, 1951), 8.
49   Lloyd George to Margaret Lloyd George, 4 Dec. 1907; Morgan, *Lloyd George Family Letters*, 149.
50   W.R.P. George, *Lloyd George, Backbencher*, 416.

Finally, when in his old age he was asked if he still adhered to Baptist beliefs, he affirmed that he did.[51]

In the ethical sphere, however, Lloyd George was in some ways lacking in adherence to Baptist and Christian teaching. His financial ventures, which attracted criticism, were the results of rashness and not corruption on his part. But the sale of excessive numbers of honours - some of them to scarcely worthy people - in order to form a personal political fund could well be stigmatized as hardly in keeping with the professions of one of the world's foremost democrats. Moreover, the personal life which he developed was not that of a model Christian. The unsatisfactory conditions of his marriage, during which he and his wife were often out of sympathy and lived separately for long periods when they could easily have resided together,led him into relationships with others. Some writers have assumed that several of these associations were adulterous, but there is no hard evidence that any of them were so until 1913. In that year he began a definite liaison with Frances Stevenson, by whom he later had a daughter (the paternity being kept secret from the public for many years).

Divorce from his wife Margaret would have ruined his political career - a consideration which Margaret, who continued to give him loyal public support until her death in 1941, appreciated as much as he did. In any case his relationship with her remained far more than nominal even though he was living sporadically with Frances. Perhaps mutual guilt-feelings continued to make the marriage a 'real' one in these unpromising circumstances.

Lloyd George's unorthodox domestic arrangements were scarcely known to the public, but they were familiar enough in political circles. The young Robert Boothby, who commenced a lasting affair with the wife of Harold Macmillan in 1929, was impressed with Lloyd George's 'ability to get away with two wives, two homes and two families'.[52] Lloyd George's elder son Richard, who sided firmly with his mother in the marital trouble, and between whom and his father tension became so great (for various reasons) that Lloyd George cut him out of his will, suggested that his father veered strongly towards promiscuity. 'My father', he wrote, 'was the greatest natural Don Juan in the history of British politics.'[53] The available evidence hardly bears out this view. Even though the press was less assiduous than today in unearthing the private lives of the famous, it is highly unlikely that a figure of Lloyd George's prominence could have lived the life suggested by his son without being exposed in the newspapers. On the other hand, though there undoubtedly were extenuating circumstances for his behaviour, his engagement in adultery contravened a basic precept of the faith which he professed.

Lloyd George's relations with the Baptist denomination and with Nonconformity as a whole were complex ones of commitment and detachment, resembling his connection with

---

51   May Lloyd, 'Baptist Political Attitudes, with special reference to the late nineteenth century' (unpublished M.Phil. thesis, University of Leeds, 1974).

52   A. Horne, *Macmillan, 1894-1956* (London, 1988), 85. Cf. the comment of A.J. Sylvester, Lloyd George's principal private secretary, when Lloyd George married Frances in 1943: 'The gods are certainly with him to a most remarkable degree. In somewhat similar circumstances as (*sic*) Edward VIII was dethroned, L.G. is elevated. He has lived a life of duplicity. He has got clean away with it...' A.J. Sylvester, *Life with Lloyd George: the Diary of A.J. Sylvester, 1931-45* (ed. C.Cross,London, 1975), 319.

53   Richard, Earl Lloyd-George, *Lloyd George*, 34.

the Liberal party and his ambivalent attitude to some questions of reform. His political life before he became a cabinet minister was largely concerned with promoting Nonconformist claims, yet he was not content with urging these and looked to broader questions of social reform which came to take the foremost place in his political concerns. He apparently did not remain consistently faithful to the religion of this fathers, but usually subscribed to Christian belief. He was anxious to uphold the ethical teachings of Christianity but did not do so completely in his own life. He was always one to scorn convention and to strike out boldly on individual lines. But though he sailed willingly from one shore to another he never burned his boats. His actions helped - against any wish of his own - to divide and weaken the Liberal party and to destroy the political cohesion of Nonconformity, yet he remained a Liberal and a Nonconformist all his life. He had periods of doubt but he apparently returned to belief after them, and he always retained the religious links forged in his childhood. While living contentedly with Frances he continued his attachment to Margaret. Though he wandered far from his roots he always remained connected with them. Perhaps the main reason for the persistent link is that he represented his home constituency of Caernarvon Boroughs for his entire parliamentary life.

LLOYD GEORGE AND THE LABOUR PARTY AFTER 1922

CHRIS WRIGLEY

On 14 October 1926 Tom Clarke, the managing editor of the *Daily News*, bluntly asked Lloyd George if he would leave the Liberals for the Labour Party. 'No. A Liberal I was born and a Liberal I die. I will not join Labour.' As Mandy Rice Davies put it thirty-seven years later, on a famous occasion concerning a prominent person's denial, 'Well he would, wouldn't he?'. Of course to such a question, in any circumstances, a leading figure in any political party would have to give a denial, let alone when the question was asked by a leading newspaperman of a key Liberal newspaper to an eminent politician on the verge of achieving sole pre-eminence in the Liberal Party as a whole (being already leader in the House of Commons).

But this was an occasion when Lloyd George's words were unambiguously and without qualification true. As Clarke himself surmised, Lloyd George 'badly wanted to be leader of a united Liberal Party'.[1] But his experience as *de facto* leader (he was never formally given the title) from 1926 was to be less than pleasant. The taste of the fruit that hitherto had been forbidden to him was to be very sour indeed.

Lloyd George's relationship with the Labour Party before the 1929 general election was one of rivalry, involving both a battle of ideas as to how to revive the economy and to make a juster society and much manoeuvring in the late 1920s to try to benefit most from the crumbling of Baldwin's government. But in 1930 and 1931, and occasionally at other times, Lloyd George acted as an external conscience to the Labour Party, urging its leadership to fulfil three decades of promises to provide the 'Right to Work'. Lloyd George hoped for more social reforms from the second Labour government than the sterile economics of Snowden or the vacuous domestic statesmanship of MacDonald permitted. Moreover, between 1923 and 1931, Lloyd George often used Labour as a counter to strengthen his position within the Liberal Party *vis a vis* the Asquithians. Yet, at other times between 1922 and 1930, he was attracted, at least momentarily, to notions of trying to form again a Centre Coalition group to fight on an anti-socialist ticket.

As for the notions held at the time and echoed by subsequent writers that Lloyd George might have left the Liberals for Labour, this was highly improbable, especially before 1931. This is so in spite of the influx of well-to-do political refugees and aspirants to office such as Sir Leo Chiozza Money, Sir Oswald Mosley, Arthur Ponsonby and Charles Trevelyan. Lloyd George's basic political philosophy and outlook, as well as his political style, were very different from those of the 1920s Labour Party. Furthermore, he had been to the very pinnacle of British politics - both as the Man Who Won The War and the Peacemaker; and then on his own political standing, not as a party leader. The prospect of becoming deputy leader of the Labour Party, even if that ever was realistic, would not have been alluring; especially not when Ramsay MacDonald was leader.

Lloyd George's political outlook was decidedly not socialist. He was a firm believer in the free market economy, except in the special circumstances of war. His fierce radical attacks were confined to landlords, monopolists and those living on inherited wealth. He was

---

1   T. Clarke, *My Lloyd George Diary* (London, Methuen, 1939), p. 23.

generally an admirer, not a critic, of businessmen. Thus in September 1919, he told Sir George Riddell, the owner of the *News of the World* and a close associate during most of his years in office,

> I am convinced that the world cannot be carried on without the aid of the skilled managerial class. You must have leaders and captains of industry if you are to have any progress. You cannot have adequate production unless you invoke the aid of the clever manufacturers and businessmen working for their own profit. But you must see that they do not get too much and that they do not grind the other classes under their heel.[2]

Riddell noted in his diary on another occasion that while Lloyd George 'has a genuine desire to improve the position of the poorer classes ... he cannot bring himself to attack the capitalist for whom, when all is said, he has lawyer-like respect'.[3]

In spite of his adoption of collectivist measures during World War 1, Lloyd George was highly critical of state socialism. Riddell, in fact, felt (in March 1920) that

> The war has shown him the value and strength of individual effort and the weakness of government departments. I have observed this conviction growing upon him during the past four years. His point of view has entirely changed, so both from conviction and expediency the No-Socialism cry appeals to him.[4]

In a major speech at the Free Trade Hall in Manchester on 28 April 1923, he told his audience that if they wanted to know what socialism was, all they had to do was to obtain a copy of the wartime Defence of the Realm Acts. He went on to declare,

> Nothing struck me so much in the war as the disappearance of the individual, of the human being, with his separate feelings and his separate affections, with his separate interests, with his separate soul. All vanished. Man was then called a unit. When men fell at the front, there was an order for units to fill their places. The units became battalions, and the battalions brigades, the brigades became divisions, and the divisions became army corps and the army corps became armies - but they are all but units in a machine ... That is what a complete Socialistic State would mean, once you carried it out ... Socialism means transferring into the area of peace the conditions of war.

---

2   Riddell's diary, 20 September 1919; Lord Riddell, *Intimate Diary of the Peace Conference and After* (London, Gollancz, 1933), p.128.
3   Riddell's diary, 2 March 1919; Riddell Papers, (British Library), Add. Ms. 629083, f.63.
4   Riddell's diary, 27 March 1920; Riddell Papers, Add. Ms. 62985, f.87.

So much did he like this analogy, that he approved its publication in a selection of passages from his speeches which was issued before the 1929 general election. Indeed this passage - along with the aphorism 'Socialism is the negation of Liberty' - constituted the section in the book on socialism.[5]

Lloyd George also viewed the strong trade unions with disfavour. While he often said that he was for the underdog in society, he meant by this the poor or the unorganised working class generally. He sometimes declared that he opposed the overmighty, whether it be aristocrats or powerful trade union leaders. The Parliamentary Labour Party after the First World War was very much dominated by the trade unions, and by the miners in particular. In 1919 out of 61 MPs who took the Labour whip in the new Parliament, forty-nine were trade unionists, and of these twenty-five were sponsored by the Miners' Federation. In the 1922, 1923 and 1924 Parliaments trade unionists continued to make up between 51 and 60 per cent of the Parliamentary Labour Party, and in these and the 1929 election 40 or more miners were returned every time.[6]

Lloyd George was not at all amenable to notions that politicians should act as delegates faithfully carrying out the decisions of trade union or Labour Party conferences (or of any other organisation), even when they personally disagreed with those decisions. Thus, like Austen Chamberlain, he had deplored J.R. Clynes' actions when, as chairman of the Parliamentary Labour Party in 1921 during the mining dispute, he carried out policies that he himself had earlier opposed. Indeed Lloyd George's style of politics could not have been further removed from that of Clynes, who really did act as a chairman of his Parliamentary group rather than as a decisive and charismatic leader.[7] With MacDonald's return to the leadership in 1922, the post of leader was recognised and MacDonald behaved with greater flamboyance and assertiveness than Clynes or Adamson. Even so, Lloyd George's personal style would have created immense friction in the Labour Party. Indeed MacDonald came close to discrediting his own style of leadership in 1924, let alone in 1931.

Moreover Lloyd George had gone too far in his anti-Labour actions and rhetoric between 1918 and 1922 for him to be acceptable to a large portion of the Labour movement. However much his Parliamentary skills and his political dynamism were admired, many could not trust the man whose premiership had seen intervention in Russia, Black and Tan terror in Ireland, the non implementation of the majority report of the Sankey Commission and tough government handling of strikes. Between 1919 and 1922 Lloyd George had based his Coalition and Centre Party politics in large part on trying to divide British politics between those for and against socialism. When attempts to label Adamson, Clynes, Henderson and Thomas as near Bolsheviks wore thin, Lloyd George had depicted Labour as a political

5   D. Lloyd George, *Slings and Arrows: Sayings chosen From the Speeches* (London, Cassell, 1929), p.15. It was edited and introduced by Philip Guedella, with a Prefatory Note, pp.v-ix, by Lloyd George. The aphorism was from a speech at Llandrindod Wells, 7 September 1923.

6   G.D.H. Cole, *A History of the Labour Party From 1914* (London, Routledge and Kegan Paul, 1948), pp.83-4, 154-55, 170-71 and 220-23.

7   C.J. Wrigley, *Lloyd George and the Challenge of Labour* (Hemel Hempstead, 1990), pp.303-06.

menace through being incapable of dealing firmly with social unrest. Either way, his attacks were much resented.[8]

So while it was not impossible that Lloyd George might have joined Labour, it was always very unlikely. Lloyd George had a real attachment to his own version of Liberalism, much more so than interwar Asquithians ever allowed - or, indeed, many subsequent historians.

Labour was a useful element in Lloyd George's political kaleidoscope. He used it - or tried to use it - in several different ways. Sometimes he used it as a Red Peril, just as he had done between 1919 and 1922. At other times he tried to exhibit it as an unimaginative and blundering rival on the Left of British politics. When it suited him, Lloyd George was also willing to use the Labour Party as an auxiliary to his wing of the reunited Liberal Party. This was to revert to his pre-1914 practice.

In 1923-4 Lloyd George's attitude to Labour was to treat it as a dangerous rival for the Free Trade and Left of Centre vote. Then he felt that the key dividing line in British politics was tariffs, not socialism, unemployment or economic recovery. His hostility to the first Labour government owed much to his desire to prevent Labour establishing itself as the undisputed radical alternative to the Conservatives and to prevent the Liberal Party disintegrating, a danger which was widely perceived in early 1924.[9] It may also have owed a little to his personal animosity for Ramsay MacDonald, whom he did not wish to see triumph in office. Before MacDonald took on the premiership Lloyd George observed in the Commons, 'He will find that formulas however unexceptional, ideas however exalted, are not so easy to translate into action when you have to deal with other nations'.[10] And from the outset of the Labour government Lloyd George went out of his way to assert British rights under the Treaty of Versailles against possible concessions by MacDonald. In part, at least, this reflected his sensitivity over his role at the 1919 Paris Peace Conference and his resentment of the criticism from the Left of the terms of the resulting European peace treaty.

It has been suggested by John Campbell that early on in life of the first Labour government Lloyd George 'became equally impatient of Asquith and of Labour, and resolved to be rid of both'.[11] If, with regard to Asquith, this was so, then it was a secondary matter to the tactical priority of minimising Labour's credibility as a party of government. More likely, Lloyd George's attitude to his party's leadership was to do what he had done during the period up to the autumn of 1916 - that is to take all the steps that he could to ensure that he was seen as the Crown Prince, ready to take over when Asquith went. As in 1915-16, in this he needed to broaden his appeal towards those normally to his Right. But Lloyd George's many and various past machinations inevitably ensured that his political manoeuvres were viewed with deep suspicion. Towards the end of the first Labour government Labour Cabinet

---

8   For example, ibid., p.251.
9   For example, Emmott to Asquith, 7 January 1924; Emmott Papers (Nuffield College Library) 2 ,Vol. 6. Also Leo Amery to Page Croft, 14 January 1924; Croft Papers (Churchill College Library); CRFT/1/2AM2.
10   On 15 January 1924; 169 *H.C. Deb. 5s*, c.110.
11   J. Campbell, *Lloyd George: The Goat in the Wilderness 1922-1931* (London, Cape, 1977), p.89.

minsters saw Lloyd George's actions as being aimed at ousting Asquith and Grey. Haldane, a former close associate of these two, felt this was the case in mid September.[12] MacDonald noted in his diary on 6 October 1924:

> I am told that LG is now working hard for his own hand. He wanted us to fall on the Russian Treaty and deliberately wishes that Liberal Party would be split so as to secure his own ascendency ... When the crisis was hastened, he supported the vote of censure policy for the same reason. He hopes Asquith will go. This I got from journalists in touch with his friends on Liberal papers. His reputation is as low as it can be.[13]

But such views probably stemmed from Asquith's staunchest supporters, such as Lord Gladstone, and from MacDonald's incapacity to grasp that his contemptuous treatment of the Parliamentary Liberals would inevitably result in the withdrawal of their support. As for the Russian treaty, Lloyd George was in step with all the Liberal leadership in denouncing it. Liberal votes against MacDonald's government in the autumn of 1924 stemmed from Labour intransigence, not from Machiavellian scheming by Lloyd George.[14]

After Baldwin and the Conservative's great electoral victory in October 1924, Lloyd George pressed within the Liberal Party for more radical policies. As in 1909-11, his proposals scared off some of the more wealthy Liberal supporters. Thus, for example, Sir Alfred Mond was outraged by Lloyd George's Land Policy and, to the astonishment of his family, joined the Tories. Mond told his daughter, '... there is no future for a third party in the world as it has become today. You must be either for Socialism or against Socialism: black or white: there will be no grey or half colours'.[15]

Lloyd George may have hoped to use Labour to tilt Liberal Party policy on the land back in a more radical direction. After the severe set-back the Liberals experienced in the 1924 general election, Lloyd George set out - as in 1912 - to revive the Liberal party's fortunes with a campaign on the issue of the land. He confided in Frances Stevenson in August 1925 that he envisaged a 'strenuous land campaign' as a means of enabling the Liberals to 'strengthen our grasp on the rural districts and the capture of a few towns where Liberalism is still a force'. He hoped to see 'the non Socialist voter turning to Liberalism as

12   Extract of a letter by Haldane, 13 September 1924; Haldane Papers (National Library of Scotland), 5916, f.150.

13   MacDonald Papers (Public Record Office), PRO 30/69/1753. The contents of his diaries were, in MacDonald's words, 'meant as notes to guide and revive memory as regards happenings' and not intended for extensive reproduction.

14   T. Wilson, *The Downfall of the Liberal Party 1914-1935* (London, Collins, 1966), pp.272-78.

15   The Marchioness of Reading, *For the Record: The Memoirs of Eva, Marchioness of Reading* (London, Hutchinson, 1973), pp.42-3.

he did towards Toryism at the last election'.[16] His land proposals, which had been in preparation for two years and which were published in the autumn of 1925 as *The Land and the Nation* and *Towns and the Land*, alarmed many in the Liberal Party.[17] The first volume on rural land called for the state to resume possession of all economically viable land. In this, and in its proposals to help the good farmer but to evict the bad, Lloyd George was looking back to the wartime controls established by the 1917 Corn Production Act. In promising to create employment by encouraging a return to the land, he was harking back to an old radical tradition. The uproar over his proposed state control of the land ensured that he had to dilute his proposals somewhat to ensure that the bulk of his proposals were accepted by a special Liberal Party Land Convention in mid February 1926.

But Lloyd George appears to have hoped to go back to his original scheme. Or, at least, he wanted to re-establish his Radical credentials with Labour's leadership. In May 1926 Commander Kenworthy (a left wing Liberal MP who joined the Labour Party later in 1926) approached Arthur Henderson on Lloyd George's behalf to offer 'a Parliamentary understanding'. Ramsay MacDonald noted after questioning Henderson about this proposed co-operation in the Commons that

> ... the only condition was that we should take up his land scheme, in its original form and not as amended by the Liberal Conference. He also pointed out the advantage of having the *Chronicle, Daily News* and *Manchester Guardian* behind us at election. Ll.G. wished for no coalition. I think he might have added 'at present'.[18]

This approach was an important indicator of Lloyd George's move to the Left, and was notable for taking place shortly after the end of the General Strike.

Lloyd George's actions in early May 1926 were an assertion by him of his importance to Asquith and his supporters. He was keeping up the pressure to see that the land campaign was not marginalised by the Asquithians. He was also warning them to think clearly how much better off they were with him than if they provoked him into leaving for Labour. This may well be the explanation for why Lloyd George let it be put about that he was moving close to Labour. Indeed Kenworthy himself thought at the time he was acting as Lloyd George's emissary to Henderson that Lloyd George was seriously contemplating joining Labour.[19] Nevertheless there is no real sign that Lloyd George or Labour's leadership saw this as probable then.

But Lloyd George was dissatisfied with the Liberal leadership's line on the General Strike. He did not attend the Liberal Shadow Cabinet on 10 May, and it was on 11 or 12 May that Kenworthy acted on Lloyd George's behalf. That Lloyd George was sounding out Labour

---

16   Lloyd George to Frances Stevenson, 20 August 1925; printed in A.J.P. Taylor (ed.), *My Darling Pussy* (London, Weidenfeld and Nicolson, 1975), pp.96-8.
17   Campbell, pp.119-31. Wilson, pp.324-38.
18   Ramsay MacDonald's diary, 14 May 1926; Ramsay MacDonald Papers PRO/39/1753.
19   M. Bentley, *The Liberal Mind* (Cambridge, Cambridge University Press, 1977), p.101.

as to a Parliamentary understanding is yet another sign that Lloyd George did not intend to cause an immediate breach with Asquith.[20] However, as in December 1916 Asquith appears to have reached the end of his tether in dealing with Lloyd George, and again misjudged both the time and the issue on which to act. In sending Lloyd George a letter effectively dismissing him from the leadership of the Liberal Party Asquith was encouraged by a meeting of other leading Liberals on 18 May at which - according to Vivian Phillipps (chairman of the Liberal Party organisation) - 'LG's action was very fully, freely and frankly discussed'. Phillipps was a purveyor of inaccurate information as to the attitude of the Liberal Party in the country, telling Lord Gladstone on 20 May that all his information from his contacts in the country showed 'that Ll.G's stock was never lower than it is at the present moment'.[21]

In fact, as Asquith and his supporters soon found to their cost, it was they who had misjudged the mood of most of the Liberal Party.[22] On the day that Lloyd George's measured response to Asquith appeared in the press alongside Asquith's letter, Ramsay Muir (a leading figure in the rethinking of Liberal policies in the 1920s) accused Sir John Simon of double standards. He wrote,

> You proposed a simultaneous calling off of the strike and the mine owners' notices. This would have been in fact an implicit bargain with the TUC. It was in substance identical with the Archbishop's proposal, which was backed by Mr Lloyd George ...I now learn, from the amazing correspondence in this morning's papers that Mr Lloyd George has been publicly rebuked and even excommunicated by Lord Oxford precisely because he took the line which you advocated, presumably with the approval of the 'Shadow Cabinet'.[23]

Once again in his career Lloyd George was very quick to take advantage of unexpected developments arising from a critical political situation which he had played a major part in creating. As with both the rejection of the People's Budget by the House of Lords in 1909 and the replacement of Asquith as Prime Minister in 1916, Lloyd George had not designed in detail what occurred. But, as Frances Stevenson noted in her diary for the week following 20 May, he knew how to make the most of other's errors. She commented,

> He will not resign. His tactics are perfect. He is giving them a long rope with which to hang themselves. He has already succeeded in driving them right into the arms of Conservatives.

---

20   Both John Campbell, pp.136-40, and Michael Bentley, pp.101-102, argue this. I agree.
21   V. Phillipps to Lord Gladstone, 20 May 1926; Herbert Gladstone Papers (British Library), Add. Ms. 46, 475, f.280.
22   Campbell, pp.141-46. Wilson, pp.331-33.
23   Ramsay Muir to simon, 26 May 1926; Simon Papers (viewed at Buckfastleigh; now at the Bodleian Library, Oxford).

She also noted, after Lloyd George saw Philip Snowden on 29 May, that the latter 'says this makes things easier for an understanding with the Labour Party'.[24]

In so far as Lloyd George had a long term view in 1926, it was surely that for the Liberal Party to survive it had to propose new social policies, and to implement these in Parliament it needed to work with the moderate majority of the Parliamentary Labour Party; Frances Stevenson noted in her diary on 15 May 1926,

> D.'s idea is to go definitely towards the *Left*, and gradually to co-ordinate
> and consolidate all the progressive forces in the country, against the
> Conservative and reactionary forces. Thus he will eventually get all sane
> Labour as well as Liberalism behind him.[25]

The nature of the new Liberal policies was pointing this way. Having swung away from supporting state intervention in the period from the autumn of 1919, Lloyd George became more attracted to it again in the mid 1920s onwards. This made sense in crude political terms. After 1924 the chances of him creating a new Centre Coalition of the 1919-22 type had largely evaporated, and Baldwin had the leasehold on Home Rule For Industry and minimising public expenditure. But the new Liberal programmes of the 1920s, which Lloyd George was quick to take up and, indeed, to foster, were calling for a certain amount of government regulation. As the introduction to the Liberal Industrial Inquiry put it,

> We have no love for State intervention in itself ... [But] The Theory that
> private competition, unregulated and unaided, will work out, with certainty,
> to the greatest advantage of the community is found by experience to be far
> from the truth. The scope of useful intervention by the whole Society,
> whether by constructive action of its own or by regulating or assisting
> private action, is seen to be much larger than was formerly supposed.[26]

Indeed, in domestic politics, Lloyd George was always better at pleading the case for helping needy groups in society or for taking action to remedy some industrial or agrarian problem than arguing for retrenchment. The 1924 Liberal programme had reflected some of his long-held concerns as well as ideas stemming from the early Liberal summer schools in its call for 'Peace, Social Reform and National Development' rather than the ancient Liberal cry of 'Peace, Retrenchment and Reform'.[27]

National Development was very much a favoured cause of Lloyd George. In his 'People's Budget' of 1909 he had set aside £200,000 for a Development Fund which he

---

24   Diary entry, 30 May 1926; A. J. P. Taylor (ed.), *Lloyd George: A Diary by Frances Stevenson* (London, Hutchinson, 1971), pp.247-48.

25   Ibid., p.246.

26   *Britain's Industrial Future* (London, Ernest Benn, 1928), p.xix.

27   M. Freeden, *Liberalism Divided* (Oxford, Oxford University Press, 1986), p.101, and for the Liberal Summer Schools of the 1920s' generally, pp.78-126.

intended should be used for light railways and harbours as well as for afforestation and agricultural research. There had also been a 'development' element in the public works that his government approved in 1920 and 1921 as part of its response to the severe post-war cyclical downturn in the economy.[28] In April 1924 he called for a major programme of public works so as to 'overhaul our national equipment', and in so doing pressed the analogy that the nation should behave like a wise businessman who 'utilises periods of slackness to repair his machinery, to re-equip his workshops, and generally to put his factory in order, so that when prosperity comes he will be in as good a position as his keenest competitor to take advantage of the boom'.[29] Lloyd George's advocacy of national development influenced Keynes' arguments for dealing with unemployment, which he first outlined in May 1924.[30]

These approaches to the role of the state and to unemployment made it highly desirable for their proponents that there should be Parliamentary co-operation between Liberals and Labour. Indeed Keynes in late 1924 saw a future in which the Liberal Party could expect to hold the balance of power 'in one election out of every two'.[31] Lloyd George appears to have taken a similar view after the 1924 general election, except, perhaps, for a period of high hopes after by-election gains in the spring and early summer of 1929. He was resigned to there being a strong Labour Party in the next Parliament, telling J.L. Garvin (the editor of the *Observer*) in October 1928 that having studied Garvin's analysis of three-corned fights in by-elections, 'I am convinced that "the triangle" will enable Labour to sweep the industrial constituencies next time'.[32] Indeed, much earlier - in 1920 - he had said of the Independent Liberals that their only opportunity of a return to office was as part of a coalition government.[33] In the late 1920s it is not easy to judge whether he hoped that another hung Parliament would lead to office or just to substantial influence on government policy making. Many of those involved in the formulation of the new Liberal policies expressed the more limited aspiration for Liberalism. Thus Keynes in 1926 observed that there was much to be said for 'supplying ... Labour governments with ideas'.[34] And E.D. Simon, when commenting in February 1927 on the Liberal Industrial Inquiry observed: 'We hope to produce a report about October which may be of some good to the Liberal Party, and may, on the

28   B.K. Murray, *The People's Budget 1909-10* (Oxford, Clarendon Press, 1980), pp.146 and 201-202. K.O. Morgan, *Consensus and Disunity* (Oxford, Clarendon Press, 1979), pp.284-88. P. Rowland, *Lloyd George* (London, Barrie and Jenkins, 1975) pp.216-17 and 543-44.
29   'The Stateman's Task', *Nation and Athenaeum*, 12 April 1924; quoted in W.R. Garside, *British Unemployment 1919-1939* (Cambridge, Cambridge University Press, 1990), pp.321-22.
30   'Does Unemployment need a drastic remedy?', *Nation*, 24 May 1924. On this see P. Clarke, 'The Politics of Keynesian Economics, 1924-31' in M. Bentley and J. Stevenson (eds.), *High and Low Politics in Modern Britain* (Oxford, Clarendon Press, 1983), pp.154-81 and his *The Keynesian Revolution in the Making 1924-1936* (Oxford, Clarendon Press, 1988), pp.75-8.
31   Clarke, *Keynesian Revolution*, p.81.
32   Lloyd George to Garvin, 31 October 1928; Garvin Papers (University of Texas, Austin), Box 11; copy in Lloyd George Papers (House of Lords Record Office), G/8/5/15.
33   In reply to Sir Donald MacLean in the House of Commons, 10 February 1920. 125 *H.C. Deb. 5s.*, c.35.
34   'Liberalism and Labour', *Nation*, 20 February 1926; quoted in Clarke, 'Politics of Keynesian Economics', p.177.

other hand, be adopted piecemeal by the other two'.[35]   But present historians can be
sceptical, just as Ramsay MacDonald was in May 1926, as to whether influence alone would
have satisfied for long Lloyd George's political aspirations before he had reached his
seventies.

    Yet if some new Liberal policies could bring Liberals close to Labour, their attitudes
to trade unionism, as well as to Soviet Russia, always remained a potential area of friction.
Lloyd George had anathematised the strong trade unions when he was prime minister after the
Armistice, and he continued to do so until after the General Strike. In this he was in line with
most Liberal opinion. As Michael Freeden has observed of the post First World War period,
there was a 'growing preoccupation of liberals with monopolies of labour rather than of
capital'.[36] When Baldwin agreed to a coal subsidy on 31 July 1925, Lloyd George was firm
in his condemnation of the government giving way to the pressure from the trade unions. In
the House of Commons he made much of the Conservatives' discomfiture, taunting William
Joynson-Hicks, the right-wing Home Secretary, Baldwin and Churchill:

> It really is no use barking at the red flag every time it cracks in the wind,
> while his chief is engaged in humbly gilding the flag-staff - and with
> standard gold. Really, it is sad to see the Chancellor of the Exchequer
> assisting in that operation. He was very eager to fight the Reds on the
> Volga. I am very sorry to see him running away from them on the Thames
> and leaving his purse behind.[37]

In this, at least in part, he was drawing attention to his government's record and to the merits
of the coalition policies of those years. At this time he was still keeping in play those on the
Right in British politics who were sympathetically inclined to him. Thus, a fortnight after his
Commons speech on the coal subsidy he wrote to Garvin in a manner clearly suggesting the
need for another 1919-22 style coalition government:

> I am very anxious to have a talk with you upon the present situation. I am
> genuinely disturbed about it, and conversations I had with J.H. Thomas
> when he was staying here with me a week ago, have deepened my anxiety
> ... As to the coal situation, I agree with you that success is the only thing
> that can possibly justify the surrender to trade union threats. I think it was
> a wild gamble, and that the risks are immeasurable. J.H.T. told me that it
> has made it impossible for him to press his men to consent to a reduction
> and yet without that reduction the railways must run at a loss. His opinion
> is that it has given an almost uncontrollable access of strength to the
> aggressive elements in the trade union world. Cook and his merry men are

---

35   Simon to F.W. Eggleston, 11 February 1927; Simon of Wythenshawe Papers (Manchester Central Library)
          M11/14/29.
36   Freeden, p.200.
37   187 H.C. *Debs 5s*, c.93; 6 August 1926.

now definitely on top. Still, serious as it is, this is only one of the elements in the outlook that provoke disquiet. I consider this country to be in greater peril than at any moment since the most critical hours of the war, not so much of immediate catastrophe, but of sinking gradually to an irrecoverable line ...

He must have been pleased at Garvin's enthusiastic response. Garvin's talk of it being 'a graver phase than the worst period of the war' and 'our 1789' must have taken him back to the heady days of 1919-1920, when he had played on the alarmist fears of the propertied classes.[38] Lloyd George went on to build a coalition castle in the air with Garvin and others at Churt on 28 August, before abandoning this political possibility.[39]

But in August 1925 Lloyd George had also been highlighting his alternative way of dealing with the long-running problems of the coal industry. This was the policy which was set out by a research committee that he had set up in March 1924 and chaired, and which was published that July as *Coal And Power*. The part of the report which dealt with coal suggested a solution broadly similar to the minority report to the 1919 Sankey Commission by Sir Arthur Duckham and which Lloyd George's government had offered to the Miner's Federation that autumn.[40] In his introduction to *Coal And Power* Lloyd George promoted the proposals in terms which harked back to his reconstruction speeches after the 1918 Armistice. He wrote,

> Today of all times, when what is needed most is work and reconstruction to make good the losses of the war and to equip the nation for that more intense competition which is inevitable in international trade, it would be almost fatal to start a struggle over the coal-mining industry which would divide the nation and involve years of turmoil and strife.[41]

In January 1926, when Lloyd George was still deploring the government's weakness in the face of pressure from the unions, Garvin continued to extol Lloyd George's middle way. Garvin wrote to him 'What about *Coal And Power* now?' - adding, 'I never thought it a party patent but you were the only statesman to give vision and energy to it, and lead the way to it'.[42]

Lloyd George's attitude to powerful unions taking steps to coerce the government remained consistent in the General Strike, a point that is obscured by the political furore within the Liberal Party over his actions at this time. Where he differed from many colleagues was that while he deplored the calling of it by the TUC he was also very critical

38   Lloyd George to J.L. Garvin, 19 August 1925 and Garvin to Lloyd George, 20 August 1925; Lloyd George Papers, G/8/5/1 and 2.
39   On this, see C.P. Scott's diary, 19 October 1925; T. Wilson (ed.), *The Political Diaries of C.P. Scott* (London, Collins, 1970), p.482 and Campbell, pp.129-30.
40   Campbell, pp.96-7. Wrigley, *Challenge of Labour*, pp.200-08.
41   *Coal And Power* (London, Hodder and Stoughton, 1924), p.viii.
42   J.L. Garvin to Lloyd George, 16 January 1926; Lloyd George Papers, G/8/5/9.

of Baldwin's government. Thus he characterised the government's actions in breaking off
negotiations before the strike as 'precipitate, unwarrantable and mischievous'.[43] As for the
unions, he stated in an article that he issued on 12 May (but which he withdrew on hearing
later that same day that the strike had been called off):

> If the trade unions inflict a defeat on the government, it will be an
> encouragement to the extreme elements in Labour to resort in future to the
> general strike as a weapon of offence whenever they find their purpose
> thwarted by the normal working of democratic institutions. Such a defeat
> would sooner or later end the experiment of popular government in these
> islands.[44]

However once the challenge of militant trade unionism appeared to be vanquished by
the calling off of the General Strike in 1926, Lloyd George and many Liberals took a more
sympathetic attitude to the trade unions. This approach was encouraged by the Baldwin
government's Trade Disputes and Trade Unions Bill of 1927, which was a naked attack on the
political activities of trade unions and placed considerable restrictions on public sector unions.
This was notably so with those Liberals actively engaged in reformulating Liberal policies.
Thus, in the case of E.D. Simon, in November 1926 he was sympathising largely with Sir
John Simon's view on trade unions, observing:

> Fundamentally the most serious thing about them is that they do not,
> generally speaking, co-operate to get the greatest and cheapest production.
> The Liberal attitude to them should ... be such as to attempt in all possible
> ways to encourage a change of outlook and spirit. However, the legal side
> is of course also exceedingly important.

But, after introduction of the Tory Bill, his emphasis changed. He wrote to William Eagar,
the secretary of the Liberal Industrial Inquiry, urging with regard to their work on trade union
legislation that 'the whole main point of the report must be to show how important strong trade
unions are, how necessary it is to get their co-operation in constructive reform, and what an
evil thing the present Bill is'.[45]
Lloyd George himself condemned the government 's failure to bring the mining
dispute to a speedy close and won praise from A.J. Cook, the secretary of the Miners'
Federation, when he denounced Baldwin for advising Americans not to contribute to the
hardship fund for miners' families on the untrue ground that there was no suffering. He also
denounced the Trade Disputes and Trade Unions Bill as the government's 'worst mistake'.

---

43   A.J. Sylvester's account remains valuable: *The Real Lloyd George* (London, Cassell, 1947), pp.146-59.
44   Davies to Runciman, 14 May 1926; Runciman Papers (University of Newcastle Library), Box 2. This
       passage was published in the *Daily Chronicle*, 13 May 1926.
45   E.D. Simon to Sir John Simon, 17 November 1926, and to W. Eagar, 6 April 1927; Simon of
       Wythenshawe Papers, M11/14/29. For Muir's similar change in emphasis, see Freeden, pp.207-08.

In the Commons on 5 May 1927 he warned, 'You may impound all the funds of the unions and imprison their leaders, you may cripple their political funds, you may do more than that, but you cannot force workmen to work better or to work more effectively by any Act of Parliament'. He condemned the Bill as a stupid move made when the trade union leaders were being conciliatory and when the revival of British industry required goodwill among the workforce.[46] This had also been the theme of the Liberal Industrial Inquiry's preliminary publication *Trade Unionism and the Trade Union Bill*, which aimed to speak for those who regarded 'trade unionism as not merely a valuable but an indispensable element in our social structure, and who had hoped its strength was going to be employed in a great co-operative effort of healing and reconstruction whereby the nation might be lifted out of its industrial troubles'.[47]

Lloyd George and the Liberal Industrial Inquiry advocated a middle way in British industrial relations that owed much to the Whitley Committee proposals of 1917, which in turn had grown out of earlier experience of joint industrial councils in many industries. The Liberal Industrial Inquiry shied away from calling for the immediate reconvening of the National Industrial Conference of 1919, or something like it; though leading figures such as E.D. Simon urged this policy.[48] Instead it called for a 'representative Council of Industry', suggesting that this might be composed of nine representatives from each side of industry, 'selected by the government from a panel nominated by representative bodies of employers and wage-earners', plus a further six persons nominated by the ministerial head of a new Ministry of Industry. But it did support joint industrial councils, and urged that procedures should be set up to give legal force to their decisions.[49] Whitleyism was something which had attracted, and still did attract, support across a wide political spectrum.[50] This included leading moderate trade union figures in the Labour Party, such as Arthur Henderson, J.R. Clynes and Ben Turner. Indeed Henderson in October 1928 was calling for a National Industrial Council to be set up, as suggested some nine years earlier by the National Industrial Conference.[51] The Liberal Industrial Inquiry also advocated schemes for profit-sharing, another old notion in some Liberal circles, and which in the past had attracted the interest of Labour figures such as Henderson.[52] So the Liberal proposals on industrial relations were

---

46   Campbell, pp.149 and 167-68.
47   Ramsay Muir, *Trade Unionism and the Trade Union Bill* (London, Williams and Norgate, 1927), p.10.
48   As in the conclusion to a typescript report on trade union legislation, forwarded by Simon to the executive committee of the Liberal Industrial Inquiry, 7 April 1927; Simon of Wythenshawe Papers, M11/14/29.
49   *Britain's Industrial Future* (London, Benn, 1928), pp.172-75, 211-13 and 222-25. Industrial relations constituted one of five 'books' (or sections) of this volume.
50   For Conservatives considering Whitleyism at this time see A. Steel-Maitland to Lord Robert Cecil, 25 May 1927; Cecil Papers (British Library), Add. Ms. 51071, f.143. More generally, on earlier enthusiastic support for Whitleyism, see C. Wrigley, 'Trade Unionists, Employers and the Cause of Industrial Unity and Peace 1916-21' in C. Wrigley and J. Shepherd (eds.), *On The Move* (London, Hambledon Press, 1991).
51   At Todmorden on 23 October 1928; *Times*, 24 October 1928.
52   For a very critical appraisal of these industrial relations proposals see A. Booth and M. Pack, *Employment, Capital and Economic Policy: Great Britain 1918-1939* (Oxford, Blackwell, 1985), pp.45-6.

far from alien to moderate Labour politicians, whereas the Baldwin government's 1927 measure enraged virtually all in the Labour movement.

However while there was a moving towards Labour by Lloyd George and many Liberal intellectuals in the late 1920s, Lloyd George himself carried with him a legacy of distrust, much of it linked to the years 1919 to 1922. He himself had spurned the 1919 National Industrial Conference, once the threat of serious industrial unrest had lessened later in the year. Similarly his government had been far from enthusiastic about implementing the Whitley Report after the end of the First World War. As for the Liberal Industrial Inquiry's proposals which would deal with unemployment, the sub-committee on which had been chaired by Lloyd George himself, Labour was to claim that Lloyd George had had the opportunity to take such action when prime minister but had failed to do so. Thus the 1929 general election Arthur Henderson responded to the Liberals' pamphlet *We Can Conquer Unemployment: Mr. Lloyd George's Pledge*, issued before the election, with the claims:

> No single proposal was now put forward which had not been publicly advocated in and out of Parliament by the Labour Party for years, and what was more to the point, they had been urged repeatedly upon governments of which Lloyd George was either prime minister or a very responsible minister. The Labour Party had appealed to Liberal and Tory governments to adopt their comprehensive proposals for dealing with unemployment which were not emergency measures only, but permanent schemes of national development and economic reconstruction.[53]

Henderson's talk of Labour's 'comprehensive proposals' was to look very hollow indeed within three years, not least because of the incubus of Snowden's financial orthodoxy. But there were inconsistencies within *Britain's Industrial Future*. As Alan Booth and Melvyn Pack have argued, it was something of 'an expansionist limb grafted onto a body of deep economic orthodoxy'.[54]

Nevertheless Lloyd George's willingness to take up new ideas and his ability to convey to the public that the Liberal Party was attempting to move with the needs of the time ensured that the Liberals did better in the 1929 general election than they probably would have done otherwise, given the appalling internecine backbiting that took place between 1924 and 1929. The 59 Liberal MPs of 1929 was a disappointing result; but better than the 20 of 1935 or 6 of 1951. However it is unlikely that the electorate as a whole took in the details of the new Liberal thinking. Indeed there always remained a problem for the Liberals of defining an area which was specifically theirs. Eagar, in the midst of the Liberal Industrial Inquiry's work, confessed to Philip Kerr:

---

53   At Cardiff, 10 April 1929; *Times* 11 April 1929. In this Henderson was enunciating the official Labour Party view, set out in *How to Conquer Unemployment* (written by G.D.H. Cole).
54   Booth and Pack, pp.43-8. For a survey of contemporary criticism of the Liberal proposals see Garside, pp.326-36.

The effect of the report, in my humble opinion, as it is at present taking shape will be:

(a)   To convince Labour men generally that Liberalism is Conservatism without the courage of its convictions.

(b)   To prove to Conservatives that Liberalism is Socialism without the moral appeal of Socialism or its intellectual tidyness.

(c)   To settle for a considerable number of Liberals that their philosophy is mainly of antiquarian interest and that they must make up their minds finally whether their intellectual home is in the Conservative or the Socialist Parties.[55]

This view was unduly gloomy as to the potential political utility of such work - but it is notable that several of the leading Liberal thinkers involved often expressed semi-detached attitudes to the Liberal Party.

Lloyd George's efforts to revive the Liberal Party and to move it to the Left were made more difficult by the activities of Asquith's supporters. E.D. Simon observed with feeling in early 1927, 'Many of our leaders have been behaving in a really disgusting manner, being far more influenced by their hatred of Lloyd George than by their love of Liberal principles'.[56] Soon after the 1929 general election some of the Asquithians were ready to indicate their disloyalty to their own leader - Lloyd George - and to offer MacDonald support, thereby weakening Lloyd George's bargaining strength in a hung Parliament. Sir George Croydon Marks, who had been the Liberal MP for North Cornwall until 1929, advised the Labour Prime Minister that Sir Donald Maclean, who had been Liberal leader in the Commons after Asquith had lost his seat in the 1918 general election and who had taken over North Cornwall from Marks in 1929, and Viscount Grey 'were joining a small band of men whose views were not those of LG and these men would decline to be controlled by anyone connected with the LG group'. In the Commons this group was said to include Isaac Foot, L.S. Jones, Sir J.T. Walters, Walter Runciman and George Lambert (all of whom represented Cornish or Devon seats). Marks commented that Maclean believed 'that there were very many of the Party who will follow him now that the country has so distinctly thrown down the Lloyd George Liberal Policy'. Marks further remarked of Maclean:

... he assures me he was more sympathetic towards you and your policy than towards L.G. He further stated that he and Viscount Grey had determined that you should have a fair chance and they would do all that was possible to support you, particularly, if they could have, sometimes in advance, some indication of the policy that was to be proposed in order that they might not be detached as they were during the 1923-24 Parliament.[57]

---

55   W. Eagar to P. Kerr, 27 August 1927; Lothian Papers (Scottish Record Office): GD40/17/229, f.317-19.
56   Simon to F.W. Eggleston, 11 February 1927; Simon of Wythenshawe Papers, M11/14/29.
57   Marks to MacDonald, 7 June 1929; MacDonald Papers, PRO 30/69/1174, f.29-31.

Given this attitude, fostered by Grey and Viscount Gladstone, it was not surprising that Lord Beauchamp, Liberal Leader in the House of Lords was to confess to Lloyd George, 'Unfortunately when we do send out a whip, a number ... come down and vote *against* us!'.[58] Little wonder that in later life Lloyd George looked back on the Liberal interparty strife of the late 1920s, along with the strain of the period of Lundendorff's breakthrough on the Western Front, as the least pleasant in his political career. From the outset of the 1929 Parliament Lloyd George's exhortation to the new Parliamentary Liberal Party was proven to be no more than wishful thinking. Then he had urged, 'In whichever lobby we decide to vote, we must go there together ... In union there is not merely strength but life itself for the Liberal Party'.[59]

Over the two years of the second Labour government Lloyd George tried to force tangible policy concessions from MacDonald. In the area of unemployment, this involved Lloyd George harrying ministers to carry out the pledges that their Party had made endlessly since its foundation. In doing this Lloyd George was adroitly reminding the electorate of the Liberal package of policies contained in *Britain's Industrial Future*. Lloyd George also took the opportunity of being close to power to try to move land as an issue to a central role in public policy. He also tried hard to extract electoral reform as his price for Liberal support.

In the sessions of Parliament in the second half of 1920, Lloyd George was at his most effective in giving Labour ministers a hard time. His questioning of their policy and his general Parliamentary command was a very clear statement to Labour that his presence could not be ignored and his support was something which struggling ministers should desire. In this period he called into question the competence of J.H. Thomas on unemployment, Wedgwood Benn on India and Margaret Bondfield on unemployment insurance.[60] However he showed Labour its need for his support when he savaged the Coal Mines Bill in December 1929.

But in doing this, Lloyd George was being consistent with his actions in 1919-20 and 1926 and with the policy of *Coal And Power*. At the outset of the Labour government, he had pointedly remarked in the debate on the King's Address:

> I do not say they are betraying the miners because they cannot carry
> nationalisation. They are going to carry what they can ... but I am bound
> to point out that they are proposing to do now what they rejected in 1919.[61]

In the case of the Coal Mine's Bill he objected to a proposal which fixed quotas and prices, thereby benefiting the economically less viable pits, as compensation to the owners for reducing the miners' working day. This gave him the opportunity to take up his fundamental

58   Beauchamp to Lloyd George, 19 July 1930; Lloyd George Papers, G/3/5/29.
59   Quoted in Campbell, p.245.
60   229 H.C. *Deb. 5s* c.141-59 and 815-21; 3 and 19 July 1929. 231 H.C. *Deb. 5s*, c.473-74 and 1313-23; 1 and 7 November 1929. 232 H.C. *Deb. 5s*, c.767-78, 1734-38 and 1983; 21 and 28 November and 2 December 1929.
61   229 H.C. *Deb. 5s*, c.155; 3 July 1929.

Liberal theme: that the Liberals were the defenders of the consumer against the self-seeking of Capital and Labour. Thus he told the Commons that the Bill

> ... contains ... the worst feature of Socialism and individualism without the redeeming features of either. It is State interference without State protection. It has all the greed of individualism without the stimulus of competition ... [It] is a complete surrender to one interest ... without regard to the general interest of the community.[62]

MacDonald was outraged. He gave vent in his diary to his views of Lloyd George as a 'sinister politician' and one who had 'degraded our public life'.[63] But this annoyance was yet another sign of MacDonald's sensitive self-centredness and inability to comprehend others' points of view. As leader of the Liberals in the Commons Lloyd George would have been a fool to have acted in any other way, unless acceptance of such a measure was part of some substantial deal on government policy.

However the growing crisis over unemployment did push MacDonald in May 1930 into seeking broader support for his government. By this time talks between the Liberals and the government over electoral reform, which had begun in earnest in early February 1930, had come to nothing. MacDonald had been willing to consider the alternative vote but not proportional representation (the change that Lloyd George sought). But on 20 May the Labour Party's National Executive had rejected that as well.[64] MacDonald, nevertheless, needed Liberal support in Parliament. This was even more desirable on 19 May 1930, with Oswald Mosley indicating to MacDonald that he was about to resign from the government over its feeble response to unemployment.

Hence MacDonald wrote to both Baldwin and Lloyd George that day asking them if they would be willing 'to attend a conference or a consultation of the three parties on the agricultural question'.[65] Baldwin declined. Lloyd George agreed, but on the wider remit of unemployment as well as agriculture, and then on the condition that he had access to all the relevant government papers and to the government's expert advisers.[66] He also urged MacDonald that

> ... in order to ensure Parliamentary co-operation free from friction it is essential that the government should not introduce measures dealing with unemployment or agriculture without first discussing them in the joint

---

62   233 H.C. *Deb.* 5s c.1672-89; 19, December 1929. Campbell, pp.256-58.

63   D. Marquand, *Ramsay MacDonald* (London, Cape, 1977), pp.526-28.

64   Marquand, pp.529-33.

65   MacDonald to Baldwin and Lloyd George, 19 May 1930; Papers of the Prime Minister's Private Office (Public Record Office), PREM 1/108.

66   Tom Jones' diary, 3 June 1930; K. Middlemas (ed.), *Thomas Jones Whitehall Diary*, Vol. 2 (London, Oxford University Press, 1969), p.262.

conference. It is important that the programme should be developed as a single whole.[67]

However Labour ministers were fearful of Lloyd George making political capital out of any co-operation. Addison, on being appointed Minister of Agriculture, observed to MacDonald, 'You don't need to be reminded but he will require careful watching ... '. MacDonald himself noted of Lloyd George in early July, after the Liberals had nearly caused the defeat of his government on the Finance Bill, 'He is the most consummate cheat and wirepuller of the time'.[68]

Whether it was distrust of Lloyd George, the sheer inertia of the government, or a combination of both, the resulting meetings proved very frustrating for Lloyd George and his two Liberal colleagues, Lothian and Rowntree.[69] On 22 August Lloyd George sent MacDonald a very long letter in which he complained about the lack of real co-operation given to the Liberals on either agriculture or unemployment, pressed again the case for a major programme of road building and demanded that the government must give proof that it would soon adopt an emergency programme and have the political will to put it into effect.[70]

In October Lloyd George appears to have still hoped that the government would take notice of the Liberal Party's ideas. On 2 October Lloyd George and his two Liberal colleagues had a private meeting with Addison, over lunch at the Langham Hotel. Lloyd George made it clear that he hoped Labour's land programme would 'be as ambitious as we can make it'. Addison reported to MacDonald that Lloyd George 'generally expressed the view that it was much better ... to go "all out" rather than to try and draft a non-contentious Bill' and that 'he was most emphatic about ... a big scheme of land development supported by a development loan'. Lloyd George also indicated that he was willing to consider agricultural marketing boards helping the domestic producer.[71] The next day he sent MacDonald an outline of the overall Liberal proposals and a week later the full 160 pages 'Memorandum on Liberal Proposals on Unemployment and Agriculture'. This was soon rushed into print for the general public, as the 104 page pamphlet, *How To Tackle Unemployment*.[72]

---

67   Lloyd George to MacDonald, 18 June 1930; PREM 1/108. the letter was drafted by Lord Lothian (formerly Philip Kerr) and approved by Seebohm Rowntree. Lothian to Sylvester, 19 June 1930; Lothian Papers, GD40/17/250, f.488-89.

68   Addison to MacDonald, 7 June 1930; Ramsay MacDonald Papers, PRO 30/69/2/676. MacDonald's diary, July 1930; quoted in Marquand, p.547. Garvin at the start of the year had urged Thomas to work frankly with Lloyd George; a letter which,curiously, is attributed to Lloyd George in G. Blaxland, *J.H. Thomas: A Life For Unity* (London, Muller, 1964), pp.234-35.

69   On this, see R. Skidelsky, *Politicians And The Slump* (London, Macmillan, 1967), pp.220-27.

70   Lloyd George to Ramsay MacDonald, 22 August 1930; PREM 1/108 and Lloyd George Papers, G/13/2/6.

71   Addison minute to MacDonald, 2 October 1930; PREM 1/108, Addison 17/5410.

72   Lloyd George to MacDonald, 3 October 1930 and A.J. Sylvester to MacDonald's secretary, 10 October 1930; PREM 1/108 and Lloyd George Papers, G/13/2/7 and G/13/3/1. D. Lloyd George, the Marquess of Lothian and B. Seebohm Rowntree, *How To Tackle Unemployment* (London, Press Printers, 1930).

With the lengthy talks with the government producing only disappointing results, Lloyd George reverted to airing the need for the recreation of something like his coalition government. In his lengthy letter of 24 August 1930 to MacDonald he had made much of there being 'no evidence of that driving energy behind the government as a whole which is essential in the emergency in which we stand'. In the autumn of that year he expressed such sentiments in public speeches, encouraged by Garvin and the Press Lords, Beaverbrook and Rothermere. But there were few senior politicians other than Churchill who were interested, and the tariff issue remained a major barrier. [73]

Indeed at various times during the existence of the second Labour government, Lloyd George indicated that if Labour rebuffed him he could try to do business elsewhere. In so doing, he was also making a wider appeal to the electorate than made by his more radical posture. As in 1924, he made much of his elder world statesman role to act as a spokesperson of British national and imperial interests. Thus, for example, in late July 1929, he raised the Young Report on Reparations, and while feeling that it was 'very stern and severe' on Germany, complained that 'the whole of the sacrifices have been made practically at our expense' and urged that 'if there is to be any abatement in the German annuity, it should be distributed fairly'. In similar vein he expressed strong concern that the Labour government was going too far in raising expectations on the subject of dominion status for India. [74] Though, equally, on occasion he did back the Labour government's foreign policy. Thus, on trade with Russia he could warmly support government policy and point to his own record on this subject when he had been prime minister. [75]

However in early 1931 the Labour government's resolve in the face of the worsening economic environment was weakening. Though MacDonald remained extremely suspicious of Lloyd George, commenting to Wedgwood Benn that Lloyd George 'quite evidently wishes that the Liberals should dominate the situation', [76] he did need Liberal support if Labour was to avoid a disastrous early general election. On 12 February MacDonald accepted a Liberal motion calling for a programme of national development backed by adequate funding for loans. Lloyd George's subsequent attack on City interests' opposition to radical measures led to George Lansbury's famous letter of 13 February 1931 in which he urged Lloyd George to join the Labour Party and even to become deputy premier. Lloyd George had no hesitation in declining to take up such a notion. But, after Liberal opposition to the government's Trade Disputes and Trade Unions Bill caused it to be dropped, there was much closer consultation between the parties. [77] By May Lothian was writing.

I am more and more coming to the conclusion that we have got to recreate a two party system and, if so, we ought seriously to consider whether a

---

73   Skidelsky, pp.278-79. Campbell, pp.275-77.

74   230 H.C. *Deb. 5s*, c.1668; 26 July 1929. 231 H.C. *Deb. 5s*, c.1313-23; 7 November 1929.

75   231 H.C. *Deb. 5s*, c.913-18; 5 November 1929.

76   This was in the context of India. MacDonald to Wedgwood Benn, 10 February 1931; Ramsay MacDonald Papers, PRO 30/69/440/1176.

77   Rowland, pp.677-79. 248 H.C. *Deb. 5s* c.179-218; 26 February 1931.

basis for gradual coalition can be found between the two parties of the Left.[78]

In late May 1931, not long before the economic crisis transformed the British political landscape, it appeared that Labour and the Liberals would be crusading yet again on Free Trade, while Conservatives again put their faith in tariffs. It also seemed likely in July that Lloyd George and some Liberal colleagues might join the Labour government.[79] But the economic crisis and Lloyd George's serious illness, which confined him to bed on 27 July 1931, ended such a possibility.

What seems clear is that direct involvement in a Labour-Liberal government or strong influence on a purely Labour government was Lloyd George's aim. When Lloyd George has pressed his policy of supporting MacDonald's government on the National Liberal Federation Conference at Buxton on 15 May 1931 he had commented,

> They say that Liberalism will be wiped out next time. I don't believe it, but
> if this were our last voyage, I would like it to be one when we are carrying
> a great cargo.[80]

There can be little doubt, for all Lansbury's effusions, that Lloyd George was determined to stay with his ship and to go down with it if necessary.

After the Liberal involvement in the National Government and the 1931 general election, Lloyd George was bitter at their performance. In a letter to his friend and former close Parliamentary associate, Sir Herbert Lewis, Lloyd George complained:

> Those who were responsible for Liberal direction after I was placed *hors de*
> *combat* surrendered all the passes to the enemy. The heights are now in
> command of the Protectionists: we are entirely at their mercy. The poor
> abject mob of Liberals are there cowering down in the swamps. They have
> ceased entirely to count. No one talks now of the extermination of the
> Liberal Party; for all practical purposes it is annihilated.

Significantly, he continued his complaint with the observation, 'When I was stricken down in the late summer we had complete control of the Parliamentary situation, and the Labour government was getting more and more into our hands'.[81]

Lloyd George was not to come close to power again. Though he did continue to pursue his major causes. Thus he raised the land as an important issue at intervals during the

---

78   Lothian to Ramsay Muir, 18 May 1931; Lothian Papers, GD40/17/259, f.433.
79   The best discussion of this possibility is in Campbell, pp.293-95.
80   Quoted in ibid.,p.290.
81   Lloyd George to Lewis, 31 December 1931; Sir Herbert Lewis Papers (National Library of Wales), (1963
        deposit), 2,f.19. He verbally lashed Sir Herbert Samuel over Free Trade in the Commons on 25 October
        1932; 269 H.C. *Deb. 5s*, c.871-74.

1930s and he pressed again his national development proposals, notably in 1935. In October 1932 he rejected MacDonald's feelers to see if he would enter the National Government to deal with unemployment,[82] and, wisely in view of his age, during the Second World War, he declined to join Churchill's government or take up any official post. In the 1930s he continued to attract the admirat. n of some in the Labour movement, as well as several of the more radical younger Conservatives. But as a major influence on the Labour movement and on British politics, apart from a few occasions such as at the time of Neville Chamberlains's fall, his hour had passed with the onset of his illness in late July 1931.

82   This was an initiative of a former Liberal candidate, Captain Frederick Boult - but which gained MacDonald's approval. The correspondence between 13 October and 4 November 1932 is in the Ramsay MacDonald Papers, PRO, 30/69/1177.

LLOYD GEORGE, JOHN SIMON AND THE POLITICS OF THE LIBERAL PARTY 1918-31

DAVID DUTTON

Most people will be familiar with Lloyd George's famous words when John Simon finally resigned the Liberal whip in the summer of 1931, a few months before the latter took office as Foreign Secretary in Ramsay MacDonald's National Government. On 3 July, during the third reading of the outgoing Labour Government's Finance Bill, Lloyd George launched his attack. Invective came easily to the Welshman, but on this occasion he almost surpassed himself. Seldom since the days of his Limehouse speech on the House of Lords had he used such venomous language. He began by comparing Simon to a teetotaller who had turned alcoholic. Then, reinforcing his argument with the long wagging forefinger which he used to such dramatic effect, Lloyd George moved on to his punch-line. He did not, he stressed, in the least object to Simon changing his opinions,

> but I do object to this intolerable self-righteousness ... Greater men ... have done it in the past, but ... they, at any rate, did not leave behind them the slime of hypocrisy in passing from one side to another.[1]

Lloyd George's outburst came at the end of more than a decade of increasingly strained relations between two of the leading figures of the British Liberal party. Yet the relationship between Lloyd George and Simon encompassed much more than a matter of personal incompatibility. Their mutual animosity helped destroy what chance their party had of surviving as a genuine contender for power in the years after the World War I. Much, perhaps too much, has been written about the causes of the decline of the Liberal party. It is now surely apparent that there exists no single all-embracing explanation for this complex phenomenon. But it may be argued that some analyses have seriously predated the inevitability of Liberalism's demise. It needs to be stressed that throughout the decade after World War One the party remained, at least in terms of the popular vote, a significant force in British politics. At the general election of 1918 the disparate strands of Liberalism secured between them 2.7 million votes, about 26% of the total. At the election of 1929 the corresponding figures were 5.3 millions and 23%. Yet the fact that throughout this period Lloyd George and Simon found it almost impossible to combine their forces in the interests of the political philosophy to which both expressed allegiance deprived the party of the chance of making the most out of its strength at the ballot box.

The two men had much in common. Both were products of the humbler end of the professional middle class. Unlike so many of their political contemporaries neither was born into a life of luxury and ease. Though, like Lloyd George, born in Manchester, Simon too could claim Welsh ancestry. At the time of the Boer War - before he had secured a seat in parliament - Simon would have regarded himself, like Lloyd George, as on the party's radical wing. Though not close in personal terms, the two men not uncommonly found themselves as political allies, most noticeably during the cabinet crisis over naval expenditure in 1913-14.

---

1   House of Commons Debates, 5th Series, vol. 254, cols. 1657-68.

Both men had made a mark in Liberal politics before the coming of the war. Lloyd George, ten years older than Simon, had been the first to rise to prominence. President of the Board of Trade in 1905 and Chancellor of the Exchequer less than three years later, he was already a figure of national if not international renown. It seemed reasonable to assume that the office of Prime Minister might be the culmination of his already distinguished career. But Simon too had made a rapid advance after his election to parliament in 1906. When war came he had for ten months been Attorney-General with, unusually, a seat in the cabinet. Barely forty, his career seemed to have assumed an irresistible momentum of its own. His expectation and that of others must reasonably have been that higher office and possibly even the premiership itself were within his grasp. The immediate succession to Asquith and his office were not out of the question. For if the control of the Liberal party were to remain in Asquithian hands there were many who saw Simon as the Prime Minister's logical successor. These same observers viewed with dismay the prospect of Lloyd George ever emerging as leader.

The war, of course, destroyed all such calculations, while at the same time effecting a dramatic change in the relations between the two men. By showing that he possessed martial qualities which Asquith self-evidently lacked, Lloyd George emerged as a war leader of the first rank, becoming Prime Minister in December 1916 and standing at the end of hostilities in 1918 as the most powerful figure seen in British political life for many years. By contrast by 1918 most of Simon's hopes lay in ruins. Despite a brief period as Home Secretary, he had fallen out of the mainstream of frontline politics, his career floundering in the turmoil of Liberal disunity. His resignation from the government in January 1916 over the introduction of conscription had proved a serious miscalculation, at least in terms of the impact on his own career. In Lloyd George's eyes Simon's brand of Liberalism was now identified with a too scrupulous regard for the niceties of political principle. He had little time for those who, like Simon, agonized in a state of intellectual anguish over the price to be paid for the victory which both men sought.[2]

The new situation was apparent in the Coupon General Election of December 1918. On the one hand the Prime Minister, at the head of a now Conservative-dominated coalition, enjoyed an immense personal triumph, recognised as the man who had won the war and who must now proceed to win the peace. By contrast Simon's personal tragedy, losing his seat at Walthamstow, mirrored the tragedy of independent Liberalism as a whole. In his election campaign Simon disparaged the Coupon which would, he insisted, only produce 'dummy members'. He called instead for the election of more independent spirits such as himself. But in his electioneering Simon could capture only one of the two largely incompatible moods of idealism and vindictiveness which infused the British voter at this time. He could neither express not identify with the intense nationalism which pervaded the public mood. It was illustrative that his Conservative opponent in East Walthamstow could proclaim, 'If you want

---

2   Lloyd George may also have resented Simon's behaviour in 1917 when the latter agreed to represent him
        in a libel case against two Liberal newspapers. Simon's conscience got the better of him and he withdrew
        from the case, leaving Lloyd George with little time to secure a substitute.

to back up the men who have won the War, vote for Johnson, the Coalition and Lloyd George'.[3]

Simon regarded the new Coalition government with total contempt and, with his relations with Lloyd George at a low ebb, set his face against the possible future reunion of the warring Liberal factions, rejecting the blandishments of those who sought such an end.[4] Some of his attacks on the Prime Minister were remarkably outspoken considering that the two men had until 1916 been cabinet colleagues. In 1921, for example, he spoke of Lloyd George's qualities:

> Cleverness, ingenuity, adroitness! There has been nothing like it in human history. But, after all, character is more than cleverness. Sticking to a principle is more than adroitly shifting from one position to another. And, in the view of Liberals, Mr. Lloyd George has shown himself a faithless trustee of their traditions and beliefs.[5]

Simon's feelings for Lloyd George were fully reciprocated by the Prime Minister, as became apparent when Simon attempted to return to the House of Commons at the end of 1919. When a vacancy arose in the Spen Valley division of Yorkshire following the death of the sitting Coalition Liberal member, Simon was adopted as candidate by the local Liberal association, which was now anxious to run an independent Liberal. In previous by-elections Lloyd George had willingly supported Coalition Unionists against Asquithians, but had stopped short of engineering a direct confrontation between competing Liberals. At Spen Valley he took a different line even though many government supporters regarded his action in putting forward a Coalition Liberal candidate as needlessly provocative. As the Liberal vote was obviously going to be split, it is clear that the desire to exclude Simon had become more important to Lloyd George than the election of a government supporter. A little earlier the Prime Minister had written:

> I want to be in such a condition that even John Simon's return won't upset me. I am rather afraid that is what is going to happen. If it does it will be a disagreeable and disconcerting fact and will take a good deal to get over for it will undoubtedly weaken my influence.[6]

With the campaign under way Lloyd George expressed the hope that Simon would come at the bottom of the poll 'as he deserved'.[7] The Deputy Chairman of the Conservative party, seeing Lloyd George before visiting the constituency, found him 'mad keen to beat Simon'.

3   C. Bechhofer Roberts, *Sir John Simon* (London, 1938) p.158.
4   J. Spender to Simon 3 May 1921, cited M. Bentley, *The Liberal Mind 1914-1929* (Cambridge, 1977) p.85.
5   *Liberal Magazine* Aug. 1921.
6   A. J. P. Taylor (ed.), *My Darling Pussy* (London, 1975) p.27.
7   J. McEwen (ed.), *The Riddell Diaries* (London, 1986) p. 297.

'I don't care who wins if that blighter is last'.[8] The result of the by-election was entirely
predictable. The Coalition Liberal drew off enough votes from Simon to deliver the seat to
the Labour candidate.

Ireland provided an important area of policy disagreement between the two men.
With the independence movement passing increasingly into the extremist hands of Sinn Fein,
the British authorities responded with measures of reprisal and punishment which did no credit
to the long history of Britain's involvement in Ireland. Simon, spurred on by his Irish wife,
felt outrage at the excesses of the Black and Tans, making a series of speeches up and down
the country condemning the government's policy. In November 1920 a Peace with Ireland
Council was formed with Lord Henry Bentinck as chairman and Simon among its backers.
In a letter to *The Times* on 25 April 1921 Simon condemned the government's policy as
'politically disastrous and morally wrong...exposing us to the scorn of the world'.

In more general terms Simon was able to profit from a growing feeling that Lloyd
George was somehow flouting the conventional norms of civilised conduct, to which misdeed
the very existence of a coalition - the prostitution of political principle - bore witness. The
time had come, Simon repeatedly stressed, for a reversion to honesty in politics. The only
Liberalism that was worth fighting for was Liberalism pure and simple. Mixed with Toryism
it produced a concoction which was ultimately unpalatable. Why, Simon asked, had the
government lost the confidence of the country?

> It was not because there were not able men in the Government or that its
> Leader was not clever. But cleverness was not everything and perhaps
> something might be said for a policy which, even if it were not quite so
> nimble, was the same policy today as it was yesterday...The fundamental
> error made by the Government was its lack of consistent devotion to political
> principle.[9]

Even so, Simon seemed to have little to offer by way of alternative except a sort of outdated
Gladstonian Liberalism which focused on free trade and 'economy' as remedies for the
nation's economic ills.

Yet the fall of Lloyd George's government at the end of 1922 and the subsequent
general election brought no respite to the internal dissensions of the Liberal movement. With
only 333 candidates for a parliament of over 600 seats, Asquith's Liberals could not
realistically expect to form the next government without the co-operation of the Lloyd
Georgeites. But the latter on the whole continued to seek accommodation with the
Conservatives. Indeed the general election of 1922 showed how difficult it would be for the
Liberal party to re-emerge as a serious contender for power in the new three-party system
which had been superimposed upon a political structure designed for only two competitors.
In rough terms the party secured a fifth of the popular vote but only a tenth of the seats in the
new House of Commons.

8   J. Ramsden (ed.), *Real Old Tory Politics* (London, 1984) p. 131.
9   *Yorkshire Observer* 13 Feb. 1922.

Once the dust of the electoral contest had settled, it was clearly time for Liberal leaders to consult as to their future strategy. Immediately after the election Simon, returned for Spen Valley, went down to Oxford to discuss the position with Asquith, who had scraped home at Paisley. The two men decided that Simon should become deputy leader of the party and Simon consented to give up all legal work that might interfere with his parliamentary duties.[10] At the end of November Simon was elected Sessional Chairman of the party by his fellow MPs to take the place of Donald Maclean who had lost his seat in Peebles. Thus, at least in terms of the internal dynamics of the Liberal party, Simon's position had been restored. Asquith was now 70 years of age and only a shadow of his former self. In preparing to abandon most of his legal work Simon clearly anticipated that he rather than the ageing nominal leader would be carrying the bulk of responsibility for parliamentary leadership.

But turning the leadership of a parliamentary rump into real political power was altogether another matter. A prerequisite was obviously a reunion of the divided forces of Liberalism, if for no other reason than that the party needed Lloyd George's money to sustain its electoral viability. On the other hand a reunion with Lloyd George would not only require many harsh words to be unsaid. It would throw into question Simon's claims to the succession when Asquith finally withdrew from the party's front line. 'The whole problem of Liberal reunion', reported the *Evening Standard*, 'will soon resolve itself into the single question of Liberal leadership. Asquith, Lloyd George or Simon?'[11]

Yet reunion seemed far from Simon's thoughts. In December 1922 he could still assert that 'our Liberals feel themselves to be closer to the Labour party than to the Coalition Liberals, for the latter is (sic) still supporting the Government on most occasions and Lloyd George remains an enigma'.[12] When C.P.Scott discussed the same question with him early in the new year, the editor of the *Manchester Guardian* was disappointed to find 'no suggestion of a big, energetic, generous Liberal movement which would sweep the whole party together and make artificial divisions...meaningless'. 'I think Lloyd George is done' was about all Simon had to say on the subject. Scott judged that Simon was clearly 'playing for the succession'.[13]

If, however, Simon would not discuss the question of Liberal reunion, he could not prevent Lloyd George from doing so, nor could he prevent spontaneous moves towards fusion in the constituencies. Two by-elections in Anglesey and Ludlow saw Coalition Liberals and Asquithians coming together and efforts towards reunion were also beginning in other constituencies. Meanwhile Lloyd George made an important speech in Edinburgh on the theme of reunion in which he stressed the need to face the common enemy of Labour and denied that he sought the leadership of a reunited party. If this represented a dove of peace, Simon was quick to shoot it down. 'You will see', wrote Simon to Lord Gladstone, 'I "let off" about L.G. and Liberal reunion yesterday'. The best way of meeting to discuss Liberal

---

10   Simon diary 18 Nov. 1922, Simon MSS, SP 5 fos. 2-4
11   *Evening Standard* 13 Feb. 1923.
12   Simon diary 15 Dec. 1922, SP 5 fos. 9-10.
13   T. Wilson (ed.), *The Political Diaries of C. P. Scott* (London, 1970) pp. 436-7.

reunion, he suggested, would be in the opposition lobby on each and every parliamentary division. That at least would test the good faith of the Lloyd Georgeites.[14] Yet in reality Lloyd George was not far from the truth when he surmised that Simon was against unity primarily because it threatened his chance of the leadership.[15] Lloyd George even believed that Simon deliberately raised issues in the House of Commons which he knew would accentuate divisions between the two Liberal factions.[16] Certainly Simon had insisted on moving a Liberal amendment to the Address, regretting that the new government had not proposed to repeal the Safeguarding of Industries Act, in the expectation that such a move was bound to create divisions among the Lloyd Georgeite Liberals.[17]

While Liberal reunion remained blocked, at least among the leadership at Westminster, Simon's position as heir apparent to the diminished throne of Liberalism seemed strong. He would, assured one supporter, 'soon be in the sort of position Gladstone was when Palmerston's sun was setting'.[18] But Simon could not have foreseen that Stanley Baldwin, the new Conservative Prime Minister, would succeed, where Liberals had failed, in reuniting the two warring factions. In a speech in Plymouth on 25 October 1923, Baldwin announced his wish for a fresh mandate to introduce tariffs. Still in the early 1920s no single issue was as likely to cement the disparate strands of Liberalism into a single whole as the defence of free trade.

When Baldwin made his statement Lloyd George was in the United States. But shortly after his return a combined committee of Liberals which included Asquith, Simon and Lloyd George managed to hammer out a joint election manifesto, agreeing to fight as a united party across the country. It was announced that Liberal candidates would be fielded in such numbers as to make united Liberalism a viable alternative to the existing government. For this to take place, of course, Lloyd George's financial support was the *sine qua non*. Not surprisingly the balance of power within the party changed almost overnight with the advantage shifting dramatically towards the former Coalitionists. As Beatrice Webb put it, the Liberals were

> reunited under the leadership of Asquith, but really under the leadership of
> Lloyd George and Winston (Simon having faded into the background),
> supplied with both oratory and money by the Lloyd George faction....[19]

The *Western Mail* confirmed that Lloyd George 'easily maintains his eminence among Free Trade orators... while as for Sir John Simon - where is Sir John Simon now?'[20]

---

14   Simon to H. Gladstone circa 28 Feb. 1924, Gladstone MSS Add MS 46085 fo. 98; C. Cook, *The Age of Alignment* (London, 1975) p. 91.
15   T. Jones, *Whitehall Diary* vol 1 (London, 1969) p. 234.
16   Lloyd George to C. P. Scott 15 March 1923, Lloyd George MSS G/17/11/6.
17   Simon diary 18 Nov. 1922, SP 5 fos. 2-4.
18   F. Hirst to Simon 29 Dec. 1923, SP 58 fo. 132.
19   B. Webb diary 19 Nov. 1923.
20   *Western Mail* 26 Nov. 1923.

Partnership with Lloyd George was not easy for Simon, but the two men did appear on a joint platform in Leeds where Simon asserted that the hatchet had been buried and that it was now time to bury it in the skull of Protection.[21] But it was noticeable that Simon did not publish a telegram of support for his election in Spen Valley sent by Lloyd George, 'for Liberal Unity only disgusted some of my keenest supporters and would not gain me a single vote'.[22]

In purely statistical terms the general election saw a marked revival in Liberal fortunes. With 30% of the popular vote, 158 members were elected and, with no party having an absolute majority, the Liberals would clearly hold the balance of power in the new parliament. When Liberal leaders met soon after the election to determine their immediate strategy, Simon strongly supported Asquith in urging that the Liberals should vote with Labour to turn out Baldwin when the new House of Commons assembled and then that, if Labour succeeded in forming a government, the Liberals should combine with the Conservatives to oust that too. Thereafter, with no one prepared to force yet another general election, the Liberals would be in a position to replace Labour.[23] Such a scenario may have been somewhat fanciful, but it at least had the merit of maintaining a Liberal identity in the eyes of the electorate. Lloyd George, however, was hostile and the meeting was adjourned without agreement being reached. By the time that it reconvened, Asquith had changed his mind (though Simon had not) and was not now prepared to go beyond voting against the existing Baldwin government. The Liberal attitude towards any resultant Labour administration would be non-committal. Lloyd George, who clearly envisaged sustaining a Labour government in power, accepted this as a step in the right direction. The change of plan did not, however, please Simon.[24] His misgivings were well founded since in effect the Liberals were now going to vote Labour into office without really considering what they would do thereafter and without seeking to extract any promises from Labour of legislation beneficial to themselves such as electoral reform.

As Ramsay MacDonald's government took office, Asquith reverted to the sort of 'wait and see' attitude which had become his trade mark, assuming presumably that Labour would make such a mess of the tasks of government that the waiting would not be greatly extended. Lloyd George, on the other hand, clearly envisaged some more positive sort of co-operation between the two parties, at least during the first months of the new government. In such a situation the Liberal party was in danger of losing its *raison d'être*. Those who had voted Liberal to resist the dangers of socialism would either realise that the Conservative party represented a more effective bulwark or else that Labour was not as dangerous as they had supposed and might even serve as the vehicle for those radical aspirations which had previously attracted them to Liberalism. The poverty of the Liberal party's last election campaign, based as it had been upon an essentially negative defence of a piece of inherited dogma of dubious relevance to the third decade of the twentieth century, now became

---

21   *Leeds Mercury* 28 Nov. 1923.

22   Lloyd George to Simon 5 Dec. 1923 and undated note by Simon, SP 58 fos. 114 and 118.

23   T. Wilson (ed.), *Scott Diaries* p. 450.

24   Ibid, p. 451.

apparent. There was a pressing need for the party to lay claim to a set of clearly defined policies, particularly in the social and economic sphere, which would differentiate it from its rivals by the time of the next general election. Such a development was unlikely without genuine party unity and effective leadership at the top. Yet neither factor emerged in 1924. The shallowness of the reconciliation achieved for the 1923 election was soon revealed. On major issues the party was still unable to present a united front.

In such a situation Simon was perhaps the man to take charge, but his attitude at the time was scarcely conclusive to effective action. Though he said that he formed 'the amalgam between HHA and LG' and that he was 'having a busy time',[25] others were less impressed by his performance. He was 'very dispirited' at losing the chairmanship of the party, a position which was allowed to lapse,[26] and, with the Liberal front bench 'speaking with two voices', Simon was 'seldom there'.[27] In May 1924 a perceptive article appeared in the *Evening Standard* which merits extensive quotation:

> Sir John Simon compromised an inestimably lucrative practice at the Bar to enter into the fight for Mr. Asquith's reversion. He became assiduous in his attendances in the House of Commons and spoke upon every available occasion. He used every artifice and wile to ingratiate himself...Sir John became unquestionably marked out as his leader's successor. All was thus serene when the clouds suddenly gathered. There was talk of Liberal unity. Sir John...opposed it tooth and nail. They hurled insults at Mr. Lloyd George...they threatened to resign if the 'Welshman were ever readmitted within the fold. Why? Partly - let us do them the credit - upon principle, partly because they know that the list of seniority must be revised. An unexpected General Election upset their plans and unity was forced upon them. Then arose the question which has yet to be answered. Would Sir John Simon have to give way to Mr. Lloyd George? He had fought, he had sacrificed so tremendously to gain his position. Was it to be snatched from him like this?[28]

Simon even hinted that he might withdraw altogether from the political scene for the time being, though there were always those who were ready to remind him that 'L.G. is distrusted by all good Liberals -by all honest men' and that Simon's own claims to the succession would ultimately meet with success.[29]

Matters came to a head when, following the government's mishandling of the Campbell Case, MacDonald tendered his resignation to the King and requested an immediate dissolution. In the constituencies the Liberal party was quite unprepared for a third general

---

25   Simon to Reading 12 March 1924, Reading MSS Eur. F 118/101.
26   Wedgwood Benn diary 20 Feb. 1924.
27   Ibid., 13 March 1924.
28   *Evening Standard* 15 May 1924.
29   Leif Jones to Simon 29 Aug. 1924, SP 58 fos. 191-2.

election in just two years. Finance remained a major problem. Throughout the 1924 session Donald Maclean and Viscount Gladstone had been engaged in difficult negotiations with Lloyd George to secure a substantial long-term contribution from the latter's private fund. In the end a less than satisfactory arrangement was reached for financing candidates. The party abandoned 136 seats fought in 1923, fielding only 340 candidates. It could not credibly present itself as a serious aspirant for power. The election result was entirely predictable. With only just over 40 seats, the party saw three-quarters of its parliamentary strength wiped out.

Within weeks of the election a decisive move in the Lloyd George - Simon struggle had taken place. Asquith had lost his seat at Paisley, a defeat which had serious implications for both Simon and Lloyd George. While no one sought to deprive Asquith of the nominal party leadership, it could not realistically be expected that he would ever again secure a seat in the Commons. Indeed early in 1925 he accepted a peerage, emerging now as the Earl of Oxford and Asquith. In such a situation there was strong pressure to revive the post of Sessional Chairman of the party in the Commons. As the general election, unlike that of 1923, had tended to favour the Lloyd Georgeite wing of the party, the implications were clear. Wedgwood Benn first heard that Simon would take no part in the leadership controversy, 'neither proposing LIG, nor opposing him'.[30] But it soon became clear that Simon intended to play a more subtle game. Speaking to the National Liberal Club he urged Liberals to forget the past and to sink their differences, but in calling for unity on Liberal issues he went on to mention every point on which in the previous parliament Lloyd George had either dissented or sided with the Conservatives. Benn concluded that Simon was 'obviously planning to come out of his dugout'. Meeting with colleagues at the home of Godfrey Collins, the new Chief Whip, Simon urged that the post of Sessional Chairman should remain vacant, with Collins himself taking the chair at party meetings.[31] This idea was put forward when Liberal MPs met at the Commons to decide the matter. It was rejected by 26 votes to 9, after which an amendment was carried to appoint Lloyd George. After the latter had taken the chair Simon called for unity and comradeship - an appeal that was a little hard to swallow for those who knew that Simon had drafted the original motion to keep Lloyd George out.[32] Lloyd George later proposed that Simon should accept nomination as vice-chairman, but the latter rejected the idea on the grounds that the post was unnecessary.[33]

In the circumstances it was hardly surprising that Simon decided not to devote himself wholeheartedly to politics for the time being. There was always his other career in the law to which he could turn. Many Liberals in the 1920s seemed to enjoy acting as if they were still a party of government. But such play-acting was not to Simon's taste. With all the potential to be a political heavy-weight, the role of supporting character -particularly in Lloyd George's shadow - held few attractions. Yet he was, he claimed, doing his best to keep the party together and cooperating cordially with Lloyd George, though there were 'many snags

---

30   Wedgwood Benn Diary 25 Nov. 1924.
31   Ibid., 26 Nov. 1924.
32   Ibid., 2 Dec. 1924.
33   Simon to Lloyd George 6 Dec. 1924, SP 58 fo.202.

in our path' and revival would be a long and difficult process.[34]   One of those snags was Lloyd George's continuing control over the Liberal party's financial reserves without which the party could not contemplate fighting another election with any realistic prospect of capturing power.   Lloyd George continued to insist that the conditions of earlier donations to his political fund prevented him from combining it with the resources of Asquithian headquarters.   As a result disbursements from the fund remained rare and almost entirely at Lloyd George's personal discretion.   In October 1925 Simon pointed out that a situation in which contributions from the fund were only made from time to time, with the possibility of strings being attached, was not one which could really go on.[35]

The event which brought Simon back into the centre of British politics was the General Strike of May 1926; it was also an event which exercised an important influence within the internal dynamics of the Liberal party.   Many believed that Simon's speeches in which he argued that the strike was illegal, and therefore not protected by existing trade union legislation, were a turning point in the dispute.   Lloyd George adopted a markedly different stance.   Though the Liberal shadow cabinet declared that society was obliged to secure victory over the strikers, Lloyd George tended to blame the government for the crisis and called for a negotiated settlement.   Many interpreted Simon's speech on 6 May as an attempt to supplant Lloyd George as the effective leader of the parliamentary party.[36]   The shadow cabinet met again on 10 May and it was in response to its decisions that Simon addressed the Commons on the following day, suggesting that both the T.U.C. and the government should act to end the conflict.   Lloyd George attended neither the meeting of the shadow cabinet nor the subsequent parliamentary debate - absences which were noted in the press.[37]   Instead he wrote to the Chief Whip, expressing his unwillingness to join in any declaration against the strike which failed also to condemn the government's handling of the situation.

There followed an increasingly acrimonious exchange of correspondence between Asquith and Lloyd George, which seemed to indicate that both sides were ready to push matters to an open rupture.[38]   The climax came when Simon took the lead, in conjunction with 11 other members of the shadow cabinet, in sending Asquith a public letter of support for his most recent epistle to Lloyd George.   Simon's letter went back as far as Lloyd George's role in the break-up of the first wartime coalition in 1916, showing that old wounds had never been fully healed.   Dealing with more recent events, it amounted to an indictment of Lloyd George's actions since reunion in 1923 and, in particular, denounced the way he had manipulated his private political fund.   Lloyd George's actions during the General Strike had 'to be regarded in the light of this general position'.   The letter concluded:

34   Simon to Reading 4 Feb.1925, Reading MSS Eur. F 118/101.
35   J. Bowle, *Viscount Samuel : a biography* (London, 1957) p. 260.
36   See, for example, A. Duff Cooper, *Old Men Forget* (London, 1953) p. 151.
37   *The Times* 12 May 1926.
38   The following year, when Lloyd George and Simon met to discuss Liberal policy towards China, Simon asked him what the expression 'Shanghaied' meant. 'It's what you and the Liberal party tried to do to me last May', retorted Lloyd George. A. J. P. Taylor (ed.), *Lloyd George : A Diary* (London, 1971) p. 249.

We have done our best in the highest interests of the cause of Liberalism to
work with Mr. Lloyd George in the consultations of the party and we regret
to say that we cannot any longer continue to work with a colleague who, in
our judgement, is not worthy of the trust.[39]

An angry meeting of Liberal MPs took place on 3 June with Lloyd George and Simon
clearly leading opposing factions. The former, however, after giving assurances that he would
not ally with Labour nor support a nationalisation policy, could still command a majority.[40]
A resolution was passed deploring the public display of internal party differences and Simon
agreed to acquaint Asquith with the feeling of the meeting. But when Simon and Asquith
spoke at the National Liberal Club the next day the situation remained unchanged. Asquith
and his supporters stood firmly by their published letters.[41] With no imminent electoral
necessity to bind the party together, it became clear that the reunion of 1923 had been a sham.
   All agreed that the annual meeting of the National Liberal Federation on 17 June
would be decisive. Less than a week before the meeting, however, Asquith suffered a serious
stroke which removed him from the political stage. An event which at another time might
have worked to Simon's advantage now stopped him in his tracks. Simon spoke twice at the
meeting, 'improving his position'.[42] But with Asquith out of action most Liberals saw that
they needed Lloyd George. The mood was for reconciliation. To be leaderless was one
matter; to be penniless was quite another. Simon's private secretary summed up the situation:

> Undoubtedly the preponderating desire of the delegates was that the recent
> published correspondence should not split the Party. While re-affirming its
> confidence in Lord Oxford as Leader, the Conference was equally emphatic
> that Lloyd George must be associated with the Party. How that was to be
> achieved I am afraid the delegates did not trouble to think about.[43]

   Simon's own position was in fact extremely delicate. 'The greatest danger arising
out of the present position', concluded this memorandum, 'is the early retirement of Lord
Oxford'. But if the latter could struggle on for a while as nominal leader, despite his physical
weakness, then the current wave of feeling for Lloyd George might recede. If during that
breathing space Simon became more and more the *de facto* leader, increasing his appeal to the
party's radical wing, then 'the question of leadership when Lord Oxford does retire will have
practically settled itself'.[44]

39   Simon and others to Asquith 31 May 1926, SP 60 fos. 91-3.
40   Freddie Guest, who led the effort to tie Lloyd George to specific commitments, confessed that 'he would
       sooner trust him than Simon'. Ramsden, *Real Old Tory Politics* p. 227.
41   *Westminster Gazette* 5 June 1926.
42   Richard Holt diary 24 June 1926.
43   Memorandum by J.Rowland Evans 20 June 1926, SP 60 fos.104-7.
44   Ibid.

Sadly for Simon, Asquith would not fall into the role assigned to him. In October he resigned the leadership. In the circumstances Simon's expressions of regret - 'I feel it as a son feels the loss of his father' -carried with them a significance beyond the realm of formal courtesy.[45] Yet if Asquith's relationship with Simon was that of father to son, there was little chance of the succession of the first born. The partisan line Simon had taken in the wake of the General Strike had offended many Liberals.[46] But, more importantly, if the Liberal party was to have any future at all it seemed to most of its members in late 1926 that it had to capitulate to Lloyd George, or at least readmit him to the Liberal fold. When Simon addressed the Eighty Club in mid-October he studiously avoided mentioning Lloyd George, but such an attitude was untenable. In November the Million Fund Administration Committee, set up after the last general election, narrowly decided to accept Lloyd George's terms for a massive grant from his political fund. In effect Lloyd George had captured the party organisation. He began to remove entrenched Asquithians from its bureaucracy.

Simon was understandably disillusioned. While Lloyd George picked up the Asquithian inheritance, he returned to his career at the bar. To serve under Lloyd George's leadership in the diminished band of just 40 Liberal MPs held few attractions for him. Declining Lloyd George's invitation to join an executive committee of the party and preferring 'informal co-operation',[47] Simon played his part in Liberal affairs during 1927 but without enthusiasm or commitment. Then, for the next two years, he found himself preoccupied as chairman of the government's Statutory Commission on India.

On his return from India in the spring of 1929, Simon could not immediately devote himself to the task of writing his report. Baldwin called an election for 30 May and Simon hurled himself back into the political fray. Almost overnight he seemed now to become a loyal acolyte of Lloyd George, whose imaginative plans to tackle unemployment had attracted much attention. Back in September, during an interval between two visits to India, Simon had warned the party not to go into the next election 'like a cheap-jack in the fair', offering a 'patent remedy' for unemployment. Coming shortly after the publication of the Liberals' famous 'Yellow Book', *Britain's Industrial Future*, Simon's words had been understandably seen as a stricture upon his own party's proposals. Now, however, he was anxious to explain that he had been referring only to protection and socialism as spurious cures for unemployment.[48] In similar vein he stressed his support for 'the remarkable man who now leads the Liberal party'.[49] Many, of course, suspected that the reconciliation with Lloyd George was purely a matter of political calculation.[50] Lord Birkenhead, for example, took mischievous pleasure in attributing Simon's change of heart to the miraculous effects of the Indian climate.[51]

---

45   Simon to Asquith 9 Oct. 1926, Asquith MSS 35 fos. 272-3
46   Arthur Crosfield to Reading 15 Sept. 1926, Lloyd George MSS G/5/7/5.
47   Simon to Lloyd George 8 Nov. 1926, Lloyd George MSS G/18/2/3.
48   J. Campbell, *Lloyd George : Goat in the Wilderness* (London, 1977) p. 230.
49   *Manchester Guardian* 16 May 1929.
50   Maclean to Gladstone 19 May 1929, Gladstone MSS Add. MS 46474.
51   J. Campbell, *F. E. Smith: First Earl of Birkenhead* (London, 1983) p. 818.

What in fact would account for Simon's change of heart? For the last time in his career he seems to have believed that the Liberal party had a realistic chance of gaining power. A split in the party's ranks would remove any such prospect. Lloyd George's policies and leadership had given Liberals a much needed shot in the arm. Trevor Wilson has suggested that 'it is unlikely that the British electorate has ever been paid the compliment of a more far-sighted and responsible party programme'.[52] But despite his optimism, Simon had not appreciated the extent to which the Liberal party had already become the victim of an electoral system designed for two rather than three contestants. Its support was too thinly spread for the party ever to regain a natural majority. In 1929 Liberals secured the backing of 23% of the electorate but only won 59 seats. On average there was one Liberal M.P. for every 91,000 votes; a Conservative for every 34,000; and a Labour member for every 28,000.

With a second minority Labour government installed, Liberals seemed for the time being agreed on the need for united action to safeguard their party's existence. At the first party meeting after the election Simon

> smote his breast and declared that except on matters which could only be fitly decided in the sacred court of conscience - or words to that effect - no matter of opinion would induce him to do other than follow the crack of the whip.[53]

In general, though, Simon was now more concerned for the immediate future with the writing of his Indian report. Its cool, indeed somewhat dismissive, reception by the Labour government was not without significance as far as domestic politics were concerned, for this turn of events brought Simon into contact and increasingly close sympathy with leading Conservatives. At the same time Simon's position within what was now clearly Lloyd George's Liberal party entered another period of crisis. In the early months of Labour government Simon followed the Liberal line that it was necessary to keep it in office. But a year later his attitude had changed. In the face of the mounting scourge of unemployment the government seemed beset by intellectual bankruptcy. In late October 1930, just before the opening of parliament, Simon wrote to Lloyd George to give him advance notice of his feelings. After 17 months in power, Simon concluded, Labour had proved a complete failure in practically every department. Liberals exposed themselves to the charge that they were trying to save their own skins by avoiding another election. Should Labour attempt to reverse the Baldwin government's trade union legislation, Simon would not be able to support them. On a vote of confidence he would go into the Conservatives lobby.

> We are in danger of carrying offers of assistance to the point of subservience and I do not believe that this is the way in which Liberalism is likely to become a more effective force in national and Imperial affairs.[54]

52   T. Wilson, *The Downfall of the Liberal Party* (London, 1966) p. 345.
53   Note by Maclean 14 June 1929, Runciman MSS 221.
54   Simon to Lloyd George 25 Oct. 1930, SP 249 fo. 93.

In effect Simon had renounced the central theme of Lloyd George's strategy since the last election. He had decided that he wished to bring the government down at the earliest opportunity. He was in fact only reverting to the line he had adopted in 1928 when surveying the prospects of the next election. To Reading he had then written:

> I could not contemplate agreeing to a repetition of what happened in 1924,
> for the result is that Labour is in power on sufferance, while we Liberals
> will have the thankless job of turning the Socialists out when we cannot
> stand it any longer.[55]

Lloyd George, on the other hand, continued to argue that the government should be kept in office until a revival in trade invalidated Conservative calls for Protection, or until the Liberals had extracted a commitment to electoral reform.

When Simon's letter to Lloyd George was published in the press Liberalism entered yet another phase of its self-destructive civil war. The extent of the party's disarray became apparent when parliament reassembled and the Conservatives put down a motion on the King's speech. The official Liberal line was to abstain, but 5 Liberals including Simon voted with the Tories, while 4 more went into the government lobby.

The leading members of the party met in Lloyd George's room in the Commons on 20 November to hear a plan from Lloyd George for a formal pact with Labour for two years. Simon spoke forcefully against this proposal. The government was already discredited and he could see no reason to put Liberal assets into a bankrupt concern. In a general election after the two year period no Liberal candidate could expect to succeed against Labour since he would be unable to criticise a party whose hold on power he had hitherto helped to sustain. The meeting broke up having established nothing but the extent of the party's divisions.[56] Discussing the situation with Lord Reading before a further meeting of Liberal leaders on 27 November, Simon ridiculed Lloyd George's latest idea of a pact for a shorter period than 2 years in return for the introduction of the Alternative Vote. Significantly, the conversation then moved on to the possible formation of a National Government, with Reading encouraging Simon to believe that he should occupy a place in such a government.[57] When the meeting of the party leaders began Simon and Reading opposed the whole notion of a bargain with the government. An arrangement for one year would in the end become a bargain for two, since after 12 months it would be said that more time was needed to secure the appropriate concessions from the government. Confusion again prevailed:

> Something was said at the end by Lloyd George about the difference
> between an agreement and an understanding and the conference ended ...
> without any clear information either as to what Lloyd George ... intended

---

55   Simon to Reading 11 Oct. 1928, Reading MSS Eur. F118/125.
56   Simon diary 20 Nov. 1930, SP 249 fos. 5-8.
57   Ibid, 27 Nov. 1930, SP 249 fo. 14.

to say to the Cabinet Ministers, or as to what account might hereafter be given of the result of their further conversation.[58]

Simon now seemed ready for a complete break with his Liberal colleagues. In advance of a party meeting on 11 December he warned the Chief Whip that he must insist that the party should declare itself opposed to changing the Trade Union Political Levy to a contracting-out basis. If the party preferred ambiguity then he would reluctantly go his own way.[59] In the event, however, an open rupture was once again avoided at the party meeting. Perhaps concerned at the amount of Liberal support he could carry with him, Simon seemed reluctant to take the ultimate step.

Simon's uneasy relationship with the Liberal party in general and Lloyd George in particular thus continued through the early months of 1931. By now Lloyd George was making no secret of his anger at Simon's behaviour.[60] When the government introduced legislation designed to undo the Conservative Trades Disputes Act of 1927, a clash was inevitable. In a major speech Simon called for the 'humane slaughter' of the bill and clashed publicly with the man who was still his nominal party leader. In an intervention Lloyd George appeared to imply that the primary motive behind Simon's actions was his own personal advancement. Though Lloyd George felt he had 'knocked [Simon's] speech endways'[61] many Conservatives were impressed by Simon's contribution to the debate.

The most obvious impediment to Simon's closer relations with the Tories was the issue of free trade. Simon gave a first public indication of movement in his thinking on tariffs in an interview with the editor of the *Sunday News* at the beginning of March.[62] As far as Lloyd George was concerned this movement indicated nothing more than blatant careerism. He was not slow to take up the challenge. Abuse came easily to him in speaking of a man for whom he had never felt much warmth. Addressing a meeting of Liberal candidates at the Caxton Hall Lloyd George cruelly asserted that Protection was 'one of the subjects to which Sir John has lent one of his countenances'.[63] Sadly for Simon's historical reputation it is Lloyd George's interpretation of this crucial phase in Simon's career which has won favour. But it is worth noting that the intellectual path which had brought Simon to abandon the sacred creed of free trade was trodden also by many others, not least by John Maynard Keynes.

A final parting of the ways was now imminent. As Simon himself put it rather graphically, Liberals could not go on poised like Mohammed's coffin between two equal attractions, or 'rather oscillating uneasily in the valley of No Meaning'.[64] He seemed almost anxious for issues to arise that would differentiate his own wing of Liberalism from that led by Lloyd George. On 19 May he spoke in the Commons against the government's proposed

58   Ibid, fos 15-17.
59   Simon to Sinclair 11 Dec. 1930, SP 249 fo 106.
60   T. Clarke, *My Lloyd George Diary* (London, 1939) p. 112.
61   Taylor (ed.), *Darling Pussy* p. 139.
62   *Sunday News* 1 March 1931.
63   *Yorkshire Observer* 27 March 1931.
64   Simon to P. Withers 16 April 1931, SP 68 fo. 14.

Land Tax, a cause to which Lloyd George had attached himself before 1914. Finally on 26 June Simon formally resigned the Liberal whip. The occasion of the breach was in itself minor. As the Chief Whip stressed in his published acknowledgement of Simon's withdrawal, the imposition of a land tax of a penny in the pound on capital values was scarcely a matter for resignation. But in truth it had been clear for some time that there was little common ground between Simon and the Lloyd Georgeite Liberal party.[65]

'The effect on the party is serious', commented one Lloyd George acolyte.[66] This was a considerable understatement. Beatrice Webb got nearer the truth in predicting the dissolution of the historic Liberal party.[67] After the formation of a National Government under Ramsay MacDonald, Simon accepted the invitation of more than two dozen Liberal MPs to lead the so-called Liberal National party.[68] He sought funds to reassure Liberal MPs that in cutting themselves off from Lloyd George's financial support they were not committing electoral suicide.[69] On 5 October his group formed a separate organisation for the specific purpose of contesting the next election in alliance with the Conservatives and with MacDonald's National Labour group.[70] When the election came in October Simon suffered again from Lloyd George's attacks, but it no longer mattered.[71] Ill during the crucial weeks of the summer, Lloyd George was now isolated not only from Simon's group but also from the mainstream party under Sir Herbert Samuel in his opposition to the National Government.

In this long story of infra-party strife it is not always easy to disentangle personal incompatibility from genuine policy differences. To an extent Simon epitomised that strand of Liberalism which could never forgive Lloyd George for his actions during the war nor welcome him back into the ranks of the party. But important policy differences did still exist. There is a curious symmetry to this story. The period began with Lloyd George in coalition with the Conservatives; it ended with Simon in the same position. Such political gymnastics reflected the central problem facing Liberalism of determining its basic line, once it had descended into the intrinsically difficult status of third party in a political system which favoured a two-party contest. In the crisis years of 1929-31 Simon's fundamental disagreement with Lloyd George over the Liberal party's attitude towards the Labour government was genuine enough. It grew out of conclusions he had rightly drawn from the experience of 1923-4. To these were added his strong feelings about the government's treatment of his report on India. In the course of the 1920s socialism emerged for Simon as the ultimate political evil, just as he came to see that the Conservative party of Baldwin and Neville Chamberlain embodied at least some of the Liberal values which he most valued. Lloyd George's thinking basically moved in the opposite direction. During the 1920s the Liberal party was already labouring under the burden of crushing difficulties and disadvantages. The Lloyd George-Simon divergence compounded these problems and destroyed any lingering possibility of political recovery.

---

65   Sinclair to Simon 27 June 1931, SP 178 fo. 2.
66   Clarke, *My Lloyd George Diary* p. 121.
67   B. Webb diary 15 March 1931.
68   G. Shakespeare, *Let Candles be Brought In* (London, 1949) p. 138.
69   Simon to Lord Inchcape 24 Sept. 1931, SP 68 fos. 127-8.
70   *The Times* 5 Oct. 1931; Lord Hemingford, *Back-bencher and Chairman* (London, 1946) pp. 152-3.
71   *Manchester Guardian* 2 Nov. 1931.

BUSINESSMEN IN WARTIME GOVERNMENT :
LLOYD GEORGE'S 'MAN FOR THE JOB' APPROACH
1915-1918

KEITH GRIEVES

Few historians have sought to deny Lloyd George's transforming power during successive wartime crises and his ambition for a government of national efficiency. In the shadow of the writings of Lloyd George, Thomas Jones and Lord Beaverbrook his ministerial record has been regarded as dynamic and his reconstruction of the higher conduct of the war in December 1916 inspired.[1] Support for Lloyd George's position as the 'architect of victory' remains strong and there is much unshakeable faith in the innumerable examples of his insight, energy and will to secure Allied victory.

However, there is a continuing necessity to rescue from obscurity the managers of the total war effort who gave Lloyd George's wartime record much substance and whose work facilitated the gradual improvement in the British government's organisation of manpower and material during the First World War. Lloyd George's interventions in high politics created significant opportunities in the quest for a total war effort but much depended on the men he secured to deliver, without delay, the improvements sought by the advocates of 'national organisation'.[2] After the war it was inconvenient for participant publicists and historians of compartmentalised spheres of the war effort to give their roles emphasis because the 'leading hustlers' had devoted much time to circumventing existing practice, had ignored the structure of party politics and rescued the management of the war effort from the unprecedented problems of mobilising the nation's resources. Their work as 'outsiders' who found ideological commitment and civil service conventions inappropriate to the task of waging total war challenged Lloyd George's insistence that wartime policies and procedures had a long-term relevance to resolving the problems of peace. For the machinery of government was found wanting on many occasions after December 1916 and improvisers resolved supply problems using business experience in the absence of a supportive political framework. Businessmen in government also had to overcome the rhetorical impediment of Lloyd George's 'man for the job' approach. A narrow line existed between fulsome praise and an invitation to Churt and departure after a shortfall between expectations and performance as another 'sacrificial lamb'.[3] Lloyd George was truly innovatory in the appointment of businessmen to the Ministry of Munitions in June 1916, but this phenomena should be reconsidered in the light of the formidable obstructions which impeded transforming actions in most phases of the war.

---

1   T. Jones *Lloyd George* (London, Oxford University Press, 1951) p.69. See also Bodleian Library Oxford, Addison mss Box 99, Mr. Lloyd George's farewell address to the staff of the Ministry [of Munitions] 1 August 1916.

2   On the purpose of the Ministry of Munitions see T. Wilson *Myriad Faces of War* (Polity Press, Cambridge, 1986) p. 231; M. Pugh *Lloyd George* (London, Longmans, 1988) pp. 86-87; C. J. Wrigley *David Lloyd George and the British Labour Movement* (Hassocks, Harvester Press, 1976) pp. 110-121.

3   A. C. Geddes *The Forging of a Family* (London, Faber and Faber, 1952) p. 228.

According to Lord Esher who liaised 'between everybody and anybody'[4] Lloyd George 'adopted with marked success the plan of cutting away red tape, and of placing reliance upon personal responsibility by bestowing extended powers upon individuals selected for their capacity, vigour and courage'.[5] These extended powers were forged by businessmen who sought to initiate change in wholly alien circumstances and survive to undertake their interventionist tasks. In 1915 Lloyd George had perceptively offered a populist challenge to 'red tape' and 'Dilly and Dally' in concluding that the War Office was in no condition to undertake large scale manpower and munitions planning for the New Armies, so wedded was its administration to the 'short war illusion'. A long war of unprecedented scale and cost did require men capable of managing 'gigantic enterprises'. However, the appointment of businessmen was too readily regarded by Lloyd George as the whole answer, instead of the first phase of a different approach requiring systematic preparation and some appreciation of the organisational implications of dismantling the *laissez faire* 'business as usual' policy.

To consider these issues in more detail two major examples of businessmen in wartime government will be considered.[6] Firstly, the Ministry of Munitions during Lloyd George's period as minister, May 1915 to July 1916.[7] Secondly, the problems which beset the National Service Department in 1917 and their eventual solution. Consequently, particular attention will be paid to the involvement of Lloyd George's leading hustlers in the two central features of conducting total war, namely the supply and allocation of munitions and manpower.

Lloyd George's 'best find from the business world' and one of his 'luckiest "discoveries" in life' was Eric Geddes, Deputy General Manager of the North Eastern Railway.[8] Geddes later recounted that Lloyd George 'asked me if I knew anything about munitions. I did not. He asked me what I could do. I said I had a faculty for getting things done. "Very well", said he, "I will make you head of department"'.[9] In wonderment Geddes

---

4   P. Fraser *Lord Esher A Political Biography* (London, Hart-Davies, MacGibbon, 1973) p. 332.

5   House of Lords Record Office, Lloyd George mss F/41/5/2, Lord Esher to Lord Murray of Elibank, 28 November 1916.

6   See also P. K. Cline 'Eric Geddes and the "experiment" with businessmen in government, 1915-22' in K. D. Brown (ed.) *Essays in Anti-Labour History* (London, Macmillan, 1974) pp. 74-104.

7   For a review of writings on the Ministry of Munitions see C. J. Wrigley 'The Ministry of Munitions : an innovatory department' in K. Burk (ed.) *War and the State* (London, Allen and Unwin, 1982) pp. 32-33. A celebratory view of the ministry will be found in R. J. Q. Adams 'Arms and the Wizard. Lloyd George and the Ministry of Munitions' (London, Cassell, 1978). Adams suggested that Lloyd George worked closely with his men of push and go who had ready access to his office (p.182). John Grigg concluded that at the Ministry of Munitions Lloyd George was able 'to carry out what was little less than another industrial revolution', in 'Lloyd George and Ministerial Leadership in the Great War' in P.H. Liddle (ed.) *Home Fires and Foreign Fields* (London, Brassey's, 1985) p.3. For one of the few studies of other leading hustlers see D. Crow *A Man of Push and Go. The Life of George Macaulay Booth* (London, Rupert Hart-Davis, 1965) Like E. Geddes, G. M. Booth was first identified by Lord Kitchener as a man of 'push and go'.

8   Lloyd George mss. F/18/4/36, Lloyd George to E. Geddes, 24 February 1922. Lloyd George continued, 'When I think of the quaffly places on the road you with strength and resource helped to lift the cart out of I always wonder what would have happened had you not been at home'.

9   9C. Cross (ed.) *The Diary of A. J. Sylvester 1931-45* (London, Macmillan, 1975), entry for 2 December 1932, p. 84.

reflected that the Ministry of Munitions was the 'craziest department ever organised by mortal man'.[10]

In fact the recruitment of leading hustlers was less *ad hoc* and less the outcome of Lloyd George's personal assessment of applicants than his *War Memoirs* would have us believe.[11] Geddes noted that Lloyd George 'interviewed applicants with a crowd of Secretaries and hangers-on around him.'[12] However, Christopher Addison, Parliamentary Secretary, provided the first stage in a systematic sift of potential talent. On 28 May he wrote, 'The arrangement was that if I thought him [Geddes] good, I was to take him up to L. G. I thought him first rate and took him up to L. G. who had sent for Girouard'.[13] Major-General Sir Percy Girouard, Director General of Munitions Supply, knew Geddes, whose availability and powers of improvisation were quickly verified by the Board of the North Eastern Railway.[14] At this stage there was no reference to specific tasks, but early in June 1915 Geddes agreed to supervise the supply of rifles, machine guns, small arms ammunition, field guns and motor lorries.

Geddes was invited to the central munitions organisation at Armament Buildings because his short interview suggested a potential for active intervention rather than any technical knowledge of munitions work. In his *War Memoirs* Lloyd George distinguished between two typologies of 'captains of industry'. He noted the careful and cautious man who gradually built up an enterprise. They would not be recruited for the Ministry of Munitions because they were less capable of initiating change than his second type who were 'great improvisers' needed for their 'intuition and decision and force'.[15]

Geddes was one of four deputy director generals in the newly formed ministry. Glynn West, shop manager at Armstrong Whitworth & Co., supervised gun ammunition production, machinery and materials; G. M. Booth, Liverpool shipowner, controlled local committees, labour, statistics, intelligence and foreign orders; and Charles Ellis, director at John Brown and Co. Ltd. later took charge of gun output from Geddes. With some complacency Addison noted, 'If the present DDG's do meet in conclave, no one is aware of it'.[16] As the biographer of G. M. Booth, Duncan Crow suggested that Lloyd George was not easy to work for and that the deputy directors met each day at the Reform Club to act as a 'clearing house' of conflicting priority orders for munitions.[17]

This problem arose because Lloyd George had tired quickly of the ambition and bombast of Sir Percy Girouard. He was determined that 'he was not going to be delivered into the hands of any one man'.[18] Consequently, Lloyd George was unwilling to allow the creation of a Munitions Board which would have facilitated the co-ordination of watertight

10   *Ibid*. p.84.
11   D. Lloyd George *War Memoirs* (London, Odhams Press, 1938 ed.) Vol. 1 pp. 138-150.
12   E. Geddes, Contribution to Family History (1920) p.12.
13   Addison mss. Box 97, diary entry, 28 May 1915.
14   Lloyd George mss. D/1/2/6, Lord Knaresborough to Lloyd George, 5 June 1915.
15   D. Lloyd George *War Memoirs op. cit*. Vol. 1, pp. 148-150.
16   Addison mss. Box 15, Memorandum on Organisation, C. Addison, 15 October 1915.
17   D. Crow *A Man of Push and Go op. cit*. p. 125.
18   Addison mss. Box 97, diary entry, 31 May 1915.

compartments with overlapping functions and eradicated the swiftly multiplying petty jealousies of unpaid temporary civil servants[19] who were intent on establishing private administrative territories manned by staff from their firms. As early as 18 July 1915 Geddes submitted a memorandum on the organisation of the department to Girouard.[20] While administrative fluidity provided benefits in the swiftly changing priorities of munitions work, the absence of interdepartmental co-ordination was heightened by Lloyd George's reluctance to secure a detailed understanding of the problems his improvisers faced in their overlapping spheres of responsibility.

In this mêlée of continuous adaptations of function and organisation, improvisers who secured improvements in the ever-changing priority areas became overburdened with further tasks, and improvisers with less visible results were usurped and became embittered.[21] The traumatic consequences of failing to delineate clear lines of responsibility were recorded by Addison, and Col. Arthur Lee, Lloyd George's Military Secretary. On 8 July 1915 Addison noted in his diary (which underwent much softening of tone to reach published form) 'There are so many big men in it that they find it difficult among themselves to subordinate their departments one to the other and generally to play the game'.[22] Lee wrote, 'There were times as the winter of 1915 grew grimmer in all its aspects, when the nerves of all of us were strained beyond endurance and the atmosphere of the Ministry became sulphurous and unhappy'.[23] The conjunction of strife among departmental heads, as they vied for increased resources and additional tasks, and the acute need to improve production levels in all munitions output was the context in which Lloyd George 'harried' the improvisers for reports of significant change. Lee noted the general use of impassioned appeals in which Lloyd George concluded, '*I must* have those guns, and I know you will not fail me'.[24]

In the summer of 1915 Geddes was charged with resolving the most appropriate relationship between the production of machine guns and rifles. Despite the promise of discussion at Cabinet level on this issue - involving Lloyd George, Asquith and Lord Kitchener - delays caused Geddes and Girouard to approach the War Office to ascertain required equipment levels. Significantly, Lloyd George's initial response to Geddes's interview with Lord Kitchener was to view the meeting as a disloyal act. Only later did he mask his irritation at this successful 'hustling' initiative by providing the overlaying interpretation that his estimate of machine guns required for each battalion was ultimately more accurate than Kitchener's response.[25]

Thereafter Eric Geddes became a prime instrument of Lloyd George's quest for increased munitions output. He took charge of Woolwich Arsenal where the methods

19   Addison mss. Box 97, diary entry, 13 July 1915.
20   PRO SUPP 12/1, E. Geddes to Sir Percy Girouard, 18 July 1915.
21   Lloyd George mss. G/252, Rough notes of an interview with Sir Glynn West, 17 November 1932.
22   Addison mss. Box 97, diary entry, 8 July 1915. See also C. Wrigley 'The Ministry of Munitions : an Innovatory Department' *op. cit.*, p.41.
23   A. Clark (ed.) '*A Good Innings*'. *The Private Papers of Viscount Lee of Fareham* (London, John Murray, 1974) p. 144.
24   *Ibid*. p. 145.
25   D. Lloyd George *War Memoirs op. cit.* Vol. 1, pp. 360-361.

employed 'were like eating soup with a fork'.[26] Geddes later recounted, 'What shells were being filled were laid out in rows on tables and were filled by pouring the filling, like treacle, by hand with a ladle and spilling it on the ground'.[27] He instigated a thorough review of existing procedures which included the collection of a detailed series of 'branch and trunk' statistics by former North Eastern Railway staff. In the stark light of reliable information flow the duplication of effort, badly designed layout, lack of trolleys and outmoded managerial regime became apparent. Consequently, this critical review procedure, which drew on elements of 'scientific management', led to enhanced accountability at each factory and the rationalisation of design, supply and production arrangements, thereafter reviewed on a weekly basis. Geddes looked to advance the state's role in industrial reorganisation in a capacity which was 'similar to that of the Managing Director of a Commercial Undertaking'.[28]

To support the re-design and enlargement of Woolwich Arsenal and other Ordnance Factories a full political understanding of the industrial consequences of an 'artillery war' needed to accompany the creation of the Ministry of Munitions. However in 1915, there was little recognition in the higher direction of the war of the altered scale of waging war necessitating the survey of production capacity and the efficient and costed delivery of large scale orders.[29] Consequently, in compiling material for his *War Memoirs* in 1932 Lloyd George had to undertake much additional research to exemplify his theme 'that it is the civilian who saved the situation when the technical soldier let you down'.[30] Geddes reminded Lloyd George of the essence of the 'businessman's organisation' at the Ministry of Munitions, notably that 'it was a matter of organisation of plotting and planning all your movements so that you had the least possible absorption into the blotting paper'.[31]

Lloyd George understood very little of these processes and failed to identify deficiencies of central organisation until December 1915,[32] yet the work of munition officials and the efficiency of the ministry were central to the enhanced authority he sought and won at Cabinet level, as the epitome of the will to victory. In January 1916 Lloyd George asked Geddes to take charge of the Gun Ammunition Section of the ministry. The well publicised shell crisis on the Western Front in 1915 had in large measure led to widespread support for a separate Ministry for munitions, but gun ammunition was strangely neglected in the first turbulent half-year of the ministry's existence.

Barely six months before the Somme offensive, Lloyd George turned his attention to shell-filling. Geddes accepted this new task without enthusiasm. Mindful of the outcome he feared, Geddes sought a definite statement on his new area of responsibility and an audit of the situation he inherited so that existing deficiencies were clear for all to see. However, time was of the essence and Geddes was asked, as he expected, 'to take this branch of duty as it

26   Lloyd George mss. G/252, Notes of an interview with Lord Chetwynd, 16 December 1932.

27   C. Cross (ed.) *The Diary of A. J. Sylvester op. cit.* p. 85.

28   Addison mss. Box 15, Transfer of Woolwich Arsenal and other Ordnance Factories to the Ministry of Munitions, E. Geddes, 19 August 1915.

29   A. Lee (ed.) *'A Good Innings', op. cit.* p. 314.

30   Lloyd George mss. G/252, Rough notes of a conversation with Sir George Beharrell, 10 November 1932.

31   Lloyd George mss. G/252, Interview with Sir Eric Geddes, 2 December 1932.

32   Addison mss. Box 97, diary entry, 23 December 1915.

stands without the usual clear definition of the position at the moment of transfer'.[33] Demands for news of instant progress were soon received at the Gun Ammunition Section. Geddes likened his position 'to a Machine Gun Section in the climax of a hotly contested battle being called upon to experiment with an entirely new type of gun and submit frequent reports explaining why it is not working better.'[34]

In this fraught situation Geddes feared that criticism of shell-filling rates would be fuelled by Lloyd George's close adherence to revised estimates without sufficient appreciation of the multiplicity of reasons why delays might occur in the assembly of the 57 components of the 4.5 inch shell. In their exchange of correspondence mutual distrust was evident.[35] Of his estimate Geddes noted, 'I have not kept it down to make it safe, it is what I think the best we can do if all goes well. I think you would be wise to discount the figures by 15% to safeguard the risks of minor dislocations of supply'.[36] For Geddes 'if all goes well' meant the absence of blizzards, air raids and explosions which turned maximum productivity into idle plant without warning.[37] Without revealing the basis of his calculations Lloyd George replied, 'Surely that must be taking rather a pessimistic view of the capacity of our filling arrangements'.[38]

During February and March 1916 Lloyd George and Geddes remained on fractious terms. They rarely met. The door to the ministerial office may have been open, but the minister was elsewhere. Lee observed that their contact was so limited that Geddes ought to write to Lloyd George to explain his working procedures which he duly did.[39] As a result of effective information flow and systematic supervisory arrangements, production of high explosive shell rose from a weekly average of 258 tons in January 1916 to 760 tons by 20 May and 1,322 tons by 1 July.[40] These figures were achieved through the gamble of assuming that the National Factories would contribute to shell output within four months of the first buildings being erected on these new sites. In March 1916 in 27 of 33 National Shell Factories this proved to be case despite the limited availability of technical staff, dismal working conditions and improvised stores. Lloyd George was not particularly anxious for his name to be associated with these new factories in this early, but utterly crucial, stage and he avoided public comment on the building programme during the first quarter of 1916. In 1920 Geddes wrote, 'Looking back on my war work, that was by far the greatest job I had, it took greater anxiety and greater toil'.[41]

In March 1916 Mrs. Ruth Lee had commented, 'Nearly everyone at Armament Buildings is in such an unhappy state from being harried by L.G. that they cannot do their

33   PRO SUPP 12/1, Lloyd George to E. Geddes, n.d.
34   PRO SUPP 12/1, E. Geddes to A. Lee, n.d. [February 1916].
35   PRO SUPP 12/1, E. Geddes to F. Black, 3 February 1916.
36   Lloyd George mss. D/3/1/7, E. Geddes to Lloyd George, 11 June 1916.
37   Lloyd George mss. D/4/2/7, E. Geddes to A. Lee, 4 March 1916.
38   Lloyd George mss. D/3/2/63, Lloyd George to E. Geddes, 20 March 1916.
39   Lloyd George mss. D/3/1/6, E. Geddes to Lloyd George, 15 March 1916.
40   Lloyd George mss. D/5/1/10 & D/5/2/12 Memoranda on Filling, E. Geddes, 26 May 1916 & 7 July 1916.
41   Quoted in A. J. Sylvester's notes of interview with E. Geddes, 2 December 1932, Lloyd George mss. G/252.

work ... L.G. has now turned against Geddes and the shell-filling department and the position is most unhappy'.[42] Two months later Lloyd George accepted Geddes's invitation to a section dinner and observed, 'I shall be delighted to break bread with your merry men. The best menu will be your Weekly Reports and the returns of the last few weeks will provide the most sparkling champagne'.[43] Lloyd George wrote this response in the knowledge that the operations planned for the Somme sector in July 1916 would be preceded for the first time in the war by a bombardment of sufficient duration and intensity. Again, the scale of this achievement was not appreciated until 1932. Lloyd George's interviews with former munitions officials during that year suggested two points. Firstly, Lloyd George's 'hands off' approach placed him at some distance from an understanding of the vocabulary of munitions work and from major projects undertaken as ministry priorities.[44] Secondly, he lacked an insightful regard for the snags which confronted officials and, in Geddes's words, 'the hair by which the sword hangs over us'.[45]

Of course, the instruments of labour control, raw materials supply and transport arrangements had legislative form because Lloyd George secured political support for the Ministry of Munitions as an early practical expression of national organisation. His political dominance in the Coalition government of May 1915 made the overthrow of the *ante bellum* departmental framework possible, but in turn he was highly dependent on his 'businessman's organisation'. Having placed little emphasis on the internal coherence of the Ministry of Munitions, it was initially doubtful if Lloyd George had established sufficiently stable conditions to allow the full potential of this innovatory department to be realised.

Nonetheless, in employing highly competent organisers who quickly accepted the necessity for industrial planning as a central feature of the war economy, the Ministry of Munitions departed from the Asquithian model of 'wait and see' non-interventionism visible at the Board of Trade. Armament Buildings provided a forcing ground for talented improvisers and on Lloyd George's appointment as Secretary of State For War in July 1916 he alerted his leading hustlers to the new opportunities, not least to improve the transport network behind the British lines in France so that an ample supply of shells could reach the artillery batteries without delay.[46]

Geddes was despatched to head a civilian mission to GHQ in France and in September 1916 he became Director General of Transportation and Haig's fourth principal staff officer. To ensure his parity of status within the military hierarchy, Lloyd George took the unprecedented step of ensuring that Geddes received the rank of Major-General and became

42   Quoted in A. Clark (ed.) *'A Good Innings' op. cit.* p. 145. See also A. C. Geddes *The Forging of a Family op. cit.* p. 229.
43   Quoted in *Ibid*. p. 230. See also Lloyd George mss. D/5/2/3.
44   For example, in 1932 Geddes reminded Lloyd George that the correct terms were 'High explosive shell *detonates*; shrapnel shell *bursts*; the propellant - the cartridge - *explodes*'. Lloyd George mss. G/252, Interview with Sir Eric Geddes, 2 December 1932.
45   Lloyd George mss. D/3/1/6, E. Geddes to Lloyd George, 15 March 1916.
46   P. Fraser, *Lord Esher, op. cit.* pp. 332-3.

a member of the Army Council, where there was formidable opposition to this arrangement.[47] The introduction of civilians into the military sphere of the war effort was a logical extension of the appearance of businessmen in Whitehall, though the outrage was greater as typified by the views of Col. Le Roy Lewis at the British Embassy in Paris. He informed Lloyd George, 'You can never get over military prejudices. The appointment of anybody who does not belong to the Military Trade Union is as welcome to soldiers, as the appointment of a bishop drawn from the ranks of stockbrokers would be to the clergy'.[48] Lloyd George ensured that Geddes's appointment was not successfully challenged and Haig was so impressed with his expertise and refusal to think in 'pennyworths' that they forged a remarkable partnership outside the usual parameters of civil-military relations.[49] The integrated control of shipping movements, port facilities, mainline railway routes and light railway construction, after statistical enquiry, made possible the adequate provision of shells for the Arras attack on 4 April 1917.

Geddes's work in 1916 formed a substantial part of the gathering evidence which suggested that dynamic change would occur in the administration of policy as well as through more inspirational leadership were Lloyd George to become Prime Minister. In late November 1916 Lord Esher reflected on Lloyd George's method at the Ministry of Munitions and the War Office. He observed that 'Mr. Lloyd George's administrative plan of selecting a Man to carry out a difficult task that baffles committees and groups of men, should be applied immediately to the greatest and most difficult problem with which he is faced'.[50] Lord Esher specifically referred to the supply and allocation of manpower which caused inter-departmental strife whenever one of numerous *ad hoc* ministerial interventions took place in this problematic sphere.

Despite the evidence that labour control was unlikely to become the uncontested preserve of one department unless the minister enjoyed seniority and had full Cabinet support, it was confidently assumed that National Service would be systematically introduced on Lloyd George's rise to the premiership. Each man and woman would be allocated to work of national importance and fit men of military age remaining in industry would be released for the army. Expectations of the total mobilisation of labour were fuelled by Lloyd George's speech in the House of Commons on 19 December 1916. He stated, 'I hope before Parliament resumes its duties in another few weeks we shall be able to report that we have secured a sufficiently large industrial army in order to mobilise the whole of the labour strength of this country for war purposes'.[51]

To this end Neville Chamberlain was appointed Director-General of National Service with the intention that another 'businessman's organisation' would be formed to supervise the

47   Lloyd George mss. F/14/4/79, Lloyd George to Lord Derby, 26 November 1917; D. Lloyd *War Memoirs*, *op. cit.*, Vol. 1, p. 474.
48   Lloyd George mss. E/3/14/26. Col. Le Roy Lewis to Lloyd George.
49   A. Geddes. *The Forging of a Family op. cit.* p. 240. See also R. Blake (ed.) *The Private Papers of Douglas Haig 1914-19* (London, Eyre and Spottiswoode, 1952) p. 161.
50   Lloyd George mss. F/41/5/2, Lord Esher to Lord Murray of Elibank, 28 November 1916.
51   88 H. C. Deb. 5s Col. 1353, 19 December 1916.

allocation of manpower on behalf of all government departments after a wide-ranging review of all categories of war work.[52] In an area where expertise was difficult to define, Chamberlain's credentials for the post were tenuous, and he was appointed in some haste several hours before Lloyd George's statement on government policy on 19 December. As Lord Mayor of Birmingham Neville Chamberlain had expressed his belief in the relevance of wartime controls to sustained harmonious relations between Capital and Labour.[53] He looked to municipal officialdom for key staff and to the War Cabinet for clear directions for his task.

As the 'New Conductor' of the '1917 Overture'[54]Lloyd George looked for early evidence of a transforming process by which all sectors of the war economy would have their labour equitably treated by the manpower co-ordinating authority. Instead, a gulf soon appeared between such misleading descriptions of Chamberlain's role as 'Civil Controller of Mobilisation' and the reality of his main instrument of policy - voluntarism. As an early example of the vagaries inherent in accepting office during Lloyd George's wartime premiership, Chamberlain wrote, 'I have never had even a scrap of paper appointing me or giving me any idea of where my duties begin and end. I don't know whether I have Ireland or Scotland as well as England. I don't know whether I have munitions volunteers. I believe I am to have a salary but I don't know what. I suppose I can be dismissed by someone but I don't know who'.[55] National Service was not a practical labour placement scheme. Instead, it presented the paradox of the raising of an 'industrial army' by the voluntary enrolment of labour in the absence of new legislative powers.[56] Chamberlain was not of ministerial rank, lacked direct accountability to Parliament and depended on the patriotic goodwill of labour in the third year of the war to transfer men outside their district to essential war work in private firms on a voluntary basis.

As General Sir William Robertson, Chief of Imperial General Staff, noted in February 1917, 'Before Lloyd George became Prime Minister he was very keen about the Man Question. He now declines to touch it'.[57] This area of deep and abiding controversy was left to Lord Milner, member of the War Cabinet, to co-ordinate during 1917 amid the welter of conflicting labour priorities. As Geddes was 'harried' in March 1916 for news of improved shell output, Chamberlain was 'hustled' in January 1917 for 'instantaneous schemes' which would achieve complete mobility of labour without contravening the pledges which were given by successive governments to allay the fear of industrial conscription.[58]

---

52   See K. Grieves *The politics of manpower 1914-18* (Manchester University Press, 1988) pp. 77-86.
53   Birmingham University Library, N. Chamberlain mss. NC2/20, Political Journal, 17 September 1916. See also Bodleian Library Oxford, Milner mss. dep. 144. A. Chamberlain to Lord Milner, 18 December 1916.
54   *Punch* 20 December 1916, p. 423.
55   N. Chamberlain mss. NC 18/1/95, N. Chamberlain to Ida Chamberlain, 24 December 1916.
56   *Punch* 20 December 1916, p. 423.
57   Liddell Hart Centre for Military Archives, King's College London, Robertson mss. I/32/52, Robertson to Monro, 1 January 1917, signed copy.
58   T. Wilson (ed.) *The Political Diaries of C. P. Scott 1911-1928* (London, Collins, 1970) entry for 28 January 1917, p. 259.

Lloyd George looked to the National Service Department as 'the instrument in charge of all nation's man-power'[59] yet the War Office was determined that it would retain responsibility for securing recruits for the army. In addition, the Admiralty, Ministry of Munitions and Board of Agriculture constantly drew attention to the complexity of distinguishing between essential and non-essential labour in their spheres of the war effort. Following the nationwide appeal for volunteers on 6 February,[60] the rise of National Service committees in each locality to organise public meetings and undertake door to door canvasses did little to enhance the department's credibility in its task of allocating industrial labour. Its message of voluntary sacrifice was more appropriate to the first year of the war than to the conditions of war weariness in 1917.[61] Successful transfers of labour via the Employment Exchanges were counted in hundreds, rather than hundreds of thousands.[62] The National Service Volunteers became an expensive 'Stage Army'.[63] Its existence highlighted the continuities of the wartime premierships and the difficulties encountered in extending the 'man for the job' approach to the new ministries.

Throughout 1917 Lord Milner complained of 'the Prime Minister's lack of method and his harum-scarum ways'.[64] Lord Riddell reflected on Lloyd George's 'Fondness for a grandiose scheme in preference to an attempt to improve existing machinery'.[65] Much sense lay in the idea of an arbiter of manpower whose recommendations would provide the foundations of government policy. However, Chamberlain's lack of access to the higher direction of the war and the absence of National Service from the War Cabinet's agenda in the first quarter of 1917 ensured its rancorous failure. Chamberlain wrote, 'The whole raison d'etre of my Dept. was that it was to control labour as between Depts. & that I could not do if Depts. appealed against me to the Cabinet & Cabinet did not support me'.[66]

The proliferation of departments - surely an impediment to the co-ordinating role envisaged for Chamberlain - and their refusal to subordinate their sectional interest to the prospect of a larger scheme nullified the role of the National Service Department. Chamberlain had no doubt where the blame lay. On his resignation in August 1917 he told Leo Amery, 'LG launched it without ever having thought out or understood what its function were to be . . . He gave me just a fortnight to collect a staff, arrange their administrative functions, make myself acquainted with the outline of one of the most difficult and complicated of problems, settle my relations with other Dept. & invent a scheme.[67]   Chamberlain

---

59   D. Lloyd George *War Memoirs op. cit.* Vol. 2., p. 1360.

60   Lloyd George mss. F/232, Speech notes, Central Hall, Westminster, National Service, Lloyd George, 6 February 1917.

61   Lloyd George mss. F/79/20/2, Memorandum relating to National Service Councils (Decentralisation) 26 March 1917, unsigned.

62   N. Chamberlain mss. NC 8/5/4/11, Memorandum, 5 April 1917, unsigned.

63   Addison mss. Box 54, Addison to Lloyd George, 6 March 1917, signed copy.

64   Quoted in Milner mss. dep 23/1, Thornton's diary, 7 July 1917.

65   Lord Riddell. *War Diary* (London, Nicholson and Watson, 1933) entry for 13 August 1917, p. 265.

66   N. Chamberlain mss. NC8/5/4/17, Diary account, 7 - 9 August [1917].

67   N. Chamberlain mss. NC7/2/30, N. Chamberlain to L. Amery, 12 August 1917, unsigned copy.

eventually understood that his department was too far removed from the prospect of widespread acceptance, despite the revised governmental structure of 1917.

Distant from benign support and vulnerable to parliamentary and press criticism, the 'Palace of Make Believe' had few friends. While acknowledging Chamberlain's problems, Lloyd George was inaccessible. Austen Chamberlain told him, 'You treated my brother very badly, and you have never forgiven him'.[68] The events of 1917 loomed large in Chamberlain's memory. The periodic suggestion that the wartime premier might return to government, notably in 1931 and 1940, was less than favourably greeted by the increasingly influential Conservative politician. After he resigned Chamberlain sought to obtain a parliamentary constituency in Birmingham,[69] while his successor, Sir Auckland Geddes, took precautions to avoid the recurrence of these problems at the reconstituted Ministry of National Service. He specified, 'That I should be provided with a seat in the House of Commons and that I should be the 'political' head of the Department in a sense similar to that in which my brother [Sir Eric Geddes] is at present the 'political' head of the Admiralty and be responsible for answering for and for defending the Department in Parliament'.[70] At the Ministry of Information Lord Beaverbrook later drew a similar conclusion.[71] Not unusually the more constructive record of the Ministry of National Service in the last year of the war followed a redefinition of its purpose initiated by its executive head in the absence of a satisfactory rationale at its inception.

After December 1916 the leading hustlers improvised in the public arena of high politics and to the qualities of determination and energy had to be added forbearance and resilience. After the dismissal of Admiral Jellicoe in December 1917 Sir Eric Geddes, First Lord of the Admiralty, wrote to Lloyd George at a time when the Prime Minister's support of administrative reforms at the Admiralty lacked visibility. Geddes wrote, 'You, I know, realise that I am feeling my position infinitely more than probably would be the case had I gone through the hardening process of some years in Politics'.[72] Here could be perceived the gulf between the first phase (at the Ministry of Munitions) which identified the quasi-autonomous public servant of 1915 and the second phase which located the temporary minister of 1917, buttressed by limited contact with a party machine and faithful to Lloyd George as the instigator of businessmen in government.

---

68 Quoted in L. S. Amery *My Political Life* (London, 1953) Vol. 2, p. 101.

69 N. Chamberlain mss. NC2/20, Political Journal, 17 December 1917.

70 Lloyd George mss. F/38/2/16. A. Geddes to Lloyd George, 13 August 1917.

71 House of Lords Record Office, Bonar Law mss., 84/6/40, Lord Beaverbrook to Lord Reading, draft letter, 22 August 1918.

72 British Library London, A. J. Balfour mss. Add. Ms. 49709, E. Geddes to Lloyd George, 8 March 1918, copy.

Lloyd George's centrality in British political life during the war years allowed a remarkable search for relevant expertise to manage the British war effort.[73] The employment of leading hustlers reflected the view of 'advanced' opinion that the demands of total war blurred the distinction between military and civil spheres of the war effort. Businessmen as managers of large scale state initiatives in industry had found favour with Lord Kitchener, but it was Lloyd George who first sought their open-ended involvement in war work.

So large is the historiography of Lloyd George that their contribution to eventual victory has been subsumed in the record of political and inspirational leadership of the Man Who Won The War, most notably through his speeches and writings. The leading hustlers contributed little to the civil-military inter-war Battle of the Memoirs, undertook substantial business commitments in the 1920s and accepted their wartime careers as atypical. The return to party politics precluded their fuller peacetime role as depoliticised hustlers. Historical accounts of the Great War had little space for personalities whose work highlighted the fragility of the British war effort and which undermined the delusions of imperial grandeur apparent at the war's end. The allied context was forgotten as were the frequent episodes of crisis management.

Most leading hustlers forged their role in adverse circumstance and did not willingly desire a post-war role. Despite his misgivings Sir Eric Geddes became Minister of Transport in 1919, but in the headlong rush to 'return to 1914' leading hustlers were quickly persuaded of the separateness of business and politics. By 1921 they had concluded that the conditions of collectivised control were only specifically appropriate to the years 1915-18.

Thereafter, they reflected on their wartime careers at the juncture of politics and administration. For Neville Chamberlain exasperation and bitterness predominated. While expectations far outran the prospects for universal National Service, Chamberlain lacked the experience necessary to attempt the control and allocation of labour. Sir Eric Geddes was more representative of the great improviser. In his contacts with Lloyd George he suffered 'feelings of disquietude and unhappiness' in a political world which he never wished to make his own. Yet as the last leading hustler to leave the government in 1922, Geddes expressed admiration and respect for Lloyd George as the embodiment of the will to victory in the Great War and of the will to initiate change in British society after 1918 in far from propitious political circumstances. Their relationship was obviously not of ministerial equals, but there grew a mutual dependency which stemmed from the imperatives of total war.

---

73   For example, other businessmen in government which demonstrated 'broad outlook' included Sir James Maclay, shipowner and Minister of Shipping (from December 1916); Sir Albert Stanley, Managing Director, Metropolitan District, Central London and City Electric Railways and President of the Board of Trade (from December 1916); Lord Cowdray, head of S. Pearson & Co. and President of the Air Board (during 1917); and Sir Andrew Weir, President of Andrew Weir Shipping and Trading Co. and Secretary of State for Air (from April 1918). In November 1917 Lloyd George agreed with C. P. Scott that 'All the men who had made reputations in the War were civilian-trained' T. Wilson (ed.) *The Political Diaries of C. P. Scott op. cit.* diary entry, 9-11 November 1917, p. 297.

Geddes told Lloyd George, 'You have a wonderful knack of calling out the best and greatest effort that one can put forward'.[74]   This was a remarkable talent which propelled Lloyd George into the premiership in December 1916, but at times the improvisers who advanced in his shadow were perilously placed - as with infantry in the early attempts at creeping-barrages - as their patron moved quickly on to tackle the next crisis.   The more autonomous, administratively efficient, politically astute improvisers survived and contributed fully to the belated emergence of the total war effort in 1918.

74   Lloyd George mss. F/18/4/34, E. Geddes to Lloyd George, n.d. [February 1922] See also K. Grieves *Sir Eric Geddes* (Manchester University Press, 1989) p.106.

LLOYD GEORGE'S LEGACY TO LIBERALISM

DAVID POWELL

Lloyd George's political legacy is, in one sense, elusive and difficult to trace. Within a few months of his death in March 1945, the Liberal party which he had once led had been reduced to a mere twelve seats in the House of Commons. Even the Caernarvon Boroughs constituency which Lloyd George had represented from 1890 until his elevation to the peerage as Earl Lloyd-George of Dwyfor was lost, going to the Conservatives. Indeed, if Lloyd George had political legatees, they seemed more likely to be found in the Conservative and Labour parties than in the small Liberal remnant. Churchill, the outgoing Conservative prime minister, had been Lloyd George's close colleague in the pre-1914 Asquith government and in Lloyd George's own coalition after World War I. There were younger Conservatives, such as Harold Macmillan, who have testified to their admiration for Lloyd George and to his influence on their political thinking. Lloyd George's son, Gwilym, was a minister in Conservative governments in the 1950s, and there seems a definite Lloyd-Georgian strand to the 'One Nation' Conservatism of the Macmillan and Butler years. Yet equally there were echoes of Lloyd George's career on the Labour side as well. Although William Beveridge, the architect of the welfare state, had been a Liberal MP from 1944-5, the Labour party of Clement Attlee rather than the Liberal party of Clement Davies seemed to have inherited the Lloyd George tradition of social reform. Many members of the Labour party admitted that Lloyd George had been an early political influence.[1] In the Labour cabinet after 1945 Aneurin Bevan embodied the spirit of vibrant social radicalism which had marked the young Lloyd George, and expressed his ideas in a similarly eloquent vein of Welsh oratory. On the Labour side, too, there was a family connection, with Lloyd George's daughter, Megan, serving as Labour MP for Carmarthen from 1957-66, following the earlier loss of her Liberal seat in Anglesey in 1951.

Lloyd George's legacy to Liberalism and the Liberal party might seem a poor one by comparison. To his Asquithian critics in the 1920s, Lloyd George was the man who bore the burden of the blame for the Liberal party's loss of its position as one of the two governing parties in the state. He was the man who had destroyed the last Liberal government, ousted Asquith from the premiership and split the Liberal party by calling the 'coupon' election of 1918. According to Sir John Simon, '"The man who won the war" was also the man who engineered the Liberal collapse'.[2] The post-war coalition was seen as representing illiberalism at its worst. In the words of Lord Grey, 'it let down and corrupted public life at home and destroyed our credit abroad'.[3] Even after the Liberal reunion of 1923, Lloyd George was still viewed with hostility as a corrupting influence, in both the doctrinal and personal sense. Walter Runciman described him as 'a millstone. He is drowning the party as well as debasing

1   F. Bealey, *The Social and Political Thought of the British Labour Party* (London, 1970), p.3, cited in K. D. Brown (ed.), *The First Labour Party (London, 1985), p. 10*.
2   Viscount Simon, *Retrospect* (London, 1952), p. 121.
3   Grey to Stanley Baldwin, 5 January 1929, quoted in Keith Robbins, *Sir Edward Grey* (London, 1971), p. 361.

it'.[4] Sir Charles Mallet's study of Lloyd George, published in 1930, was redolent with satisfaction at the failure of Lloyd George's last great bid for office, since this would enable the Liberal party to recapture the purity of its Liberalism, even if it meant the continuing exclusion of the Liberals from the highest councils of the nation.[5]

These views were obviously the product, in part, of the thwarted hopes and frustrated ambitions of the Asquithians and of their desire to find a scapegoat to blame for the problems which the Liberal party faced in the inter-war years. The one-sidedness of such an analysis can be countered by demonstrating that other individuals - notably the leading Asquithians themselves - shared the responsibility for the Liberal party's plight, or by emphasising the long-term social, political and economic factors which may have undermined the viability of Liberalism as an effective governing force. Yet even the most extreme partisan of Lloyd George's career would have to admit that the charges levelled at him were not entirely without foundation. He was a major participant in the events which led to the downfall of the Liberal party during and after World War I. His personality inspired considerable (and understandable) resentment and mistrust in Liberal ranks. There were undoubtedly times when he appeared to place his own career above the interests of the Liberal party or the principles of Liberalism on which its platform was supposedly based. However favourable a gloss is put on some of his actions, legitimate doubts about Lloyd George's relationship with Liberalism remain. Did he ever see the Liberal party as more than a flag of convenience for his personal ambitions? Was his idea of 'Liberalism' too elastic to fit comfortably into any meaningful philosophical definition of the term? Was he, in the final analysis, really a Liberal at all?[6]

Lloyd George's essential commitment to Liberalism in the pre-1914 phase of his career should not seriously be questioned. He campaigned enthusiastically for most causes which the Liberals of late Victorian and Edwardian Britain held dear. He defended the rights of Nonconformists to religious and educational freedom, from his early revolt against the catechism in the village school at Llanystumdwy to the later battles in favour of Welsh Disestablishment and against the Education Act of 1902. As a backbencher, he spoke frequently on temperance platforms in England and Wales. He was an advocate of a wide range of social and constitutional reforms, including old age pensions, Welsh devolution ('Home Rule for Wales'), the restriction of the powers of the House of Lords and the introduction of adult suffrage. He was also a voice in favour of the Gladstonian principles of morality and conciliation in international and imperial affairs. In all of these respects, he

---

4   Runciman to Harcourt Johnstone, 3 October 1928, quoted in John Campbell, *Lloyd George, The Goat in the Wilderness* (London, 1977), p. 215.

5   Sir Charles Mallet, *Mr Lloyd George, A Study* (London, 1930).

6   On this last point, one recent biographer of Lloyd George has written:
        '[Lloyd George] simply cannot be fitted neatly into a Liberal scheme of things ... [H]e was, from the start, detached, freelance, something of a buccaneer in politics ... deficient in some of the attitudes that, in the twentieth century, go to make up the quintessential Liberal. His lack of interest in matters of individual rights and freedoms, in constitutional reforms, and in the rights of subject peoples to self-determination, cuts him off from the central stream of British Liberal principles from the early nineteenth century to the present day'.
        Martin Pugh, *Lloyd George* (London, 1988), p. 188.

exhibited the distinguishing characteristics of a radical Liberal of his time. More than that, while he had a political style that could be combative in the extreme - as in the controversy over the 'People's Budget' in 1909 - he was for the most part an exponent, too, of the Liberal manner in politics, a believer in the power of persuasion and reasoned argument, even in the face of public hostility and physical danger, as witnessed by his courageous defence of his actions at meetings during the South African War. This engrained belief in the virtue of campaigns of public education and propaganda, a constant feature of his career from the days of *Cymru Fydd* in the 1890s to those of the Councils of Action in the 1930s, placed him firmly in the tradition of Liberal politicians from Cobden and Bright onwards.

These basic Liberal attitudes which he had imbibed in his early career gained renewed importance for Lloyd George following the reunion of the Liberal party in 1923. He had to be able to demonstrate his soundness on the traditional tenets of Liberal policy, notably Free Trade. He was also trying to reactivate his former sources of support following the confusion of the coalition years. The suspicion remained, however, that between 1914 and 1922 Lloyd George had abandoned Liberalism, or, to put it another way, that he had revealed during the war and immediately afterwards his true political character, which was in some respects profoundly at odds with the principles of Liberalism and what they were deemed to represent. His critics, who included many of his former supporters and admirers, pointed to various stages of apostasy, determined according to their own political and ethical precepts and their personal interpretation of Liberal doctrine. For some, Lloyd George should have opposed the decision to go war in 1914, to the point of resigning from the cabinet when war was declared. For others, he had been wrong to advocate conscription or to connive at the restrictions on civil liberties imposed by the wartime emergency powers legislation. After his assumption of the premiership in 1916 the barrage of criticism grew steadily louder, focusing on Lloyd George's style and tone of government, his increasing intimacy with his Conservative colleagues at the expense of his Liberal ties, and on the illiberal policies of the Coalition in Ireland and the frustrated hopes for post-war reconstruction at home and abroad. Even the diaries of as ardent a Lloyd Georgeophile as C. P. Scott, editor of the *Manchester Guardian*, record the progressive disillusionment with Lloyd George which set in after the outbreak of war in 1914 and deepened in the post-war period.[7]

Some of the criticisms of Lloyd George were justified. Asquith's denunciations of Coalition policy in Ireland, especially the use of the 'Black and Tans', were particularly telling. At the same time, a measure of balance is necessary. For example, Lloyd George had never been an out-an-out pacifist, even during the Boer War. He was not an enthusiast for war in 1914, but, like most Liberals, he accepted it as unavoidable if Britain was to protect its own interests and uphold its moral and treaty commitments to its allies. Conscription was certainly an affront to Liberal sensibilities, but there were actually principled arguments in its favour, based on Liberal concepts of fairness, equality of sacrifice and the duty of the individual to defend the social community of which he was a part. Arguments of this kind should perhaps not to be taken too far, but the point is worth making that the war of 1914-18

7   Trevor Wilson (ed.) *The Political Diaries of C. P. Scott, 1911-1928* (London, 1970).

posed a fundamental challenge to the developing ideas of Edwardian Liberalism, and it was a difficult matter for individual statesmen to apply those ideas in circumstances of extreme national emergency, as Asquith found to his cost. Moreover, there were within the Liberalism of the pre-war period distinct and differing strands. There were those Liberals who clung to older, Gladstonian, notions of minimal state interference, voluntaryism, and individual liberty founded on guaranteed political rights and freedom from unnecessary restraint. On the other hand, there were the more collectively-inclined 'New Liberals' (supported by the former Roseberyite Liberal Imperialists) who had more complex ideas of citizenship and for whom the state had a democratic moral authority which for more individualist Liberals it did not possess. Although it is true that many of the New Liberals of pre-1914 opposed some of the extremities of policy which were involved in the mobilisation of the country to fight a total war, there was an inherent assumption in their earlier writings that the state was entitled to call upon the resources of the community to protect the interests of its members. Without being overly sophistical, it could be argued that, even according to their own ideas, the supreme test of wartime required the temporary sacrifice of individual liberties to which so many Liberals were opposed.

The First World War accelerated an ideological and organisational fragmentation of Liberalism which had been in train since the 1880s. In intellectual terms, as has been seen, this involved the emergence of competing schools of Liberal thought - Gladstonian, New Liberal, Liberal Imperialist. Organisationally it meant the loss of supporters both to the right (with the Liberal Unionist breakaway of 1886) and to the left (the Labour and socialist parties). Lloyd George was as much a victim as an agent of this process. He had done his best to provide a unifying platform for the party under Asquith's leadership before 1914. He had worked hard to sustain the effectiveness of a Liberal government during the early part of the war. Even under the Lloyd George Coalition, as Professor Morgan has shown, Liberal objectives were not entirely lost sight of, despite the deep divisions which by that time existed in Liberal ranks in parliament and in the country.[8] Lloyd George may have been a prime mover in the disaster which overtook Liberalism at the polls, but the post-war Coalition did pursue some traditional Liberal goals such as Welsh Disestablishment, Irish self-government and social reform. Its industrial and foreign policies may have been ultimately unsuccessful, but again they were capable of being presented as part of a Liberal synthesis, designed to promote international conciliation and a domestic harmonisation of the interests of capital and labour.[9]

---

8   Kenneth O. Morgan, *Consensus and Disunity: the Lloyd George Coalition Government, 1918-1922* (Oxford, 1979).
9   *Ibid.*, chapters 3 and 5. On the industrial side, however, the government was also forced into a confrontation with organised Labour, with Lloyd George personally guilty of encouraging fears of the 'red menace' and at times adopting an anti-Labour posture which did not accord well with a stated desire to achieve industrial harmony. Even here, though, such anti-Labour bias (albeit less hysterical in tone) was not impossible to detect in some pre-war Liberal thinking on the Labour question. In other words, the fact that Lloyd George was in favour of restraining Labour is not necessarily proof of a departure from Liberal norms, however damaging an impact it had on Lloyd George's relations with the Labour movement.

Lloyd George's major political weakness as prime minister, of course, was that he was a leader without a secure party base. This has led to the widespread view that in some senses he was never a party politician at all, that from his early days he felt uncomfortable in the straitjacket of party politics and that he was always looking for a means of escape, most likely by indulging his preferences for coalition or for a 'centrist' government of national efficiency.[10] Yet although Lloyd George flirted briefly with the idea of a separate Welsh Nationalist party in the 1890s, before 1914 his loyalty to the Liberal party was never really in doubt. The coalition scheme of 1910 was an improvised expedient rather than the maturing of a long-term plan. It has to be set beside Lloyd George's undeniable partisanship for Liberal causes and the repeated references, in his speeches and elsewhere, to the need to preserve the Liberal party as an effective political force.[11] Only when the Liberal party was no longer a viable vehicle for the attainment of Liberal goals would other political combinations have to be sought. But this was only what other politicians of the left had been saying since the 1890s.[12] The idea of 'realignment' had been very much in vogue at the time of the South African War, although significantly it was the Liberal Imperialists rather than radicals like Lloyd George who were most in favour of it. In the pre-war period, Lloyd George, along with other Liberals, considered the possibility of various alliances - with the Conservatives, with Labour, with the Irish. But none of these was intended to lead to the permanent supersession of the Liberal party as the organised expression of Liberal opinion in the country or to its disappearance as an independent party of government.

The war, and particularly the circumstances of Lloyd George's assumption of the premiership in December 1916, transformed the political situation. Despite attempts by followers of Asquith and Lloyd George to avoid an 'organic division' of their party, inevitably Liberals found themselves split into two opposing camps. Lloyd George's decision to prolong the Coalition beyond 1918 hardened the division and did much to destroy any hope of the Liberal party once again exercising sole responsibility for the government of the country. His attempt to fuse the Liberal and Conservative supporters of the Coalition into a 'Centre' party under his leadership must be seen in this context. It was on one level a plan to supply Lloyd George with a power base which otherwise he would lack, drawing upon the mood of national unity generated by the war. But it could also be seen as a means of sustaining a form of Liberalism in a 'post-Liberal' world, rallying the non-socialist (or anti-socialist) forces of moderate and progressive opinion while isolating the extremists of right and left. In practice, given the imbalance between Liberals and Conservatives in the Coalition, such a scheme was

---

10   Trevor Wilson, *The Downfall of the Liberal Party* (London, 1966), p. 54, refers to Lloyd George's craving for coalition. On the theme of national efficiency, see Robert J. Scally, *The origins of the Lloyd George Coalition* (Princeton, 1975).

11   For example, his speech on 'Liberals and the Labour Party' at Cardiff in October 1906, reprinted in Herbert Du Parcq, *The Life of David Lloyd George* (London, 1912-13), vol. IV, pp. 627-631.

12   Lord Rosebery had written to Canon Scott Holland on 21 August 1895 that, 'The Liberal Party had become all legs and wings, a daddy-long-legs fluttering among a thousand flames: it had to be consumed in order that something more sane, more consistent, and more coherent, could take its place ...' Quoted in R. R. James, *Rosebery* (London, 1963), p. 386.

never likely to succeed, but its aims in principle were not dissimilar from those which the pre-war Liberal party had always espoused.

With the collapse of the fusion plan in 1920, Lloyd George was left with only his personal National Liberal party on which to rely.[13] It was in this phase of his career that Lloyd George's relationship with Liberalism - both organisational and intellectual - seemed at its most tenuous. He appeared to prefer the big stage, and the quasi-presidential style of a politician above party, to the role of a conventional party leader. This was a stance that accorded well with the reality of his position, yet which did little to improve it. Nor did Lloyd George himself seem quite clear about his own political identity in these years. At one point he could be found playing to the gallery of his Liberal supporters, at another taking a hostile anti-Labour, anti-Bolshevik (sometimes anti-Asquithian) line indistinguishable from that of the most extreme Conservatives. He could still strike the chord of Liberal rhetoric, but he sometimes gave the impression that he believed the Liberal party was dead. Only as the clouds gathered over the Coalition in 1922 did Liberalism once again offer a psychological as well as an ideological lifeline. Yet while Lloyd George's assertion to C. P. Scott in October 1922 that he was a 'Liberal pure and simple'[14] may have been a trifle disingenuous (on another occasion he described himself to Lord Riddell as a 'Nationalist-Socialist'), in party-political terms it contained a fundamental truth. After the end of the Coalition in 1922, Lloyd George may have gone back to the Liberal party because he had nowhere else to go, but his very homelessness was a reflection of the enduring Liberalism of his position. His Welsh radical background made it inconceivable that he could ever join the Conservative party, while his deep suspicions of class interest and the sectionalism of the trade unions would have made the Labour party an equally uncongenial home. If any party could engage his emotional and intellectual energy, the Liberal party alone was likely to be able to do so.

A case can thus be made for portraying Lloyd George, through most, if not all, of his career, as a Liberal, in both the ideological and the party-political sense. If his view of party was functional, and if he put 'getting things done' above purely party considerations, in this he was following the precedent set by Gladstone over the Irish Home Rule. Gladstone, though, had succeeded in shaping the Liberal party of his day largely in his own image and in creating a Gladstonian brand of Liberalism which left a lasting legacy for his followers. Did Lloyd George leave any remotely comparable legacy, or is the monument to his Liberalism to be found in a 'shattered party'[15] and a few, fading, relics of nostalgia in his native North Wales?[16]

Certainly to talk of Lloyd George's intellectual legacy to Liberalism requires some justification. In the past, Lloyd George has had the reputation of being a supremely

13   On the National Liberals, see Kenneth O. Morgan, 'Lloyd George's Stage Army' in A. J. P. Taylor (ed.),
        Lloyd George: Twelve Essays (London, 1971).

14   Trevor Wilson (ed.), *Diaries of C. P. Scott*, p. 429, 23 October 1922.

15   The phrase is taken from Kenneth O. Morgan, *The Age of Lloyd George* (London, 1971), p. 110, although
        it should be added that, according to Professor Morgan, Lloyd George's permanent legacy lies 'rather in
        a more just and civilized society'.

16   The faded exterior of the Caernarvon Liberal Club now provides the facade for a snooker hall.

unideological politician - an improviser and an adapter rather than a man at home with abstract theories and intellectual blueprints. Up to a point, the image is a correct one. When compared with figures like Balfour and Haldane, with university-trained 'New Liberals' like Herbert Samuel, or even with his Welsh contemporary, Tom Ellis, Lloyd George did not have a particularly academic or philosophical approach to politics. He did not join discussion groups like the Rainbow Circle (the crucible of 'progressivism') in the 1890s, nor did he frequent the meetings of the Fabian Society or the socialist soirees of the Webbs. He did not write, or for that matter read, political treatises of the kind which abounded in the Edwardian period and which younger Liberals like Samuel and Masterman spent much of their time producing. Neither did he offer any extended written statement of his own political views. Most of his published works before 1914 were short, journalistic pieces on issues of the moment, while his major writings of the inter-war period were in the form of the extended justification of the *War Memoirs* and *The Truth About The Peace Treaties*. The nearest he came to a personal manifesto was in the volume of speeches reprinted as *Better Times* at the height of the political crisis precipitated by the 'People's Budget' in 1910.

For all that, Lloyd George was a politician deeply interested in ideas (at least those with a practical application) and he possessed a keen, fertile and creative mind of his own. His speeches and occasional writings show him to have been alive to the importance of new ideas and sensitive to the intellectual movements of the day, and he was sometimes capable of achieving a personal synthesis which clarified contemporary issues in a way that more academic writers found it difficult to do. Furthermore, as a statesman of the first rank, he forged a vital link between the world of ideas and the world of governmental politics. On at least two occasions in his career, he was able to provide the focus for a redefinition of Liberal priorities in a way that no other leader of the party could.

The first example of this was in the heyday of the New Liberalism before 1914.[17] The ideas of the New Liberalism had been developed gradually by various Liberal politicians and theorists since the late 1880s. The MP for North-West Durham, L. A. Atherley-Jones, had called for a 'New Liberalism' which would embrace the concept of state-sponsored social reform in an article in the *Nineteenth Century* in August 1889, at the time of the London dock strike. In the 1890s, influenced by the rise of Labour and by successive revelations about the extent of contemporary poverty, writers such as L. T. Hobhouse and J. A. Hobson took it upon themselves to provide the theoretical basis for a Liberal rationale of state intervention based on a new view of the state as the democratic centre of an organically-evolving human community.[18] Younger Liberal politicians such as Herbert Samuel, C. F. G. Masterman and L. G. C. Money, who also contributed to the theoretical debate[19], were keen to apply these

---

17   For the background to the New Liberalism and a consideration of its ideas see Michael Freeden, *The New Liberalism* (Oxford, 1978). On the development of Lloyd George's own ideas and his role in shaping the policies of the Liberal government see, Bentley B. Gilbert, *David Lloyd George, The Architect of Change, 1863-1912* (London, 1987), John Grigg, *Lloyd George, the People's Champion* (London, 1978), and Bruce K. Murray, *The People's Budget* (Oxford, 1980).

18   The best mature statement of this view is L. T. Hobhouse, *Liberalism* (London, 1911).

19   Herbert Samuel published *Liberalism* (1902), L. G. C. Money, *Riches and Poverty* (1905) and Masterman various works including *The Condition of England* (1909).

ideas to the work of social reform, advocating the redistribution of wealth and even, under certain conditions, the public ownership of industry. Leaders of the party like Asquith were sympathetic to some extension of state intervention in the social sphere, and the governments of Gladstone and Lord Rosebery in 1892-5 had made some hesitant but significant steps in this direction.[20]

However, it was not until the formation of Asquith's government in 1908 - in which Lloyd George became chancellor of the exchequer and Winston Churchill president of the Board of Trade - that the social reforming impetus of the New Liberalism began to be felt in earnest. It would be wrong to portray the subsequent reforms as the work of Lloyd George alone. In the cabinet Asquith and Churchill were key figures; Samuel and Masterman were energetic junior ministers and civil servants like Beveridge and Braithwaite played an important part. From outside parliament there was pressure and advice from the *Nation* group of journalists and writers, and from senior figures in the poverty movement, notably Seebohm Rowntree. Churchill entered the propaganda struggle with his 1908 letter to the *Nation* on 'The Untrodden Field of Politics' and with collections of speeches on *The People's Rights* and *Liberalism and the Social Problem*. Yet Lloyd George was particularly concerned about the wider implications for Liberalism of the shifting focus of the political agenda. In language similar to that employed by J. A. Hobson in his seminal *Crisis of Liberalism*[21], Lloyd George assured the Welsh Liberal Convention at Swansea in October 1908 that, 'British Liberalism is not going to repeat the errors of Continental Liberalism'. Continental Liberalism, he said, 'has been swept to one side before it had well begun its work, because it refused to adapt itself to new conditions.' It had 'concerned itself exclusively with mending and perfecting the machinery which was to grind corn for the people. It forgot that the people had to live while the process was going on'. British Liberalism, he told his audience, 'had been better advised. It has not abandoned the traditional ambition of the Liberal party to establish freedom and equality; but side by side with this effort it promotes measures for ameliorating the conditions of life for the multitude'. In a passage which defined the essence of the difference between the 'old' Liberalism and the 'new', he went on:

> The old Liberals in this country used the national discontent of the people
> with the poverty and precariousness of the means of subsistence as a motive
> power to win for them a better, more influential, and more honourable status
> in the citizenship of their native land. The new Liberalism, while pursuing
> this great political ideal with unflinching energy, devotes a part of its
> endeavour also to the removing of the immediate causes of discontent. It is
> true that man cannot live by bread alone. It is equally true that a man
> cannot live without bread. Let Liberalism proceed with its glorious work of

20   David Powell, *The Liberal Ministries and Labour, 1892-1895, History*, October, 1982, pp 408-426.
21   This was published in 1909, but the various chapters had mostly been published as newspaper articles over the previous two years.

building up the temple of liberty in this country, but let it also bear in mind
that the worshippers at the shrine have to live.[22]

Not only did Lloyd George have a dynamic understanding of the reforming potential
of Liberalism. He was also in a position to give the concept of New Liberalism political
credibility by showing how its theory could be translated into practice. In so doing, he
injected his own prejudices and preferences into the Asquith administration's scheme of
reform. He it was, in effect, who determined the financial and political strategy of the New
Liberalism with his 1909 Budget, incorporating the idea of land taxes and plans for 'national
development'into the broader programme of fiscal reform. He was the moving spirit behind
the Health Insurance scheme of 1911. Almost single-handedly in the government, he was
responsible for launching the Liberal land campaign in 1912-14.[23] In pursuing these policies,
as Kenneth Morgan has shrewdly observed, Lloyd George was skilfully blending the old
Liberalism and the new, providing a personal synthesis which seemed calculated to enhance
the political prospects of Liberalism as the general election of 1915 drew nearer. It might also
be observed that by bringing the diverse strands of Liberal thinking together in the way that
he did, he had given the New Liberalism of the Asquith years a distinctively Lloyd Georgian
stamp.

The same intellectual inventiveness was displayed by Lloyd George later in his career,
following the merger between the Asquithian and Lloyd Georgeite wings of the party in
1923.[24] He was quick to align himself with the progressive Liberals of Manchester and the
intellectuals of the famous Liberal Summer Schools - E. D. Simon, Ramsay Muir, John
Maynard Keynes and others - who had been trying unsuccessfully to persuade the Asquithian
leadership to adopt a more constructive policy of social and industrial reform since 1919-20.
From 1924, Lloyd George deployed the seemingly inexhaustible resources of his Political
Fund to finance a series of expert enquiries into aspects of Britain's economic problems in the
post-war world. The results of these investigations were seen in the report on *Coal and Power*
and in the publication of the so-called 'coloured books' - *The Land and the Nation* (the 'Green
Book'), *Towns and the Land* (the 'Brown Book') and finally the famous 'Yellow Book' of
1928, *Britain's Industrial Future*. This last was the product of the 'Liberal Industrial Inquiry'
inaugurated after Lloyd George took over the leadership of the party in 1926. Described by
one sympathetic historian as 'the outstanding achievement of Lloyd George's political
exile'[25], it has been widely seen as representing a major breakthrough in certain areas of
economic policy, not least because sections of it were informed by ideas which later provided
the basis of 'Keynesian' thinking. Although the final report rested heavily on the contributions
of others, however, (notably Keynes, Rowntree and E. D. Simon), Lloyd George himself
played an active part in the proceedings of the committees which produced it, chairing working
parties and drafting sections of the final version. He was also largely responsible for the

---

22   Speech, 1 October 1908, reprinted in Du Parcq, *op. cit.*, p 640.
23   On the land campaign, see Ian Packer's chapter in this volume.
24   John Campbell, *The Goat in the Wilderness* provides a detailed study of this period. See above.
25   Campbell, *The Goat in the Wilderness*, p 204.

abridged version of the report, the 'Orange Book', *We Can Conquer Unemployment*, which formed the basis of the Liberal party's appeal to the voters at the 1929 election.

The revitalised Liberalism of the 1920s represented in many ways an extension, or a culmination, of the New Liberalism of pre-1914, especially insofar as its ideas were a response to the emergence of the 'Labour Question' in British politics in the early twentieth century. The 'Yellow Book', with its concentration on questions such as industrial democracy, the development of industry and the problem of unemployment, finally provided what the New Liberalism of the Edwardian era had lacked, namely a comprehensive economic and industrial strategy. But although its roots were to be found in the pre-war period, it was influenced also by the experience of the years since 1914 - by the experiments of the Lloyd George Coalition in industrial policy and by the perceived need for Liberals to provide an alternative to the confrontation between Labour and Capital which threatened to dominate the political and industrial life of the country. To what extent the resulting policies amounted to a kind of 'Lloyd Georgeism' comparable to the 'Gladstonianism' of the late nineteenth century is a moot point. Domestic and international realities had altered considerably since Gladstone's day. In the changed circumstances of Liberal politics it was difficult for any one individual to achieve the kind of ascendancy which Gladstone had enjoyed. What is clear, though, is that with Lloyd George's encouragement and guidance the Liberal party in the 1920s was beginning to address itself to the problems which had faced Britain since 1918. Lloyd George's personal role in that process - as contributor, catalyst and conductor - was of crucial importance. Masterman's comment that 'when Lloyd George came back to the party, ideas came back to the party'[26] may underestimate the intellectual vitality of a Liberal party without Lloyd George, but it testifies to the energising effect which Lloyd George's inspiration and leadership could have, even in difficult times.

Even so, as far as the Liberal party itself was concerned, reunion with Lloyd George was perhaps more of a mixed blessing. Liberal politics in the 1920s were largely dominated by the running feud between Lloyd George and his Asquithian opponents, a feud which was a struggle both for control of the party machine and of the Lloyd George Fund, which was the only major source of finance available to the Liberal party for propaganda and electoral purposes. Even during Lloyd George's period as leader of the party from 1926-31, the Asquithians in the Liberal Council (a 'party within a party' organised by Viscount Gladstone and Lord Grey somewhat on the lines of Lord Rosebery's Liberal League of the early 1900s) worked hard to undermine his position and weaken his authority. Lloyd George, for his part, gave them some reason for their mistrust, adopting a rather *grand seigneurial* manner towards the party and its organisations and at times seeming reluctant to place himself fully at the disposal of the party's cause. Nevertheless, here too there are more positive aspects of Lloyd George's legacy which, as in the realm of ideas, are worthy of comment, and which have a particular relevance to the history of the Liberal party after 1945[27].

---

26   Lucy Masterman, *C. F. G. Masterman* (London, 1939), p 346.
27   For general histories of the Liberal party, see Roy Douglas, *The History of the Liberal Party, 1895-1970* (London, 1971) and Chris Cook, *A Short History of the Liberal Party* (3rd ed, London, 1989).

First, Lloyd George can be credited with helping to ensure that the Liberal party survived at all in the difficult conditions of the 1920s. Divided and overtaken by Labour at the Election of 1922, the Liberals failed to escape from their third-party position in 1923, despite being reunited in defence of Free Trade. In 1924, after the fall of the first Labour government, the Liberals were routed at the polls, causing Sidney Webb to remark that he had witnessed 'the funeral of a great party'[28]. So, too, it might have been. The Liberals were weak in organisation, short of money and their morale was low. Asquith, out of parliament and visibly in decline, was in no condition to offer inspirational or innovative leadership. If the party had fallen into the hands of a figure such as Sir John Simon, who saw himself as Asquith's natural successor, it would in all likelihood have become little more than an appendage of the Conservative party and might have disappeared altogether. In a real sense it was Lloyd George who ensured the continuing independence of the Liberal party as a political force, and perhaps its very existence as a political party. He provided inspiration, money and ideas. Above all, from 1924 until 1931, he ceaselessly tested the possibilities of the Liberal party's third party position, striving to establish an identity for the party which would distinguish it from socialism and Toryism and to develop a strategy which would return Liberals to office. His efforts were only defeated in the end by the endemic disunity of the Liberal MPs in parliament and by the cruel accident of timing which produced the political crisis of 1931 just when Lloyd George was too ill to participate in the negotiations which led to the formation of a National Government.

Before 1931, though, Lloyd George had genuinely offered the Liberal party a new political role. After the experience of 1923-4, when the Liberals had reaped public humiliation from keeping in office a Labour government over which they had no control, he realised the dangers as well as the opportunities that were inherent in holding the balance of power in the Commons. He pondered long and hard on what the Liberal party should do if it found itself in such a position again. Of course, the best answer was for the Liberals to win enough seats to form a government of their own, but there were few who thought this was possible in 1929, nor did it prove to be so. The most the party could hope to do was to establish a solid bridgehead of MPs and, in the event of a 'hung' parliament, use its voting strength to influence the other parties. For this reason it was important that the Liberals should carve out a distinctive identity for themselves independent of the right-left polarities of Conservative and Labour. Here the updated New Liberalism of the 1920s provided an answer - a platform that was at once 'centrist', in the sense of being neither socialism nor Toryism, yet at the same time radical. It thus enabled the Liberals to present themselves as a moderating influence in the struggle between capital and labour while still offering a programme of progressive, left-of-centre measures of reform. On a charitable reading, it could be said that this was what Lloyd George's Coalition had offered between 1918 and 1922, but in reality the Coalition was too heavily dominated by the Conservatives and too anti-Labour to fit the bill. There were other differences as well between the strategy of the Coalition and that of the Liberal party in the late 1920s. In 1919 and 1920 Lloyd George was

---

28   Quoted in Margaret Cole (ed), *Beatrice Webb's Diaries, 1914-1932* (London, 1956), p 48. Only 40
      Liberal MPs were elected in 1924, compared with 158 in 1923.

thinking in terms of a dominant Centre party which could monopolise government and marginalise the two extremes of 'revolution'and 'reaction'. By 1928-9, the talk (assuming the failure of the Liberals to win an electoral majority on their own) was of organised cooperation with one of the other parties, probably Labour. There was still a commitment to moderating the excesses of socialism, but a new sub-text had emerged. The Liberals were presenting themselves not just as a middle party but as a radical alternative to a system of politics derived from industrial conflict. They were also reaffirming their reforming credentials. How deep the change went in practice it is hard to say. In one sense, 'radical centrism' was what the Liberal party had always offered; the rise of Labour simply made this more explicit. Again, there were Liberals who did not accept the new line and preferred a right-wing alliance with the Conservatives. But arguably it was Lloyd George who reconciled the strategic demands of the political situation with the inherited traditions of Liberalism more effectively than any of the other potential leaders of the party at this time.

Admittedly, in 1929-31 the strategy was no more than partially successful. The Liberals did win the balance of power in 1929[29], but there were formidable obstacles in the way of the implementation of Lloyd George's long-term plans. One was that Ramsay MacDonald and his colleagues in the Labour government were opposed to any open acknowledgement of their dependence on the Liberals, whom they hoped to supplant as the sole party of the left. Another was that Lloyd George's Liberal MPs were deeply divided, with Sir John Simon and others on the right of the party against the idea of cooperating with the Labour government and preferring a deal with the Conservatives. The Liberals were also unable to maintain electoral pressure on Labour because of the poor state of their party organisation and their dismal record at by-elections from 1929 on. In these circumstances, it was a testimony to Lloyd George's political skills that he was able to manoeuvre the Labour government into promising to introduce a measure of electoral reform in return for Liberal support. By the summer of 1931, as the economy plunged towards collapse, he was on the verge of concluding a broad agreement with MacDonald to deal with the problem of unemployment which might have led to the formation of a Liberal-Labour coalition government. Then two unexpected disasters struck. First, MacDonald's administration split over the issue of public spending cuts and was replaced by a National Government under MacDonald's leadership, ostensibly to deal with the immediate financial crisis. Secondly, at the moment of crisis, Lloyd George was incapacitated following a serious operation, leaving Samuel as the chief Liberal minister in the coalition cabinet that came into existence. When, under pressure from its Conservative members, the National Government decided to seek a popular mandate at a general election, any Liberal satisfaction at regaining office was soon cut short. The Samuelite and Simonite factions began to organise separately within the government while Lloyd George and his small 'family party'remained on the opposition benches. Samuel and his colleagues eventually left the National Government in 1932 in protest against the abandonment of Free Trade by the Ottawa conference, but the Simonite Liberal Nationals remained in the coalition. By this time, in any case, the Liberal party's immediate

---

29   The Liberals won 59 seats and 5.3 million votes. Labour emerged as the largest party but without an
          overall parliamentary majority.

prospects had been shattered. An increase in the total number of Liberal MPs returned in 1931 could not disguise the party's underlying weakness. At the election of 1935 (at which Lloyd George launched his Council of Action campaign) only 21 independent Liberals were elected, with the hopes of any sustained revival relegated to the dim and distant future.

Liberal fortunes did not revive in the last ten years of Lloyd George's life (though Samuel's successor as leader, Sir Archibald Sinclair, served with distinction in Churchill's wartime government), nor in the first decade after his death. As has been said, if Lloyd George left a permanent legacy it seemed in these years to be in the form of a general diffusion of his ideas into the policies of the other two parties. The years of the post-war consensus were unfavourable for third-party politics, nor did the Liberals themselves, their minds dwelling on the legacy of dissension and decline, make much use of Lloyd George's memory, preferring to hark back to the safely more distant days of Gladstone and Bright[30]. Neither Sinclair nor Clement Davies, who led the party from 1945-1956, were men cast in the Lloyd George mould, nor did they seem to have any clear idea of where the party was going. Not until the Grimond era of the 1960s, and more especially the Thorpe-Steel decades of the 1970s and 1980s, did things begin to change. At about the time when the historiographical rehabilitation of Lloyd George began to get under way in the early 1960s (coincidentally at the same time as the Orpington by-election victory in 1962), younger Liberals became more likely to look to the career of Lloyd George for political inspiration[31]. More importantly, Grimond's strategy for realignment of the left marked the beginning of a new quest for power. In the 1970s, Jeremy Thorpe and David Steel returned to an essentially Lloyd Georgeite strategy for rebuilding a Liberal presence in politics, drawing on mounting disillusionment with the two-party system which Lloyd George had condemned. In the election of February 1974, the best Liberal result since 1929, Thorpe's flamboyant style of campaigning echoed that of Lloyd George. His talk of finding a middle way between capital and labour - the need for which was demonstrated by the Heath government's confrontation with the miners - was reminiscent of Lloyd George's line during the General Strike of 1926. There was even discussion of the possibility of the Liberals entering a coalition government, either with the Conservatives or as part of a government of national unity. In 1974 this came to nothing, but in 1977 the new Liberal leader, David Steel, led the Liberal party into the Lib-Lab pact with James Callaghan's Labour government, bringing back memories of 1929 and 1931. In the same year, the 'Yellow Book' was reissued, with many of its ideas still incorporated into Liberal party policy. As political developments and historiographical trends moved in parallel directions, the Lloyd George legacy began to be more favourably assessed and its relevance to the politics of the late twentieth century was openly acknowledged.[32]

---

30   Gladstone's legacy was certainly an enduring one, as Jo Grimond discovered in Orkney and Shetland in 1945 when one of his elderly supporters promised to vote for 'Mr Gladstone's man'. Jo Grimond, *Memoirs* (London, 1979), p 118.

31   Lloyd George was one of the two great heroes of David Penhaligon, the late MP for Truro. (The other was Isambard Kingdom Brunel.) Annette Penhaligon, *Penhaligon* (London, 1990), p 172.

32   For example in Ian Bradley, *The Strange Rebirth of Liberal Britain* (London, 1985).

Lloyd George himself could take posthumous pleasure from these later events which had been foreshadowed and to some extent made possible by his own career. Although there had been times when he was politically detached from the Liberal party, and although the party had sometimes been more harmed than helped by his actions, he retained the character of a dedicated Liberal to the end of his life. As that life drew inexorably to its close his faith in the mission of Liberalism was still undimmed. In 1943, at a gathering to celebrate his eightieth birthday, Lloyd George summed up his complex relationship with Liberalism thus:

> He had been born a Liberal, had always been a Liberal and was too old to change now. He felt convinced that the Liberal Party, wholly independent from any vested interest, had still much of importance to say which could not be said by either the Conservative or the Labour Party, and he advised it to keep its armour bright and be prepared for what may come out of an unknown future.[33]

33   Viscount Samuel, *Memoirs* (London, 1945), p 293.

THE TREATY THAT NEVER WAS:
LLOYD GEORGE AND THE ABORTIVE
ANGLO-FRENCH ALLIANCE OF 1919

A LENTIN

Lloyd George est très versatile; son esprit est vif mais choquant. Lloyd George promet une chose, s'engage et retire sa parole, se dégage le lendemain. Georges Leygues, Diary, 11-12 March 1919 (J Raphael-Leygues, *Georges Leygues*, Paris, 1983, p. 216).

I

On the morning of 28 June, 1919, the day of the signing of the Treaty of Versailles, Lloyd George, for Britain, and Clemenceau, for France, set their hands to another international agreement, to all appearances hardly less momentous than the former in the postwar settlement of Europe. This was an Anglo-French alliance, or treaty of guarantee to France, stipulating that 'Great Britain agrees to come immediately to her assistance in the event of any unprovoked movement of aggression against her being made by Germany'. Ratification by Britain followed in July, when Lloyd George and Curzon successfully steered it through Parliament as the Anglo-French Treaty (Defence of France) Act 1919. In the autumn, Clemenceau likewise secured approval from the National Assembly. Formal ratifications were exchanged between London and Paris in November. A new era of Anglo-French solidarity seemed to have been inaugurated. A month later, the treaty no longer existed, except as a historical memory. Britain's guarantee to France, which Clemenceau described as 'nothing less than the ultimate sanction of the Peace Treaty' and 'the keystone of European peace', turned out to be a damp squib, a half-forgotten footnote in the annals of the Paris Peace Conference.[1]

Most historians have been content to leave it at that: an unfortunate mishap in Lloyd George's foreign policy, a bold but ill-fated initiative, frustrated by circumstances ultimately beyond his control. The failure of the alliance to become operative, it will be remembered, was occasioned by the failure of the United States Senate to ratify an analogous American treaty of guarantee, which President Wilson had signed on the same day and in the same ceremony as that in which Lloyd George committed Britain to the side of France. Blame for this débâcle tends therefore to fall on Wilson for his political ineptness in failing to secure senatorial approval, rather than on Lloyd George.[2] There were, it is true, critics like Lord Hardinge of the Foreign Office, who singled out the Anglo-French treaty as the most egregious of Lloyd George's attempts to run foreign policy as a 'one man band'; and who

---

1   'Notes of a meeting held at President Wilson's House', 28 June 1919, Bonar Law Papers, House of Lords Record Office, Box 88; *British and Foreign State Papers*, Volume CXII, H.M.S.O., 1919, pp. 213-215; R. A. Lansing, *The Peace Negotiations. A Personal Narrative*, 1921, p. 162; G. Clemenceau, *Grandeur and Misery of Victory*, 1930, pp. 225, 230, 232; L. A. R. Yates, *United States and French Security 1917-1921*, New York, 1957, p.xx.

2   The American treaty was not even submitted to the Senate. According to E. Ambrosius *(Woodrow Wilson and the American Diplomatic Tradition. The Treaty Fight in Perspective*, 1987, p. 214) 'indifference of the Democratic president and senators, even more than opposition from some Republicans, killed this alliance'.

fulminated against his airy indifference to the professionals, and the ready resort to 'stunts'and spur-of-the-moment improvisations which the Permanent Under-Secretary was not alone in seeing as characteristic of Lloyd George's conduct of foreign affairs. 'I doubt if any treaty of such vital and far-reaching importance', he wrote, 'has ever been negotiated in such a thoughtless and light-hearted manner'.[3] Now whether justified or not - and as this essay hopes to demonstrate, Lloyd George's underlying approach to the treaty was neither thoughtless nor light-hearted - such criticisms relate to the Prime Minister's methods, not to his policy as such. They are about means, not ends. While most historians of Lloyd George, including such admirers as Professor Morgan, readily concede his unorthodoxy of method in foreign policy, few have questioned his good intentions in the matter of the Anglo-French alliance.[4] Professor Northedge, indeed, claims that 'the revolutionary offer to France ... was the greatest achievement of the personal diplomacy of the British Prime Minister'.[5] Others have had their doubts, but have not followed them up in detail. The current revival of interest in Lloyd George's activities at the Peace Conference,[6] however, invites a closer consideration of the treaty that never was.

II

It is common knowledge that Lloyd George devised the notion of an Anglo-French alliance in order to resolve the grave diplomatic crisis arising from French demands over the Rhineland. The crisis, which emerged in January and February 1919 and came to a head in March, was seemingly unbridgeable. The French insisted that Germany's western frontier be relocated on the Rhine and that all German territory on the left bank be detached from the Reich as a separate buffer-state under French control. They regarded the Rhine as an indispensable strategic frontier and bastion against Germany, the minimum guarantee of French security, without which France would in effect have lost the war. Clemenceau announced that he could sign no treaty which did not include this essential provision. Lloyd George and Wilson, for their part, refused to countenance it. For Wilson, the severance of German territory was a naked violation of the principle of national self-determination. For Lloyd George, it signified the creation of what he called an Alsace-Lorraine in reverse. For both it meant laying up fresh tensions for the future and as such was absolutely inadmissible.

---

3   Lord Hardinge of Penshurst, *The Old Diplomacy*, 1947, p. 242.
4   K. Morgan, *David Lloyd George. Welsh Radical as World Statesman*, 1964, p. 63. L. A. R. Yates, author of the leading work on the subject, claims (*op. cit*, p. 18) that 'the aims of the pacts were high and the motives praiseworthy'. Dr Alan Sharp, on the other hand (in his forthcoming study, *The Versailles Settlement. Peacemaking in Paris 1919*), remarks: 'it is tempting to ask if they were ever intended to operate'.
5   F. S. Northedge, *The Troubled Giant. Britain among the Great Powers 1916-1939*, 1966, p. 105.
6   A. Lentin, *Guilt at Versailles. Lloyd George and the Pre-History of Appeasement*, 1985. (First appeared as *Lloyd George, Woodrow Wilson and the Guilt of Germany. An essay in the Pre-History of Appeasement*, 1984); A. Sharp, 'Lloyd George and Foreign Policy 1918-1922: The 'And yet' Factor', *The Life and Times of David Lloyd George*, (ed) Judith Loades, 1991, pp. x-y; *The Versailles Settlement. Peacemaking in Paris 1919*, 1991.

There was deadlock between France and the Anglo-Saxons. The Conference came close to a breakdown that threatened the entire work of peacemaking.[7]

Then came Lloyd George's intervention. On the morning of 14 March, President Wilson returned to Paris from the United States, where he had been obliged to attend the opening of Congress. Barely had he reached his residence on the Place des Etats-Unis than he was visited at noon by Lloyd George. Precisely what arguments the Prime Minister used in the private interview with the President that ensued, we do not know. No official record was made of their discussion, nor of that held in the afternoon at the Hôtel Crillon, where the two leaders proceeded for an urgent confidential exchange with Clemenceau. What is known is that Lloyd George made Clemenceau the offer of an immediate military alliance with Britain, undertaking to guarantee France against any future unprovoked aggression on the part of Germany. Wilson for his part volunteered to put a similar proposal to the American Senate. In return they required Clemenceau to give up all thought of detaching the Rhineland. On the strength of these pledges, Clemenceau eventually agreed to abandon his demand for a separate Rhineland, though he insisted that the territory remain a demilitarized zone in perpetuity, with a fifteen-year military occupation by the Allies to protect France in the immediate term. The promise of alliance with Britain and America thus replaced the Rhine frontier as the basis of French foreign policy at the Peace Conference. Lloyd George's initiative enabled the Conference to resume its work, not without difficulties during the next weeks and months over the terms of the treaties of alliance and particularly the length of the Allied occupation. But thanks to Lloyd George, the immediate crisis was over. The peacemakers could proceed to other matters.[8]

The importance of the Prime Minister's personal role in the resolution of the Rhineland crisis cannot be exaggerated. He broached the issue of alliance with France at the highest possible level, with Wilson and Clemenceau direct, and, in Hankey's words, 'under very "hush-hush" conditions ... without the presence of any official or secretary', not even Hankey himself.[9] He raised it on his own initiative, without prior consultation with any of his colleagues either in the British Empire Delegation or in the Imperial War Cabinet. Not, apparently, until several weeks later did he inform the Foreign Secretary, Balfour, and even

---

7   M. L. Dockrill and J. D. Gould, *Peace without Promise. Britain and the Peace Conferences 1919-1923*, 1981, pp. 34-38; G. Terrail, *Le Combat des Trois. Notes et documents sur la Conférence de la Paix*, Paris, 1922, pp. 191-200.

8   D. Lloyd George, *The Truth about the Peace Treaties*, 1938, vol. I., p. 403; A. Tardieu, *The Truth about the Treaty*, 1921, pp. 176-177. Yates (*op. cit.*, p. 17) stresses that the pledges of British and American alliance 'served as the key factor in making possible the Versailles Treaty'.

9   Lord Hankey, *The Supreme Control at the Paris Peace Conference 1919*, 1963, p. 144.

then he treated him as a mere drafting amanuensis.[10] The Anglo-French treaty was his own brainchild; and it was his personal offer of a British guarantee to France that made by far the greater impression on Clemenceau. It was, Clemenceau recalled, 'an unprecedented historical event. What a stroke of fortune for France! The American agreement was secondary'.[11] Lloyd George's démarche was understood as an extraordinary departure in British foreign policy, 'an astounding innovation' in the words of Tardieu.[12] Never before had a British Prime Minister in peacetime offered France or any other Great Power a military guarantee of her territorial integrity. When making this sensational offer to Clemenceau on 14 March, Lloyd George also gave the convincing assurance that he would lose no time in authorising the construction of a Channel tunnel, to expedite the transfer of British troops to France, should she ever again be threatened by a German invasion.[13]

To the French, the offer was irresistible.[14] It was meant to be. Clearly, Lloyd George understood that nothing less than a *quid pro quo* on the scale of a full, defensive alliance against Germany could ever induce Clemenceau to abandon his claim to the Rhine. 'It was proffered', he admitted, 'as an answer to those who claimed that the left bank of the

---

10   T. E. Jones, *Lloyd George*, 1951, p. 180. Lord Hardinge, (*op. cit.*, pp. 241-242), suggests that neither Balfour nor 'any other member of the Cabinet' was aware of the treaty's existence until 6 May. It certainly appears that the Cabinet was not informed of Lloyd George's offer to Clemenceau until after the event (Lloyd George to Bonar Law, 31 March, 1919, Lloyd George Papers, House of Lords Record Office, F/37/3/40). A draft agreement was first submitted for Balfour's approval on 22 April ('Papers respecting Negotiations for an Anglo-French Pact', Cmd. 2169, *House of Commons Sessional Papers*, H.M.S.O., 1924, p. 287). Lloyd George did not notify the British Empire Delegation until 5 May ('Minutes of a meeting of the British Empire Delegation' 5 May, 1919, *British documents on Foreign Affairs. Reports and Papers from the Foreign Office Confidential Print, Part II, Series I, The Paris Peace Conference of 1919*, (ed) M. Dockrill, vol 4, 1989, p. 65). On 6 May, he told Clemenceau that 'he had already informed the Imperial War Cabinet' (*Papers relating to the Foreign Relations of the United States. The Paris Peace Conference 1919*, vol. V, Washington, 1946, p. 475). On 5 May, Lloyd George requested Balfour to draft a further text for signature by Lloyd George and himself (Lloyd George Papers F51/1/22), which the Prime Minister handed to Clemenceau the next day. This is no doubt the occasion witnessed by Hardinge and of which he notes (in a remark attributed to Philip Kerr): 'Lloyd George had only sent the paper to Mr Balfour to put the phraseology into proper shape' (p. 241).

11   D. R. Watson, *Georges Clemenceau. A Political Biography*, 1974, p. 347.

12   '*Une éclatante innovation*', Tardieu, *La Paix*, Paris, 1921, p. 225.

13   L. Loucheur, *Carnets Secrets 1908-1928*, (ed) J. De Launey, Brussels, 1962, p. 72. Lloyd George had mentioned the Channel tunnel to Colonel House on 12 March and he repeated his undertaking to Foch on 31 March (*The Intimate Papers of Colonel House*, (ed) C. Seymour, vol. IV, 1928, p. 360; P. J. Mantoux, *Les Délibérations du Conseil des Quatre: Notes de l'officier interprète*, Paris, 1955, vol I, p. 95.) H. J. Nelson (*Land and Power: British and Allied Policy on Germany's Frontiers 1919-19*, 1963 p. 220) comments: 'the ebullient Welshman surely jested!' This is possible, perhaps likely; but he was not fantasizing. Lloyd George included the tunnel as a corollary to the guarantee to France in a statement of policy on 23 March. (Lloyd George Papers F/147/3/2/2). The Channel tunnel was under active consideration by the Cabinet at the time (A. Sharp, 'Britain and the Channel Tunnel 1919-1920', *The Australian Journal of Politics and History*, vol. xxx No. 2, 1979, pp. 210-215).

14   Loucheur (*loc. cit*, p. 72), to whom Clemenceau revealed Lloyd George's offer on the evening of 14 March, noted in his diary for that day: '*il paraissait impossible de refuser une pareille offre*'.

Rhine should be annexed to France'.[15] In the succeeding days and weeks, until the treaty was finally concluded, Lloyd George followed up his original offer with further, supplementary assurances. On 27 March, he expressed his readiness, in the event of a German attack on France, 'to place all our forces at her disposal'.[16] His words suggest the kind of unified Allied command under French leadership that had been entrusted since the spring of 1918 to Marshal Foch. He also hinted at Anglo-French military conversations on the pre-1914 model.[17] Whatever the particular details, Lloyd George also reiterated his overall pledge. On 25 March, he renewed it in his celebrated Fontainebleau Memorandum.[18] On 28 March, attempting to dissuade Clemenceau from his policy of annexing the Saar, Lloyd George cited the inviolability of his own plighted word. Clemenceau must understand, he said, that Britain and America could no more break their word to Germany over self-determination for the Saar than they could go back on their promise to defend France against German aggression.[19] On April 2, he wrote to Clemenceau to remind him of 'the pledge I offer on behalf of Britain to come to the support of France if the invader threatens'.[20] On 22 April, he formally assented to a written memorandum of agreement with Clemenceau, incorporating the outlines of an Anglo-French convention,[21] offering, two days later, 'to publish in full our agreement with France to guarantee her against the risk of invasion'.[22] On 6 May, at Clemenceau's urgent request, he and Balfour signed a further protocol of alliance, which Lloyd George formally handed to Clemenceau later the same day after its terms had been publicly announced by Tardieu at a plenary session of the Conference.[23] On 21 May, to Clemenceau's complaints of British bad faith in the Syrian question, Lloyd George indignantly retorted: 'I do not think that France has the right to complain of Great Britain's loyalty ... British opinion freely offers to place the whole of Great Britain's strength at France's disposal if she is in danger'.[24] What more could Lloyd George have said or done by way of assurance to Clemenceau before both Prime Ministers put their signatures to the final draft of the Anglo-French treaty on 28 June?

But there was more to Lloyd George's assurances than met the eye. Or rather, as it turned out, there was less. A variety of important qualifications and reservations crept into his original clear undertaking. Not all of them were drawn to Clemenceau's attention, and

15   Lloyd George, *Is It Peace?* 1922, p. 8.
16   Mantoux, *loc. cit.*, p. 48.
17   Mantoux, *loc. cit.*, p. 51.
18   Lloyd George, *The Truth about the Peace Treaties*, vol. I, pp. 411, 413-414.
19   Mantoux, *loc. cit.*, p. 73.
20   'Prime Minister's Reply to M. Clemenceau', Lloyd George Papers F/Box 147/Folder 2.
21   'Papers respecting negotiations for an Anglo-French Pact', *loc. cit.*, p. 287.
22   Mantoux, *loc. cit.*, p. 352.
23   *Papers Relating to the Foreign Relations of the United States. The Paris Peace Conference, 1919*, vol. V, Washington, 1946, pp. 474-5, 494; vol III, Washington, 1943, p. 379.
24   Mantoux, *op. cit.*, vol II, p. 140.

none of them was communicated to him before 6 May at the earliest, a fortnight after he had formally and definitively committed himself, on 22 April, to giving up the Rhine frontier.[25]

How long, to take an elementary stipulation, was the treaty to remain in force? On 27 March, Lloyd George appeared to intimate to Clemenceau that the guarantee would be of unlimited duration,[26] and the draft agreements of 22 April and 5 May stated that the treaty would remain in force until 'the contracting parties' agreed that the League of Nations afforded 'sufficient protection' to France.[27] Since by definition there could be no such agreement without France's consent, this gave France the final word in determining the duration of the alliance. Briefing the British Empire Delegation on 5 May, however, Lloyd George gave a different account. The treaty, he informed them, would be 'for a period of fifteen years, coterminous with the military occupation of the Rhineland'.[28] 'Had the Prime Minister intended to deceive?' asks Professor Nelson. 'Or had he inadvertently revealed a private misunderstanding, or was he simply confused?'[29] Forgetfulness or confusion seems the most likely explanation, since the plain words of the draft convention were there for all to hear; indeed, Lloyd George read them aloud to the Delegation. Even so, the incident reveals a certain casualness towards a salient term of the alliance.

When Lloyd George pledged Great Britain to come to the defence of France, what did he mean by Britain? On the face of it, there could be no doubt: Britain meant the British Empire; and 'the British Empire' is specified in the Fontainebleau Memorandum and indeed in the treaty itself.[30] When Britain went to war in 1914, the Empire automatically marched with her. But the war had brought ideas of a looser relationship with the mother country. Lloyd George informed the Empire Delegation on 5 May that 'Clemenceau desired the Dominions to join in his guarantee'; but on hearing the hostile reaction towards the treaty at once expressed by the Prime Ministers of Canada and South Africa, he assured his colleagues there and then that the Dominions would not be bound by it.[31] In the signed protocol which he presented to Clemenceau the next day, a clause was added stating that 'the obligation imposed under this treaty shall not be binding on the dominions of the British Empire until the

25   Clemenceau further committed himself to accepting the British guarantee and dropping France's claim to the Rhine frontier at a Cabinet meeting at the Elysée on 25 April, at which his policy was unanimously approved by the Council of Ministers.

26   Mantoux, *op. cit.*, I, p. 51.

27   'Papers respecting negotiations for an Anglo-French Pact', *loc. cit.*, p. 287; Lloyd George Papers F/51/1/22; Balfour Papers, British Library, Add Mss 49750/16.

28   'Minutes of a Meeting of the British Empire Delegation', 5 May 1919. *loc. cit.*, p. 65. A fifteen-year term was also mentioned by Henry Wilson to Lloyd George on 27 April, 1919 (G. Riddell, *Lord Riddell's Intimate Diary of the Peace Conference and After*, 1933, p. 61). In the final draft of the treaty, agreed on 27 June, it was stipulated that the treaty could be terminated by a majority decision, if necessary.

29   H. J. Nelson, *op. cit.*, p. 246.

30   Lloyd George, *op. cit.*, pp. 411, 414. *British and Foreign State Papers, loc. cit.*, p. 213. Cf. Lloyd George Papers F/147/3/2/2.

31   'Minutes of a Meeting of the British Empire Delegation', 5 May 1919, *loc. cit.*, p. 66.

treaty is ratified by the Parliament of the Dominion concerned',[32] Lloyd George explaining to Clemenceau on the eve of final signature that he was not authorized to sign for the Dominions.[33] The implication seems to have been, not that the Dominions would not sign in due course, merely that, as British Prime Minister, Lloyd George could not from a constitutional point of view sign for them. Given his realisation of Dominion feeling against the alliance, this surely suggests some degree of disingenuousness. In any event, South Africa, Canada, Australia and New Zealand, whose men had fought in their tens of thousands on French soil, were exempted by him at a stroke of the pen from his original promise to Clemenceau, express and implied, of aid from a united Empire.

The definition of a *casus foederis* also turned out to be less clear-cut in private than appeared from the Prime Minister's promise to Clemenceau, as engrossed on the face of the treaty. The treaty laid down that British military intervention on France's behalf would be activated 'in the event of any unprovoked movement of aggression'; and 'movement of aggression' was defined in relation to specific German violations of the demilitarized zone.[34] At the same meeting of the British Empire Delegation, however, chaired by Lloyd George, Bonar Law observed that 'the words "unprovoked aggression" protected us': whether an 'aggression was provoked or not' would be for Britain to decide for herself.[35] Bonar Law would never have given such an assurance without the Prime Minister's assent. And indeed, in a letter to Botha of 26 June, two days before signing the final treaty, Lloyd George himself confirmed that 'we ourselves shall be the sole judge of what constitutes unprovoked aggression'.[36]

We have noted Lloyd George's repeated assurances to Clemenceau in March, April, and May, of Britain's absolute commitment to France. However much whittled away in detail, his overall pledge was clear and unambiguous: if Germany attacked France, Britain would go to France's defence. Between 14 March, when he first produced his offer, and 27 June, the eve of the signing, at no time did he suggest that it might be in any way contingent on the American treaty. Writing to Bonar Law on 31 March, Lloyd George stressed the unilateral nature of the British guarantee, adding: 'Wilson is inclined to join if he can persuade the Senate'.[37] Certainly Wilson never intended any connection between the two pacts. On the contrary, he was particularly anxious to dissociate them. He repeatedly deprecated any link between the British and American guarantees, on the grounds that such an association

---

32   Balfour Papers, Add Mss 49750/18; Lloyd George Papers F/30/3/40. Cf. Lloyd George to Dominion
     Prime Ministers, 10 May 1919, Lloyd George Papers F/5/3/56. The final version stated that the treaty
     would not bind any of the Dominions 'unless and until it is approved by the Parliament of the Dominion
     concerned', *British and Foreign State Papers, loc. cit.*, p. 215.
33   *Foreign Relations of the United States. The Paris Peace Conference, 1919*, volume VI, 1946, p. 735.
34   British and Foreign State Papers, *loc. cit.*, p. 214.
35   'Minutes of a meeting of the British Empire Delegation', 5 May 1919, *loc. cit.*, p. 66.
36   Lloyd George Papers F/5/5/14/2.
37   Lloyd George Papers F/30/3/40

would be anathema to the isolationist Senate and likely to prove fatal to the American treaty.[38] Wilson's aide, Colonel House, moreover, while doubting that the Senate would ratify Wilson's pledge, believed that 'England was resolved to give this guarantee, whether the United States did or not'. Lloyd George had told him so on 12 March, two days before approaching the President.[39] Moreover, when revealing to the Empire Delegation on 5 May the existence of the British guarantee, and admitting that he was 'apprehensive lest the United States Senate might refuse' to ratify its American counterpart, Lloyd George gave no indication that he regarded the two treaties as in any way connected other than in their subject-matter.[40]

Clemenceau was undoubtedly under this impression. As has been noted, Clemenceau set considerably greater store by Lloyd George's offer than by Wilson's. In an emergency, only British troops could reach France, with or without a Channel tunnel, in time to stem a German invasion. The promise of immediate British aid was therefore absolutely crucial to French security. Clemenceau was clear in his mind that the British and American proposals comprised two distinct offers, of related but unequal importance. 'Do not forget', he recalls in *Grandeur and Misery of Victory*, 'that it was Mr Lloyd George who had made the original proposal, offering to do all he could to induce the American President to agree to it. Mr Wilson merely came in in the second line as the defender of interests less immediately concerned with us'.[41] Lloyd George's guarantee, then, was in Clemenceau's eyes the one that really mattered. Wilson's, if it materialised, would be an additional bonus. Lloyd George confirmed Clemenceau's understanding of the matter. When, on 21 May, Clemenceau pointed out how much France had conceded at the Conference, Lloyd George retorted: 'If M. Clemenceau has agreed to sacrifice certain claims, it is because England has promised to come to France's aid if she were attacked'.[42] The Prime Minister here acknowledged - and correctly acknowledged - that the overriding consideration, the *sine qua non* for Clemenceau in his reluctant agreement to abandon the Rhine frontier was - the British alliance.

Although drafted in similar terms, therefore, the two treaties, British and American, were quite distinct. How, then, did the British treaty come to be dependent on the American? The link came about at Lloyd George's instigation, by virtue of what eventually became Article 2 of the Anglo-French treaty.[43] The draft convention which Lloyd George signed and presented to Clemenceau on 6 May included a clause stating that the British treaty 'will be in

38   Mantoux, I, pp. 319; *Papers Relating to the Foreign Relations of the United States. The Paris Peace Conference*, vol V, Washington, 1946 p. 475. All three official United States Commissioners at Paris opposed a Franco-American treaty (*Papers Relating to the Foreign Relations of the United States. The Paris Peace Conference* vol. XI, Washington, 1945, p. 133).
39   House, diary, 12 March, 1919, *The Intimate Papers of Colonel House, loc. cit.*, p. 360.
40   'Minutes of a meeting of the British Empire Delegation', 5 May 1919, *loc. cit.* p. 65. Nelson (*op. cit.* p. 245) argues that 'Lloyd George's reference to the Senate clearly explains the British reservation that the guarantee would only come into force for Great Britain when the United States had also ratified it'. It does nothing of the sort, though it may suggest a *mental* reservation on Lloyd George's part.
41   Clemenceau, *op. cit.*, p. 228.
42   Mantoux, *op. cit.*, II, p. 140.
43   Yates, *op. cit.*, II, p. 271.

similar terms to that entered into by the United States and will come into force when the latter is ratified'.[44]   An innocent addition on the face of it, signifying no more than that the two treaties, British and American, both having the same purpose, both containing virtually identical provisions, would come into effect simultaneously. It was essential to specify when the British treaty would become operative, and it was not in itself unreasonable to synchronize that date with the ratification of the American treaty. There was no obvious or necessary implication that the one would not come into being without the other.[45] Yet President Wilson dropped a curious remark to one of his delegates. Lloyd George , the President observed, 'had slipped a paragraph into the British note about ratification by the United States and ... he did not think Clemenceau had noticed it'.[46] What was there that required notice by Clemenceau?

The answer becomes startlingly clear if we turn to the final draft of the Anglo-French treaty, presented by Lloyd George, be it noted, at one of his very last meetings with Wilson and Clemenceau. It was the late afternoon of 27 June, the day before the Anglo-French treaty and the Treaty of Versailles were to be signed. At 4.30, the three leaders withdrew briefly to a private room. Lloyd George called in Cecil Hurst, legal adviser to the Foreign Office, who, he explained, 'had prepared a text' of the alliance.[47] After discussion of some relatively minor amendments, which were duly agreed, Hurst's amended copy of the treaty, according to the official record of the meeting, was 'read to and approved by' the three leaders.[48] The final draft, then, of which there was only one authoritative copy - Hurst's - was read aloud, in English only, presumably by Hurst. No translators were present. Into this draft another word had been inserted - the word 'only'. The operative phrase in Article 2 now read that in relation to the American guarantee, the Anglo-French alliance would come into force '*only* when the latter is ratified' (my italics - A. L.).[49] One word completely altered the sense of the British undertaking, making its fulfilment wholly dependent on the fate of the American treaty. Whether Clemenceau, or his foreign Minister, Pichon, the only Frenchmen

---

44   Lloyd George Papers F/51/1/22.

45   This was apparently the understanding of Tardieu and Clemenceau. Tardieu's assertion (*The Truth about the Treaty*, p. 214) that the effect on Article 2 of America's failure to ratify was that 'the treaty with Great Britain is also pending' suggests a belief on his part that the ostensible purpose of Article 2 was to synchronize the date when the treaties should come into effect Cf. p. 207). Clemenceau's account (*op. cit.*, p. 226) also states simply that 'Article 2, which provided for the "simultaneous" coming into force of the two treaties, could not take effect'. Botha was under the same impression with regard to the draft of 6 May: 'I think it would be a most dangerous thing for the British Empire to bind itself ... unless the Senate of the U.S.A. ratifies the treaty and the U.S.A. is, therefore, also bound'. Botha to Lloyd George, 6 May 1919, *Selections from the Smuts Papers*, (ed) W. K. Hancock and J. Van Der Poel, vol. IV, 1966, p. 150). Nelson's gloss (*op cit.*, p. 247) on the 6 May draft that 'this text made British participation in the guarantee dependent upon that of the United States' is made with benefit of hindsight.

46   D. H. Miller, Diary, 5 May, 1919, *My Diary at the Conference of Paris*, New York, 1924, vol. I, p. 294.

47   *Papers Relating to the Foreign Relations of the United States. The Paris Peace Conference*; volume VI, 1946, p. 735; Hankey, *op, cit.*, p. 736.

48   *Papers Relating to the Foreign Relation of the United States, loc. cit.*, p. 736.

49   *Ibid.* The French version, produced after the meeting from Hurst's fair copy, reads: '*Le présent Traité ... n'entrera en vigueur qu'au moment où ce dernier sera ratifié*'.

present, appreciated or even noticed Lloyd George's surreptitious introduction of the vital qualifying word, is not known.[50]   It seems inconceivable that Clemenceau would have assented to the final draft or still less have signed the treaty the following morning, had his attention been drawn to the force of Lloyd George's last-minute interpolation.   But Clemenceau never went back on his word - 'he was', Lloyd George noted, 'a man who kept faith in any bargain he entered into'[51] - and once having signed, he was bound by the treaty whether he had read the small print or not.

III

Lloyd George's manner of negotiating the treaty with France, his repeated assurances to Clemenceau, and the reservations with which he later hedged them once Clemenceau had acted on the strength of those representations, are bound to raise doubts as to his intentions. Tardieu voiced his private suspicions in a conversation in 1920.   While acquitting Wilson of any taint of sharp practice, he added: 'I am not so sure of the good faith of Lloyd George. Why should he have made the assistance of Britain contingent upon the ratification of the pact by Washington'?[52]   Why indeed?

Answers are not far to seek.   If the Senate ratified the American treaty, then, in the event of another German attack on France, Britain and France would again have the support of the United States.   American intervention would no doubt prove no less decisive in a future conflict than in the late war.   But, as Lloyd George suggested to Foch, faced with the certainty of American and British retaliation, it was surely unlikely that Germany would ever again venture to attack France.[53]   In all probability, therefore, Britain would never be called upon to fulfil the Prime Minister's promise.   If war did come, however, America would automatically and immediately intervene on Britain's side.   In this sense, the American commitment was as much a guarantee to Britain as to France.   If, on the other hand, the Senate declined to ratify Wilson's guarantee, Britain would not have to act alone.   Britain would not be bound to do anything at all.   She would be discharged altogether from her treaty obligation to France - paradoxically, by the terms of the treaty itself.   Lloyd George would be absolved from what a recent historian rightly calls his 'solemn pledge',[54] and the blame

---

50   According to S. Bonsall (*Suitors and Suppliants. The Little Nations at Versailles*, Port Washington, New York, 1964, pp. 216-217), Clemenceau and Tardieu both denied having been deceived by Lloyd George. Tardieu told Bonsall in 1920: 'We knew that such a pledge required parliamentary sanction in both countries, and while I fear we have been left "holding the bag" ..., we were not hoodwinked'(p. 216). This does not answer the question whether the Frenchmen were aware of the link between the British and American treaties introduced in the final draft of Article 2.   Tardieu, however, does seem to hint at subterfuge on Lloyd George's part.   Arguing that Lloyd George foresaw the rejection of the American treaty, Tardieu adds: 'he saw to it that in this event Britain would be free to act or stand aside as she desired'. (p. 217).   How did he 'see to it', unless via Article 2?

51   Lloyd George, *The Truth about the Peace Treaty* vol. II, p. 1409.

52   Bonsall, *op. cit.*, p. 217.

53   Mantoux, *op. cit.*, p. 93.   Cf. Lloyd George to Botha, 26 June 1919, Lloyd George Papers F/5/5/14/2.

54   W. A. McDougall, (*France's Rhineland Diplomacy 1914-1924*, Princeton, 1978), p. 60.

could be laid entirely at the door of the United States. As he confirmed in the House of Commons on 18 December: 'If there should be such a possibility as the United States not ratifying the compact, undoubtedly we are free to reconsider our decision'.[55] Either way, Britain's liability was limited. Either way, Lloyd George was indemnified. Whether the Senate would ratify the American pact remained to be seen. Meanwhile, Lloyd George's promise had served his immediate purpose of resolving the Rhineland crisis, so enabling the work of the Conference to proceed and the Treaty of Versailles to be concluded.

Whatever the outcome in Washington, Clemenceau's formal abnegation of the Rhine frontier on 22 April was irrevocable. Lloyd George knew the man he was dealing with when he made his offer. As he recalled, 'Clemenceau had already accepted our proposals and he never went back on an arrangement to which he had assented - however reluctantly'.[56] It is tempting indeed to ask whether Lloyd George did not positively hope and intend that the Anglo-French alliance should come to nothing. Viewed in terms of Realpolitik, it might not be wholly to Britain's geopolitical disadvantage to abandon her ally. Major differences between the two countries, especially over reparations and colonial issues, arose at the Conference. Clemenceau recalls that no sooner was the war with Germany over, than Lloyd George began to assume an antagonistic attitude to France and to reassert Britain's traditional hostility.[57] What is certain is that in the event, Lloyd George did leave Clemenceau in the lurch. Clemenceau staked all on the treaty with Britain - and he lost all - the American alliance, the British alliance and the Rhine frontier. In reliance on Lloyd George's promises, Clemenceau had done what his critics feared most: he surrendered the substance for the shadow, the strategic frontier for a scrap of paper.[58] It helped to destroy him politically. More important were the consequences for French foreign policy. More than any other single consideration, it was the evaporation of the Anglo-French alliance, France's principal deterrent against Germany, which intensified French feelings of vulnerability and alarm at the inadequacy of Versailles. Under Poincaré, France clutched desperately at the letter of

55   123HC Deb 5s, p. 762. Even to the veteran French Ambassador in London, Paul Cambon, the effect of American non-ratification on the Anglo-French treaty remained unclear until December 1919 (Paul Cambon, *Correspondance 1870-1924*, vol III, Paris, 1946, p. 366).

56   Lloyd George, *op. cit.*, p. 433.

57   Clemenceau, *op. cit.*, p. 113. Cf. Lloyd George to Clemenceau, 18 October, 1919, Lloyd George Papers F/51/1/41.

58   J. Néré, *The Foreign Policy of France from 1914 to 1945*, 1975 p. 16; G. Wormser, *La République de Clemenceau*, Paris, 1961, p. 356; J. B. Duroselle, in *Clemenceau et la justice*, Paris, 1983. p. 176. It is true that under Article 429 of the Treaty of Versailles, Clemenceau secured provision for a possible delay of the final evacuation of the Rhineland if 'the guarantees against unprovoked aggression by Germany are not considered sufficient by the Allied and Associated Governments'. As Tardieu observed on 25 April *'Sans alliances, pas d'évacuation'* (G. Terrail, *op. cit., p. 228*); Article 230 also gave the right to reoccupy the Rhineland after 15 years as a security against Germany default on reparations. However decisions here would require fresh agreement with Britain and France, and the policy of the Rhine frontier had still been irrevocably abandoned in return for Lloyd George's pledge of alliance.

Versailles because, as a Frenchman put it, 'England and America would give France nothing else to stick to'.[59]

Let it be assumed in his favour that Lloyd George was sincere in his promise of aid to France in the event of German aggression, however remote such a prospect might seem to him in 1919. Certainly he persuaded the Commons to approve the treaty without a division, using language of passionate moral conviction.[60] Why, then, did he hedge his bet by making Britain's commitment contingent on America's? We are impelled to confront the same insistent question.

Lloyd George was well aware - as were almost all the participants at the Peace Conference, of the real possibility that the Senate might not ratify Wilson's guarantee. The Republicans had won the recent congressional elections. Their opposition to his foreign policy was well known. Republican senators on the Foreign Relations Committee denounced his pledges of overseas commitments as a breach of American neutrality and even of the American constitution. Lloyd George knew that the main object of Wilson's return to America in February 1919 was to arrest this isolationist trend, and he knew that Wilson had failed.[61] It was plain to Lloyd George, as he told the British Empire Delegation on 5 May, that American rejection of a Franco-American treaty was on the cards. Was this perhaps the very reason why he made Britain's commitment conditional on it?

Was Lloyd George a thorough machiavellian, who planned from the start to trick Clemenceau into giving up the Rhineland in return for a worthless promise? Or a casual opportunist, who played the diplomatic game by ear, and adapted his tactics in accordance with shifting circumstances? In support of the latter view, it may be argued that in making his original offer to France, he acted in good faith, hoping that renunciation by Clemenceau of the Rhine frontier would remove that problem permanently from the Conference agenda; but that when Clemenceau insisted on Allied occupation of the Rhineland, and it later emerged that this was the point which aroused most strenuous opposition in the British Empire Delegation as likely to drag Britain into war under the treaty[62] - Lloyd George changed tack and determined to qualify his original commitment.

Even if this interpretation is correct, it follows that Lloyd George represented as an inducement to Clemenceau a set of circumstances which he then found himself constrained, or inclined to abandon. He offered alliance with the British Empire; he subsequently excluded the Dominions. He portrayed the treaty as of unlimited duration; he eventually engineered that

59   D. Saurat, 'How the Treaty looks to France today', *The Versailles Treaty and after*, 1935, p. 103; A. Wolfers, *Britain and France between two wars. Conflicting strategies of peace since Versailles*, 1940, p. 16.

60   117 Hc Deb. 5s, 1123-4.

61   Riddell, diary, 1 March 1919. *The Riddell Diaries 1908-1923*, (ed) J. M. McEwan, 1986, p. 258; Lloyd George to Bonar Law, 31 March 1919, Lloyd George Papers F/30/3/40.

62   'Minutes of a meeting of the British Empire Delegation' 5 May, 1919, *loc. cit.*, p. 66; 'Minutes of a meeting of the British Empire Delegation'1 June, 1919, *ibid.*, pp. 99-103, 112-115, 'Minutes of a meeting of the British Empire Delegation'10 June 1919, *ibid.*, pp. 121, 124; Botha to Lloyd George, 6 May, 15 May, 1919, Lloyd George to Botha, 10 May, 1919, *Selections from the Smuts Papers*, loc. cit., pp. 150-151, 155, 158-159; Lloyd George to Botha, 26 June 1919, Lloyd George Papers F/5/5/14.

it could be terminated by majority decision, unilaterally terminated, that is, by Britain and America. On paper, he promised instant retaliation against German aggression; to his colleagues he confided that it would rest with Britain to define what 'aggression'was and when it should be deemed to have taken place. He mentioned military conversations and a Channel tunnel; they never materialised. Above all, he held out the treaty as independent and free-standing; and by what looks suspiciously like a last-minute sleight-of-hand, he made it contingent on the dubious outcome of American domestic politics.

'Had the Prime Minister intended to mislead?' asks Professor Nelson.[63] Whether Lloyd George intended all along that the British guarantee should hinge on Wilson's ability to sway the Senate, or whether this was an inspired afterthought, makes no difference to the outcome for France. Either way, France had reason to complain of *Albion perfide*. For if Lloyd George took seriously his pledge to France, why, when it failed to become legally binding, did he not recommend acceptance of what remained on his own admission a moral obligation?[64] To this it may perhaps be contended that by the end of 1919 political opinion in Britain had turned against the alliance, that circumstances alter cases and that, as Lloyd George observed to his confidant, Sir George Riddell: 'if you want to succeed in politics, you must keep your conscience well under control'.[65] But was Lloyd George ever serious about the alliance? His original state of mind is of crucial concern to the student of his psychology, strategy and tactics at Paris. At one stage or other, he decided to go back on his word to Clemenceau. Was it before or after he gave it? And was it a question of innocent, or, as Nelson legitimately asks, of fraudulent misrepresentation?

The suspicion of premeditated guile must be strong. Is there evidence to substantiate it? There is the evidence of Lloyd George himself. First, the negative testimony: the absence in *The Truth about the Peace Treaties*, of any attempt to explain, or even to mention the sequel to his promise to Clemenceau. His silence on the point in that lengthy apologia of his conduct of affairs at Paris, is in itself suggestive. But there is also positive evidence of his intentions. It was at a Cabinet meeting on 4 March 1919 that he first mooted the idea of a treaty with France. 'If the United States and ourselves would guarantee France against invasion' he declared, 'she would be satisfied. This, however,' he continued, 'was impossible, as the President would not hear of any entangling alliances, as he put his faith in the League of Nations'.[66] On 4 March, then, Lloyd George contemplated a solution to the Rhineland crisis in terms of an Anglo-American undertaking to France, but apparently had no belief that America would adhere to one. Nothing suggests that he had changed his mind ten days later, when he put his proposal to Wilson. Indeed by that time he was well aware of the hostility to Wilson's policy in the United States. In other words, when, on 14 March, he approached Wilson about an American guarantee, he was, at the least, open-minded about the

---

63   Nelson, *op. cit.*, p. 246.
64   Mantoux, *loc. cit.*, p. 73; Lloyd George to Botha, 26 June 1919, Lloyd George Papers F/5/5/14/2.
65   G. Riddell, Diary, 23 April 1919, *Lord Riddell's Intimate Diary of the Peace Conference and After*, 1933, p. 57; Northedge, *op. cit.* p. 160.
66   Watson, *op. cit.*, p. 347.

prospect of its ever materialising.[67]   Why, then, did he bring Wilson into it at all?   Why make a point of awaiting the President's return from America and securing his promise of a guarantee on the morning of March 14 before making his own pledge to Clemenceau in the afternoon, unless it was that he intended all along that the two offers should be linked?   He admits as much in *The Truth about the Peace Treaties*: 'I then conceived the idea of a *joint* military guarantee by America and Britain' (my italics - A. L.).[68]   He also indicated at the time that this was his intention.   On 23 March, 1919, nine days after making his offer to Clemenceau, in a policy statement marked 'secret', he specified a '*joint* guarantee by the British Empire and the United states'. (my italics - A. L.)[69]   Lloyd George had good reason to believe that Wilson's promise would come to nothing, and that consequently, he would be relieved of his own.   The treaty which he devised was a masterpiece of legerdemain, a contradiction in terms: a 'joint guarantee' in the sense that it was underwritten by America, but by virtue of Article 2, not severally binding on Britain, so that when the underwriter backed out, the principal guarantor could also default.

    If this interpretation is correct, then as far as Lloyd George is concerned the Anglo-French alliance was an illusionist's trick from start to finish; and its disappearance represented not the failure, but the consummation of his real policy.   Frances Stevenson once charged him with being 'a past master in craft';[70] Lloyd George did not deny it.   Was it not part and parcel of his professional repertoire, his stock-in-trade as a political escapologist?   It would not have been the only occasion at the Peace Conference when he fashioned for himself a convenient exclusion-clause behind which to evade the consequences of previous solemn commitments once they had served his purpose.[71]   He gloried in such agility as marking 'the chief difference between ordinary and extraordinary men.   When the extraordinary man is faced by a novel and difficult situation', he told Riddell, 'he extricates himself from it by adopting a plan which is at once daring and unexpected.   That is the mark of genius in a man of action'.[72]

---

67   On 12 March, two days before Wilson's return, Lloyd George asked Colonel House whether America would join Britain in the guarantee. House said he did not know. (*Intimate Papers of Colonel House, loc. cit.*, p. 360).

68   Lloyd George, *op. cit.*, p. 403.

69   Lloyd George Papers F/147/3/2/2.

70   Quoted in A. Lentin, *op. cit.*, p. 120.

71   Lentin, *op. cit.*, p. 107.

72   G. Riddell, Diary, 3 April 1919, *Lord Riddell's Intimate Diary of the Peace Conference and After*, 1933, p. 45.

LLOYD GEORGE AND FOREIGN POLICY, 1918-1922.
THE 'AND YET' FACTOR

ALAN SHARP

David Lloyd George has an impressive claim to be regarded as a British statesman of the first rank. He was a principal author of the Treaty of Versailles, one of the Council of Four responsible for the most comprehensive redrawing of the world map ever effected to that date. He represented the victorious British Empire as it approached its widest territorial limits, at a moment when it was still a world power and when the ultimate inadequacy of its resources to sustain its pretensions was still hidden. To no other British premier has fallen such an opportunity to remake international boundaries on such a scale and even to transform the whole basis of international relations as it did to Lloyd George in Paris in 1919. And yet ... when he left after the triumph at Versailles on 28 June 1919, he may have had a 'wonderful time' at the conference but the signature of the German treaty was little more than the end of the beginning of peacemaking, and both the prime minister's record and the treaty were disappointing. Within a year of leaving office he would admit to the veteran British diplomat Charles Hardinge, ' ... If I had to go to Paris again I would conclude quite a different treaty'.[1]

When the peace conference ended he retained enormous prestige as the last political survivor of the Big Four and, in the negotiations to execute the treaties, he dominated conference after conference. His breadth of vision could be immense, few documents in British foreign policy are more impressive than the Fontainebleau memorandum or even his memorandum for the Cannes conference in 1922. Equally beyond question were his grasp of detail in negotiation, his feel for compromise, his political instinct and his command of language. He was a master of conference diplomacy, a brilliant conciliator of apparently irreconcilable positions, a skilful manipulator of facts, figures and personalities, an instinctive tactician whose ability to engage the most effective and persuasive arguments and emotions rarely failed. And yet ...

And yet ... the balance of contemporary and historical opinion lies against Lloyd George. Two respected correspondents, Sisley Huddleston and Valentine Chirol, attacked his record at the time. In April 1922 Huddleston dismissed him as 'a great political force perpetually producing disappointing results'. In 1923 Chirol disparagingly compared Britain's outstanding position in November 1918 with her situation in November 1922 and concluded ' ... if he is to go down in history as the man whose great qualities did at any rate very much "to win the war", he will also go down to history as the man whose great defects went far "to lose the peace"'. Two ministerial colleagues with a strong interest in foreign affairs were also forthright in their condemnation. Robert Cecil declared ' ... I am personally convinced that

Acknowledgements:
I am indebted to John Hemery, Ruth Henig, Tony Lentin, Zara Steiner and Chris Wrigley for points made during the discussion of this paper in Bangor and Cambridge. I am grateful to the Faculty of Humanities research committee for its assistance. The FO and Cab papers cited are held in the Public Record Office at Kew and are quoted with the permission of the Crown Controller.

1   Lord Hardinge *Old Diplomacy: The Reminiscences of Lord Hardinge of Penshurst* (1947) p. 240.

there has never been a less satisfactory directory of our foreign policy in this country', whilst George Curzon wrote bitterly that, at the Paris peace conference, 'Lloyd George was supposed to be holding up the flag of Britain ... with sustained vigour and brilliance ... In reality (he) was sowing the seed of European disaster'. Recent historical debate on foreign policy questions has also inclined against Lloyd George. Michael Dockrill and Douglas Goold have contrasted the short-term successes of the British peacemakers in 1919 with the long-term reality and concluded that 'beyond any question, the peace settlement after the first World War was a peace without promise'. For this Tony Lentin ascribes much of the blame to a prime minister who 'was every inch the political animal, frisking to the thrill of the game. His ruling passion was a passion for brilliant improvisation'. In the key area of reparations Marc Trachtenberg and Bruce Kent have stressed Lloyd George's responsibility for the undefined nature of Germany's debt at the Paris conference and have questioned the motivation and results of his later policies.[2]

Lloyd George has not, however, lacked champions. David Lindsay, the Earl of Crawford and the First Commissioner of Works, wrote, in May 1921, that 'Lloyd George has been a pillar of strength to the country. It is little short of marvellous what an influence he exercises on Europe. During the last fortnight he has extracted us from two terrific dangers - Ruhr and Silesia - and although the little man is surrounded by sycophants who discount all his great personality, yet he remains our really big asset'. Arthur Balfour, who had enormous admiration for Lloyd George's resilience and courage during the dark days of 1917, paid him a characteristically double-edged tribute, 'I've often been surprised when Lloyd George has come to what I thought was the right decision on some complicated issue, to discover afterwards how little he appears to have known about the essential facts. All I can say is that if I had known as little as he appeared to do, I should certainly have gone wrong'. In the historical debate Dr Martin Pugh has tried recently to rescue Lloyd George's reputation as a figure of moderation and sense in foreign and domestic affairs.[3]

The most spirited defence of the coalition's record in foreign policy, however, comes from Professor Kenneth Morgan who argues that the Coalition attempted to create a national consensus behind positive foreign and domestic programmes. On most issues he sees Lloyd George (sometimes, admittedly, almost despite himself) as the apostle of conciliation and

2   S. Huddleston *In My Time: An Observer's Record of War and Peace* (1938) p. 145. V. Chirol 'Four Years of Lloyd Georgian Foreign Policy' *The Edinburgh Review* vol. 237 no. 483, January 1923. Cecil, quoted by Kenneth O. Morgan *Consensus and Disunity: The Lloyd George Coalition Government 1918-1922* (Oxford, 1979) p. 111. Morgan has an informative section on contemporary opinion *Ibid* pp. 1-9. Memorandum by Curzon, Dec. 1922/Jan. 1923, Curzon Papers, India Office Library, (CPIO) Mss EUR f112/319. Michael L. Dockrill and J. Douglas Goold *Peace Without Promise: Britain and the Peace Conferences 1919-23* (1981) p. 258. A. Lentin *Guilt at Versailles: Lloyd George and the Pre- History of Appeasement* (1985) pp 121-3. Marc Trachtenberg *Reparation in World Politics: France and European Diplomacy, 1916-23* (New York, 1980) pp 64-71. Bruce Kent *The Spoils of War: The Politics, Economics, and Diplomacy of Reparations 1918-23* (Oxford, 1989) pp 374-5.

3   John Vincent (ed.) *The Crawford Papers: The Journals of David Lindsay twenty seventh Earl of Crawford and tenth Earl of Balcarres, 1871-1940, during the years 1892 to 1940* (Manchester, 1984) diary 26.5.21 pp 411-2. Sir Austen Chamberlain's recollection of Balfour's remarks during the peace conference, *Down the Years* pp. 244-5. Martin Pugh *Lloyd George* (1988) pp 132-9.

international security. 'Throughout the Paris peace conference, Lloyd George had been the leading advocate of moderation'. Later his administration, 'Alone of the post-war governments in Europe or North America, ... sought an active dynamic foreign policy. It tried to reconcile Franco-German rivalries, to assuage fears of the French for their national security, to reduce to credible proportions German reparations payments, and to bring the great pariah, the Soviet Union, into the international community. From Versailles to Genoa, Lloyd George sought to give Britain a creative role of leadership, appropriate for a major victorious power which was not, like France, paralysed by the impact of physical catastrophe and the Pétain mentality, and which had not, like the United States, defaulted on its international responsibilities'. A powerful defence which suggests that Lloyd George mounted a concerted effort to carry through a programme which bore a close relationship to the principles and policies of the Fontainebleau memorandum.[4]

This had been drafted by Philip Kerr, Lloyd George's private secretary, at a crucial stage in the peace conference when a log-jam of issues - reparations, the Rhineland, Danzig, the Saar, the League and war criminals, not to mention Anglo-American naval antagonism or Anglo-French rivalries in the Middle East - all threatened the possibility of further progress. The 25 March memorandum was the result of a weekend conference between Lloyd George and his principal advisers, Smuts, Hankey, Kerr and Henry Wilson and represented, in Lloyd George's words, ' ... the kind of Treaty of Peace to which alone we were prepared to append our signature'. Its overall thesis was that, whilst it might be easy to patch up a peace for thirty years, what was required now was a more durable settlement based on justice and acceptance. Germany must be punished but within the limits of fairness, ' ... injustice, arrogance, displayed in the hour of triumph will never be forgotten or forgiven'. She must not lose more of her nationals to foreign rule than was absolutely necessary, she must be given no excuse to prefer the chaos of bolshevism to the settlement and the reparations bill must be one she could pay in a reasonable time with the resources left to her by the treaty. The settlement must be one which Germany herself would execute without constant pressure from the victors. Furthermore France was entitled to security and the settlement must encompass Russia. 'It is idle to think that the Peace Conference can separate, however sound a peace it may have arranged with Germany, if it leaves Russia as it is today'.[5]

These ideas were to be constant themes in Lloyd George's post-war declarations and many of the sentiments and phrases recurred in the January 1922 Cannes memorandum. Thus Morgan's list of his achievements, or at least his ambitions, seems to indicate a consistency of programme and purpose in Lloyd George's foreign policy. And yet ... there must be at least an element of doubt in such an assessment. At one level Fontainebleau was open to Clemenceau's criticism that here was a typical piece of British pragmatism posing as principle. Britain had achieved most of her major objectives - the destruction of Germany as a naval,

---

4   Morgan *Consensus and Disunity* p. 132 and pp. 370-1.
5   S. Roskill *Hankey: Man of Secrets* (3 vols. 1970 onwards) vol. 2 pp. 72-3. Lloyd George *The Truth about the Peace Treaties* (2 vols. 1938) p 404. 'Some consideration for the Peace Conference before they finally draft their Terms'. *Papers respecting Negotiations for an Anglo-French Pact* is printed in Cmd. 2169 (1924) pp. 78-87.

mercantile and colonial competitor, and a share in any reparations - and could now advocate concessions to Germany at others' expense. Lloyd George naturally refuted such a suggestion, but the more fundamental question of the extent to which he was seriously advocating moderation in Paris remains. Huddleston tells how Lloyd George's attempts to introduce some of the memorandum's concepts to British journalists were treated as jokes. Only he took them seriously, spoke to Lloyd George later and produced the *Westminster Gazette* story of 31 March 1919, based on an interview with a 'high authority', stating that Britain was seeking a moderate settlement. This, adding to the existing unrest amongst government supporters, provoked the famous telegram to the prime minister and the House of Commons debate on 16 April. Diverting the discussion away from the *Westminster Gazette* article, and claiming that the whole attack on his position had been orchestrated by Lord Northcliffe, Lloyd George savaged the Northcliffe press and enjoyed a parliamentary triumph whilst avoiding the substantive points at issue.[6]

In the discussion which followed the original version of this paper, Chris Wrigley suggested that the *Westminster Gazette* story was a deliberate political manoeuvre by Lloyd George to provoke a debate on the peace terms at a time of his own choice. Such could well have been the case, but where does this leave the Fontainebleau memorandum? Was it also part of an elaborate hoax played on his right-wing critics or is the truth less sinister, that the prime minister did flirt briefly with moderation but changed his mind when the political consequences of such a stance became clearer? Tony Lentin suggests that Lloyd George's appetite for a spectacular battle was, for a short time, whetted, but that political realism soon reasserted itself. The long term aims might be splendid but were they worth the political suicide of one who took the pragmatic view that it was necessary to 'deviate for political reasons ... to keep afloat in order to give effect to his principles'? Instead the immediate triumphed over the future in the hope that the ends would justify the means, and this is perhaps the most consistent aspect of Lloyd George's record.[7]

Part of any assessment of that record must rest on what one judges to have been his options and opportunities to influence the relationship with France. It is not an easy question to resolve, given the complex and diverse nature of that relationship but even though the Foreign Office sometimes suspected that Lloyd George wished to substitute an *entente* with Berlin for that with Paris, there is no serious evidence to suggest that this was ever his policy. There was no real flexibility of choice after 1919 and the French connection was a vital element which, however reluctantly, most British observers perceived to be at the heart of almost every aspect of post-war diplomacy: Germany; the Soviet Union; the Near East; the Middle East; disarmament and the financial and economic problems of the world.

To what extent was it possible for the prime minister to create a working partnership between two powers whose world views and aspirations were so different? It could, for

---

6   The Cannes memorandum from Lloyd George to Aristide Briand, 4.1.22, *Ibid*. pp. 116-122. Clemenceau's rejoinder to the Fontainebleau memorandum, 31.3.19, *Ibid* pp 90-3. Huddleston *In My Time* pp. 141-150.

7   Lentin *Guilt at Versailles* pp. 50-3. Lord Riddell *Lord Riddell's Intimate Diary of the Peace Conference and After, 1918-1923* (1933) p. 57.

example, be argued that a man with Lloyd George's vision might have penetrated the facade of Britain's imperial position and recognised that the late-Victorian record of detachment from Europe was not the norm in British foreign policy. Yet such reshaping of British attitudes would indeed have been visionary, running contrary to the advice the prime minister received from his advisers, both amateur and professional. Even in the wake of a second major conflict it has not always seemed an obvious course to his successors. His policy was rather to create a self-enforcing peace settlement which would produce a stable, self-regulating and balanced continent with which Britain could trade but for which her responsibilities would be limited. An yet ... unless Britain recognised herself as a European power, she had little hope of maintaining the confidence and trust of a France which feared she would be abandoned to face German resentment alone. If Lloyd George was to be effective as a European and world statesman he had to find some way of cooperating not only with Aristide Briand, with whom he at least shared a history of Celtic enmity towards the English, but also with the dreaded Raymond Poincaré, Britain's least favourite Frenchman. If this was to be achieved Britain had to offer something to France and it may be interesting to consider two questions upon which Lloyd George might have engaged in a constructive dialogue with France - an alliance or financial concessions in the tangled area of reparations and Allied debts.[8]

The revolutionary idea of a British guarantee to France was Lloyd George's: he made it to Clemenceau on 14 March 1919 without even informing Arthur Balfour, the foreign secretary. His objective was to end French demands for the Rhine as a military frontier, either through the outright annexation of the German left bank provinces, or by the establishment of one or more independent Rhineland republics. The offer, made in conjunction with President Wilson, was accepted by Clemenceau, who, after further concessions, abandoned the Rhineland schemes, a decision for which he was bitterly attacked by Foch and Poincaré. From the outset the pact was part of a bargain but Lloyd George's subsequent insistence on the link between the British and American guarantees, and House's grave doubts as to Wilson's ability to achieve the approval of the Senate, pose the question as to whether Lloyd George ever intended to honour that bargain. For the moment it achieved at least some of its ends and his government passed a bill authorising the ratification of the guarantee, remarkably without dissent in the British parliament. Wilson, however, never presented the American treaty to the Senate and thus the British offer lapsed, leaving the government with a moral, but no legal, obligation to France.[9]

There was no rush to honour that obligation. Instead a debate developed in Britain as to the best way to influence French policy, particularly over matters of treaty execution and

8   See for example Philip Kerr's memorandum, 2.9.20, in which he advised the prime minister that ' ... we had better leave Europe to itself with such help as the League of Nations can give to it ...' and to ' ... turn your whole attention to the problems of Great Britain and the British Empire ...' Lloyd George Collection, House of Lords Library (LGC) F/90/1/18. Geneviève Tabouis *Perfidious Albion - Entente Cordiale* (1939) p. 1. Few had a good word for Poincaré, Hardinge declared him ' ... a dirty dog, a man of very mean character'. Hardinge to Curzon, 5.5.22, Hardinge Papers, Cambridge University Library, col. 45.

9   Edward House's diary for 12.3.19 and 20.3.19, Charles Seymour *The Intimate Papers of Colonel House* (4 vols. 1928) vol. 4 p. 370 and p. 409. S. P. Tillman *Anglo-American Relations at the Paris Peace Conference of 1919* (Princeton, 1961) pp. 189-193. See also Tony Lentin's contribution to this volume.

the key relationship with Germany. Partnership with France was both psychologically and practically an uphill task. Geography played a vital role but historical perception was also of enormous significance. Curzon wrote on 2 December 1918 'I am seriously afraid that the great power from whom we have most to fear in future is France', whilst Clemenceau accused Lloyd George of reverting to an anti-French policy as soon as the armistice was signed. Lloyd George was not alone in his ambivalent attitude towards France, there were many British decision-makers who, for a variety of reasons - colonial rivalry, traditional enmity, a concern for the balance of power - tended to believe that German militarism was dead, but that the French still harboured ambitions of a Napoleonic domination of Europe. Curzon told the Imperial Conference in 1921 'There has never disappeared from her imagination the lure of the Ruhr Valley ... with Lorraine, the Saar and the Ruhr Valley in her occupation she becomes the mistress of Europe'.[10]

Britain's role was thus to act as a moderating influence on a France she regarded with suspicion. 'We go about arm in arm with her', said Curzon, 'but with one of our hands on her collar', but was France driven by fear or ambition and what was the most effective way of restraining her? There were those like Smuts who advised a retreat into Imperial isolation, but they were in a minority - as Churchill remarked, 'There are thousands of graves in France ... '. The question for most members of the cabinet was whether it was better to offer France a guarantee or alliance and to hope for a relaxation of French insecurity and hence a more generous attitude towards Germany, or whether France would be more restrained if she was uncertain as to Britain's support. Some British advisers were firmly committed to an alliance: Lord Derby, ambassador in Paris 1918-1920; Sir Henry Wilson, Chief of the Imperial General Staff; Austen Chamberlain and Winston Churchill. The Labour party and some advisers, well represented by Sir Maurice Hankey, the secretary to the cabinet, were opposed. Most, however, were uncertain but wanted proof that an alliance would pay dividends, for very few intended to give France a guarantee without adequate returns, usually seen in terms of greater cooperation in Europe and the Middle East. 'I earnestly hope it will not be proposed to give the guarantee for nothing', wrote Curzon in December 1921 and indeed Lloyd George's offer of an alliance to Briand at the Cannes conference in January 1922 was seen as the price for French support for his proposals for a wide-ranging economic and political conference at Genoa that spring.[11]

Thus both substantive offers of a guarantee or alliance were made - and dropped - as a result of short-term negotiating needs rather than as part of any overall strategy in Anglo-French relations. Curzon's conclusion in his voluminous paper of December 1921 that,

---

10   Eastern Committee minutes, Cab 24/27. Georges Clemenceau *Grandeur and Misery of Victory* (1930) p. 113. Meeting 22.6.21, E4 in Cab 32/2.
11   *Ibid.* Smuts told the Imperial Conference, ' ... I would rather assume a position of independence, putting the British Empire entirely aside from all of them ...'. Meeting 24.6.21, E6 *Ibid.* Meeting 27.6.21, *Ibid.* Arthur Henderson to Lloyd George, 7.1.20, LGC F/27/3/39. Hankey declared, 'We should constantly be in the dilemma of having to choose between breaking off an Alliance and associating ourselves in a policy utterly distasteful to us and liable to lead to a breach of the peace'. Hankey to Lloyd George, 25.6.21, *Ibid.* F/25/1/48. Curzon memorandum, 28.12.21, E. L. Woodward and R. Butler (eds.) *Documents on British Foreign Policy, 1919-1939* (DBFP) (First Series, 1947 onwards) vol. XVI pp. 869.

despite the advantages he recognised in European terms, such a pact would have only dubious value in an imperial or world context and was thus not worth pursuing, reflects three strands in British policy which Lloyd George did little to alter: the imperial theme; hostility towards France and the desire to retain a free hand in foreign policy. Austen Chamberlain asked, ' ... if it be once admitted that we cannot afford to see Germany dominating Belgium and Holland or overwhelming France, is it not far better that this vital object of British policy should be consecrated and defended by a public treaty ...?' but his colleagues did not agree. Britain's resistance to the construction of a Channel tunnel in 1919 and 1920 was symbolic of a similar atavistic urge to distance herself from the continent. Even though he was aware of the crucial role of the French in British affairs, Hardinge, the permanent under-secretary at the Foreign Office could still write in 1920, 'The whole question is dependent upon the stability of friendly relations between France and this country ... our relations with France never have been, are not and probably never will be sufficiently stable and friendly to justify the construction of a Channel Tunnel'.[12]

Reparations were a crucial area in those relations with France. There has been a general agreement amongst both contemporaries and historians that the reparations settlement did much to set the moral and practical tone of the peace conference, as well as becoming one of the most difficult and persistent problems of treaty enforcement. It has always been a difficult area for those who wish to present Lloyd George as a force for moderation at the conference and after but it is possible to produce evidence to support various interpretations of his words and actions. Those who argue for moderation see the 1918 election campaign, the association with Cunliffe and Sumner (the 'Heavenly Twins'), and certain episodes in the drafting of the settlement as aberrations, disguising the prime minister's underlying wish to support a more moderate, perhaps more realistic, settlement. He is portrayed as caught up in a tide of anti-German feeling and constrained by a vindictive and inexperienced parliament, thus being forced to buy time for passions to cool. Such an interpretation has a certain plausibility and could be said to fit the chronology of events. After the conference his apologists would see Lloyd George as a reasonably consistent advocate of a downward revision of reparations and they could argue for his success by the summer of 1921.[13]

Again there would appear to be some justification for this claim. By the London schedule of payments of May 1921 the undisclosed demands placed upon Germany by the treaty had been quantified at 132,000m gold marks (£6,600m). This liability was divided into three sets of bonds, A, B and C, of which the C bonds made up over 80,000m gold marks (£4,000m). The C bonds were really what the Americans at the peace conference had called 'phoney money', camouflage to produce an impressive but meaningless reparations bill. Only once (in December 1922) did anyone argue seriously that the C bonds would ever be paid, thus the London payments reduced, in effect, the German liability to 50,000 gold marks

---

12   *Ibid*. pp. 860-70.   C.I.D.   Paper 246-B, 28.6.20, in Cab 4/7.   Hardinge memorandum (n.d.)
        187042/183192/17 in F0371/3765, see also Alan Sharp 'Britain and the Channel Tunnel 1919-1920',
        Australian Journal of Politics and History vol. 25, no. 2 (1979) pp. 210-15.

13   Morgan *Consensus and Disunity* p. 132 and pp. 139-42. Pugh *Lloyd George* pp. 133-4 and p. 138.
        Trachtenberg *Reparation* pp. 46-8.

(£2,500m). The London conference itself had been a triumph for Lloyd George: he had reduced the reparations bill and yet left Briand sufficient shelter against the storms raised by Poincaré, Barthou and right wing diehards; he had forced the German government to agree to the schedule of payments and yet he had kept the French out of the Ruhr.[14]

And yet ... the prime minister's 'moderation' could also be seen in terms of an arsonist claiming credit for calling the fire brigade, a further example of short-term improvisation to deal with immediate political needs. It was, in large measure, Lloyd George's fault that the reparations section of the treaty left the final bill unspecified. He did nothing during the 1918 election campaign to discredit the wildly exaggerated claims of Cunliffe and Sumner that Germany could pay an indemnity of £24,000m, event though he knew that the highest estimate of the Treasury was £3,000m, and, more importantly, that the pre-Armistice agreement with the Germans ruled out the legitimacy of any demand for an indemnity. Professor Morgan argues that 'It was not electorally necessary for Lloyd George to concentrate on a punitive post-war settlement ... it was clear that Lloyd George would have won the election whatever line he took on indemnities'. Nonetheless, given the massive increase in the electorate and the uncertain circumstances, it was a difficult election to predict and, without the benefit of hindsight Lloyd George was taking no chances. David Lindsay's diary entry for 28 December 1919 is revealing:-' ... The electoral process has been significant. Lloyd George's original campaign fell rather flat. He pulled himself together on realising that he was being left high and fry on the shore. He revised his programme, or rather enlarged it by adding items about indemnities, aliens, punishment of the Kaiser, and pledges to end conscription. Then he got on to the wave again and with an advancing tide has been borne to victory. But can these expectations, these pledges be fulfilled?' There can be no doubt that the perception of many Conservative candidates was that they had gained a mandate for a punitive peace and the Lloyd George shared their views. This was not important to Lloyd George; he had won the election and that was the pressing concern of that moment.[15]

Lloyd George was thus expected to extract large sums from Germany and the hopes of the British public were encouraged when he appointed Cunliffe, Sumner and the Australian premier, Billy Hughes, as the British reparation delegates. All three were notorious indemnity extremists capable of conjuring overnight astronomical estimates of Germany's ability to pay and hence an odd choice for a leader set on moderation. Quite why he should have appointed them has been a matter of speculation though Keynes wrote to the *Sunday Times* in 1938, ' ... I can confirm his [Lloyd George's] claim that he never honestly believed in the advice given him by Lord Cunliffe, Lord Sumner and Mr Hughes ... ' and stating that the appointments were due ' ... not to conviction, but to a supposed political expediency'. As

14   Trachtenberg *Reparation* pp. 208-11. Kent *Spoils* pp. 129-38.
15   In simple terms reparations meant a demand for Germany to restore the damage she had done to Allied civilians and their property, an indemnity implied a policy of demanding both reparations and an element to cover all, or part of, the Allied war costs. Morgan *Consensus and Disunity* pp. 40-1. Robert E. Bunselmeyer *The Cost of the War 1914-1919: British Economic War Aims and the Origins of Reparation* (Connecticut, 1975) pp. 149-70. Vincent *Crawford Papers* p. 399 16 Letter 30.10.38, Elizabeth Johnston (ed.) *The Collected Writings of J. M. Keynes: Activities 1914-1919, The Treasury and Versailles* (1971) vol. XVI pp. 335-6.

Lentin suggests, this political hedging of his bets left him with a self-imposed handicap which made it difficult for Lloyd George to make any positive steps towards moderation in Paris. Instead, despite the Fontainebleau memorandum's sensible suggestion that reparations should disappear with the generation that made the war, Lloyd George resisted attempts to impose a time-limit on reparations payments or to name a total sum for Germany's debt. Most dubiously of all he induced Smuts to persuade Wilson to 'damn logic' and to include pensions and allowances paid to Allied soldiers and their dependants as legitimate civilian damages, thus doubling the eventual bill to Germany. Even during his rearguard action in June 1919, despite stressing the dismay of the British cabinet at the reparations settlement, he was, according to Cecil, 'curiously reluctant to make any changes' to the reparations clauses. Norman Davis, the American reparations expert, believed that the conjunction of Lloyd George's disquiet and the German offer of a lump sum had represented an opportunity to agree to payments totalling £5000m under a plan which could have been rapidly executed. Instead Lloyd George shied away from his own success in persuading Wilson to renew the attempt to name a definitive sum in the treaty, much to the president's disgust.[16]

    After Paris Lloyd George portrayed himself as one who sought a possible settlement rather than an impossible bill but this apparent moderation has to be judged against both the overall thrust of British financial policy and the figures of the various schemes which were suggested as alternatives to the treaty. It is not easy to do this, particularly in a restricted space, because the sums discussed were deliberately inflated and politicians, either from ignorance or choice, often confused the raw arithmetical figures of the proposed annuities whereby Germany would discharge her debt with their present value. Thus the July 1920 Boulogne agreement annuities, spread over 42 years, totalled 269,000m gold marks (£13,450m) but had a present value of 101,000m gold marks (£5,050m). In private the British and French were discussing figures of between 100,000m and 120,000m gold marks (£5,000m to £6,000), though the French were reluctant to accept the British raw arithmetical figures - declaring the minimum they would accept were payments with a current value of 120,000m gold marks. It is thus difficult to extract comparable figures from the 'phoney money' and financial obscurity of the proposals. Nonetheless the January 1921 Paris conference proposal of 42 annuities totalling 226,000m gold marks plus a variable annuity amounting to 12% of her exports, was an increase on the Boulogne agreement with a present value of 124,000m gold marks (£6,200m). Lloyd George was trying to gain French and to force German acceptance of these figures, once again reached for short-term political reasons, when news filtered through that the Reparation Commission was likely to present a much lower bill to Germany. With Allied losses assessed at 169,000m gold marks (£8,540m) the Belgians were

---

16   Lentin *Guilt at Versailles* pp. 112-5 and p. 96. Kent *Spoils* pp.66-82. Trachtenberg *Reparation* pp. 46-72. *The Treaty of Versailles and After: Annotations of the Text of the Treaty* (1968 reprint of 1944 U.S. Government original) pp. 470-5. Klaus Schwabe *Woodrow Wilson, Revolutionary Germany, and Peacemaking 1918-1919: Missionary Diplomacy and the Realities of Power*, translated by R. and R. Kimber (North Carolina, 1985) pp. 363-4.

proposing between 130,000m and 150,000m gold marks, the British less and the French more.[17]

From the outset Lloyd George had distrusted the Reparation Commission, established by the treaty to assess Germany's liability by the spring of 1921. The absence of the Americans and the casting vote of the French chairman seemed to disqualify it as a vehicle for moderation particularly since the first chairman was the implacable Raymond Poincaré, but in April 1921, Lloyd George found himself advocating a return to the letter of the treaty, having spent nearly two years trying to circumvent it. His performance at the ensuing London conference was masterful but the history of the reparations problem does seem to suggest that the prime minister had never worked out the details to link the desired end of a more moderate settlement to a strategy which had a realistic hope of ensuring its achievement. Had he ever established in his own mind the figure for a 'moderate' settlement? It seems unlikely and thus he found himself arguing for the 'moderate' Paris proposals in the spring of 1921 which were far in excess of the 'punitive' settlement which he anticipated, incorrectly, the Reparation Commission would produce.

The question is broader than Lloyd George's British reparations policy. Closely linked was the problem of the inter-Allied debts contracted during the war between the Europeans and from the United States. These were seen by the Europeans, but not by the Americans, as part of the total financial legacy of the war. The position in 1920 was that Britain's European allies owed her £1,6000m, she herself owed the United States £800m but, whereas the Americans expected to recover their loans, there was little prospect of Britain receiving more than a fraction of the sums owed to her. Austen Chamberlain, both when Chancellor of the Exchequer and later, consistently advised the cabinet to renounce their claims upon France and Italy and to fund Britain's debt to America, in the hope that the Americans would respond by an all-round cancellation of debts. The government would have welcomed such an American initiative but Lloyd George balked at the unilateral gesture Chamberlain proposed and sought assurances of reciprocal American generosity before renouncing the European claims. The cabinet had to balance the value of its European credits as a means of putting pressure on its allies, particularly in their treatment of Germany, with the prestige and moral pressure upon the United States that a cancellation would bring. Lloyd George tended towards the former option.[18]

The two issues came together in 1922 when, on the one hand, the Germans claimed that they could not fulfil their obligations under the London schedule of payments agreed in May 1921 and requested a moratorium, and, on the other, the Americans began pressing for the repayment of their debts over twenty five years at a minimum of 4.5% interest. On 29 April 1922, at the Genoa conference, Lloyd George suggested to Barthou, the French delegate, that, if America would forgo her claims on Europe, including Britain, then Britain would wipe

17   Etienne Weill-Raynal *Les Réparations Allemandes et la France* (3 vols. Paris, 1947) vol. 1 pp. 547-60, pp. 593-600. Trachtenberg *Reparation* pp. 136-44, pp. 201-2. Kent *Spoils* pp. 95-6, pp. 123-6. A. McFadyean, (Controller of Finance, Treasury) memorandum 16.4.21 C.P. 2843 in Cab 24/122.

18   Chamberlain memorandum 12.5.20 C.P. 1259 in Cab 24/105. Discussions in Cabinet 25 (20), 21.5.20, in Cab 23/21.

out all government debts owed by European states and drop her pensions claims against Germany. In return France should also drop her pension claims and seek to recover only the costs of restoring the devastated regions. With remarkable nerve, admitting implicitly Keynes' condemnation of the pensions fraud, Lloyd George declared that 'If this plan were adopted, the position would be that ... the claims against Germany would be confined to reparation', but the plan depended on American participation.[19]

There was little prospect of this and the cabinet began to develop an alternative strategy, requesting Arthur Balfour, the acting foreign secretary, to draft a despatch to Britain's European debtors pointing out the nature of the American demands on Britain, the seriousness of the British economic position and regretting the necessity of exacting payment on similar lines from them. The blame was pinned firmly on the Americans. The practicality and tactical effectiveness of this policy were questioned by the Chancellor, Sir Robert Horne, and the Controller of the Treasury, Sir Basil Blackett. On 12 July 1922 Blackett wrote to Chamberlain claiming that the British policy was 'insincere'. If Britain demanded European payments of £43m each year to fund her American debt, France would seek to recover this from Germany as well as the cost of restoring the devastated regions. Germany would also have to cover the debts of the smaller allies to Britain, assuming that the Americans cancelled the European debts. He projected annual German payments of £139m over 50 years, only marginally less than the present schedule, and clearly beyond her capacity. 'Our policy being to persuade France to agree to a big reduction in the total of Reparation in the interest of European civilisation, can we reasonably expect Europe to fund what we pay to the U.S.A.'? Pillorying American selfishness was not sensible policy.[20]

The cabinet did make minor adjustments to the draft but the Balfour Note, which Lloyd George claimed as his own, was sent on 1 August 1922. It was a splendid piece of drafting, its logic and argument were impeccable, it had obvious political attractions but it was an international disaster: it castigated the Americans and left them little room for manoeuvre; its logic was that the less the Germans paid in reparations the more France would have to repay of her debts to Britain; it wrecked whatever slim chance of success was left to the London reparation conference in August. It was an abdication of all responsibility for European economic affairs, a denial of the possibility of any European solution to the problems arising from the war, and a partly conscious decision that Britain's status as a major world power was illusory. 'How' asked Lloyd George's private secretary, Sir Edward Grigg, 'can we demean ourselves so much as to range ourselves with the pitiful European bankrupts and to declare our credit dependent on theirs'? By the end of the coalition its reparations policy was in tatters and, although the French had not yet occupied the Ruhr, it was unlikely that this would be long delayed.[21]

This brief discussion of reparations and war debts shows the best and the worst of Lloyd George. The vision of the Fontainebleau memorandum, the negotiating skills of the

---

19   *DBFP* vol. XIX p. 625.
20   Blackett memorandum 12.7.22, LGC F/86/2/8.
21   Lloyd George *The Truth about Reparations and War Debts* (1932) p. 111. Grigg note 6.7.22, LGC F86/2/4. Trachtenberg *Reparation* pp. 257-8. Kent *Spoils* pp. 188-9.

peace conference or the London gathering of May 1921 contrasted with the short-term expediency of the appointment of Hughes, Sumner and Cunliffe as the reparations delegates and the ineptitude and lost touch of the Balfour Note. Which was the real Lloyd George? It may indeed be that he did desire a punitive peace against Germany and it would certainly be unwise to deny the streak of Calvinism in his soul which believed in retribution - 'It was not vengeance but justice,' he told his cabinet colleagues, ' ... whether we ought not to consider lashing her [Germany] as she had lashed France'. Yet the balance of probability is that he believed he preferred a moderate reparations settlement, though it is less clear if he had a firm idea of what that meant. Even less clear is whether he had worked out what price he was prepared to pay to gain French acceptance of revision. He resisted French attempts to gain any priority of payment - a concession which might have helped the overall cause - he approached an alliance always with a balance sheet in hand and he shied away from any radical solution of the reparations and war debts problem. Instead, Trachtenberg suggests, 'Lloyd George ... was inclined to treat international politics as a kind of game, the goal of which was to solve the problems that presented themselves while obtaining the maximum advantage for one's own side. To him difficulties were basically subjective in nature: the important thing was to bring France and Germany together, but the exact terms of agreement hardly mattered in themselves'.[22]

This idea certainly helps to explain Lloyd George's passion for summit diplomacy. He had an unquenchable faith in his ability to conjure agreement in the most unlikely situations and he revelled in the intimacy and excitement of rapid decision-making and debate - conferences were fun. There can be no doubt as to his ability to think quickly on his feet and to adjust his arguments rapidly and with consummate skill. And yet, as James Headlam-Morley, the historical adviser to the Foreign Office pointed out, 'Looking back over the last two years it would be difficult to point to a single problem of real importance that has been settled; what has been done is to postpone the problems, to effect a temporary makeshift or *modus vivendi*; this no doubt is often the best thing to do, but the fact remains that our relations with France have been getting steadily worse ... Conferences are no more a sovereign specific for avoiding international conflict than avoiding a coal strike'. Valentine Chirol was perhaps uncharitable to suggest that the only successful conference of the Lloyd George era was that at Washington which the prime minister did not attend, but the collapse of the 1922 Genoa conference, and of his illusions of European prosperity based on Russian trade, did illustrate the folly of ill-judged and ill-prepared conference diplomacy.[23]

---

22   Cabinet 491B, 26.10.18 in Cab 23/14. See also Lentin *Guilt at Versailles* pp. 111-22. Trachtenberg *Reparation* p. 104.

23   Keynes' biographer, Sir Roy Harrod, recalls one notable example: 'On certain occasions Keynes was able to work closely with Lloyd George. Mr Dudley Ward recalls an episode. There was a very tangled question concerning shipping in the Adriatic, which had to be settled by the Council of Four one afternoon. Over lunch Keynes and Ward reached the conclusion that they had briefed Lloyd George for the meeting in a sense diametrically opposed to British interests. They rushed round to the meeting. Lloyd George was at his seat in the semicircle round the fire and already speaking to the subject; Dudley Ward judged that, since the arguments were so tangled and British self-interest must not be too blatantly advanced, nothing could now be done. Keynes, however, took up half a sheet of notepaper on which, having advised

Somewhere between the breadth of vision necessary to evolve a widely based programme for British policy and the ability to negotiate and execute that policy there was a gap which Lloyd George was unable to bridge. He disparaged the detail of diplomacy and yet saw himself as both the initiator and the coordinator of policy. This left him exposed to disasters like Genoa, when the machinery fell apart, and made the position of the foreign secretary ambiguous at best. Had Lloyd George's relationship with Curzon been closer it is possible that here might have been the link between vision and minutiae which his handling of affairs lacked, but Curzon had no intention of granting the 'little man' a free hand as Balfour had in Paris and their relationship became notorious both at the time and later. Curzon regularly and bitterly complained about the second Foreign Office at Number 10 and yet proved curiously reluctant to resign - a situation which led, inevitably, to Lloyd George bullying or disregarding his foreign secretary. A lack of any coherent mechanism for sustained foreign policy decision-making and implementation was the hallmark of the Lloyd George era. Instead there were confused and confusing divisions of responsibilities, with the Cabinet Office and the older Offices of state vying with the Foreign Office for control.[24]

Lloyd George was not without principles, though he was never fastidious in their observance, and many of his contributions to the peace conference and later gatherings were sensible, often admirable, but part of his failure to achieve his objectives can be attributed to the lack of any consistent British policy or programme caused by administrative confusion exacerbated by Lloyd George's intermittent interventions followed by long periods of Micawberish inactivity. He could not resist the temptation to score small successes, to produce temporary solutions and to effect short-term reconciliations or ruptures at the expense of longer-term aims. In many ways the game was more important to him than the result and the inevitable result of his dexterity and cleverness was that he came to be distrusted by everyone with whom he dealt. In every aspect of his life Lloyd George had a blind faith that the half-truths (or worse) of today would not be exposed tomorrow, that he would not be found out, and that even if he was that he could either persuade people to cover up for him or that he could convince them that there had been a mistake, a terrible injustice, or a gross misrepresentation of the real case.

Lloyd George to reverse the British demand, he summarized with a brevity Ward would not have believed possible the arguments supporting this change. Keynes passed the paper to Lloyd George, who looked at it quickly and proceeded. He continued on the same lines as before. Ward was confirmed in his idea that it was too late to do anything. But gradually, as they listened, a gentle trickle of thought of a new kind began to appear in Lloyd George's pleadings. And then slowly, as he took plenty of time in making his case, the whole trend was transformed, and he was soon using all Keynes arguments on the opposite side; he added an admirable one of his own. He carried the day, and Ward is sure that the others did not perceive the change of front. It was the finest example which he ever knew of cooperation between two master minds to achieve what at first seemed quite impossible. If only there could have been like cooperation between them in the whole business of peacemaking!' R. F. Harrod *The Life of John Maynard Keynes* (1972 paperback ed.) pp. 280-1. Headlam-Morley note, 18.10.20 in FO 800/149. Chirol 'Four Years' p. 20.

24   Alan Sharp 'The Foreign Office in Eclipse 1919-22', *History* 61 (1976), pp. 198-218. I am grateful to Dr Ruth Henig for information on the arrangements for handling the British delegation to the League of Nations which supports this view.

It would be naive to suggest that Lloyd George was the only international statesman who told lies, but he does seem to have attracted a reputation for duplicity which undermined his effectiveness. Somewhere in every archive or frank assessment the sentiment is expressed in more or less picturesque form. The Belgian statesman, Henri Jaspar, himself no novice in the use of language, jotted his notes for a 1937 article on the Cannes conference and outlined Lloyd George's qualities thus:- 'brilliante intelligence; rapporte extreme et comprehensive, homme d'état; celte peu un anglo-saxon, menteur'. The article itself was more subtle:- 'Et le culte de la veracité comme la suite dans les idées n'obsédèrent jamais Lloyd George'.[25]

In the last analysis Lloyd George's record is a disappointing one. Fontainebleau may have set the agenda for his foreign policy but there must be serious doubt as to whether he had any consistent or coherent strategy for its implementation. He was adept at pillorying French politicians for their reluctance to face their electorate with unpalatable truths and at delivering homilies on statesmanship, but he showed a curious reluctance to follow his own advice. His circumstances were always difficult and there were no assured answers to the dilemmas he faced, only conflicting, often confusing, advice. Even allowing for this his policies towards Germany and France in 1920 and 1921 smacked of petty opportunism and did little to alter a situation that was rapidly becoming, if it had not already become, intolerable. By 1922 his touch, his luck and, some would say, his judgement, had deserted him. Kemal was only the final straw. There was no cure for Europe's ills in Lloyd George's prescriptions, only a postponement of the crisis in the hope that it might never happen. It is typical that his own defence of the government's record six months after its fall should be plausible rather than strictly accurate: 'As long as we were in office we prevented the Turks from going to Constantinople, the French from going into the Ruhr, and the American hand from coming into our till. Now they have all got there'. And yet ... at what cost to Britain's long-term prospects and international reputation had these 'advantages' been achieved? The trouble with Lloyd George is that there is always an 'And yet ... '[26]

25   Dossier 209 Papiers Henri Jaspar, Archives du Royaume, Brussels. See also Sherif Hussein who spoke
        scathingly of 'Luweed Jurj'. 'The English, my son, are an honourable kind, in word and in deed, in
        fortune and in adversity ... Only his Excellency the estimable, energetic Luweed Jurj is something of an
        acrobat and a fox. I say a fox, saving your presence'. G. Antonius *The Arab Awakening* (Beirut, 1969)
        p. 183. According to Lord Derby, the British ambassador in Paris, Clemenceau was very bitter about
        Lloyd George: 'He says that he had been tricked by him ... he says he can't believe a word the P.M.
        says!' Derby to Curzon, '16.10.19, CP10 MSS EUR F112/196.

26   Lord D'Abernon *An Ambassador of Peace: Pages from the Diary of Viscount D'Abernon (Berlin 1920-
        1926)* (3 vols. 1929-1930) vol. 2 p. 185.

LLOYD GEORGE AND THE LAND CAMPAIGN 1912-14

IAN PACKER

Once Lloyd George had become a major figure in the Liberal Cabinet, upon his appointment as Chancellor of the Exchequer in 1908, he twice chose an assault on the landlords to reinvigorate the Liberal Party and provide the spearhead of its attack on the Unionists. The first occasion was the introduction of the land taxes in his 1909 Budget. The second, and much less studied, was the Land Campaign Lloyd George launched in 1913 as the central Liberal initiative to win the General Election that would have occurred in 1914 or 1915 if war had not broken out. Earlier biographers of Lloyd George had little problem in explaining their subject's concentration on the land question in Edwardian politics. To them, it merely reflected Lloyd George's upbringing in the tradition of Nonconformist radicalism, which regarded landowners as 'allies of the devil'.[1] Frank Owen believed 'he had long had in mind' such an attack, 'from his earliest years'.[2] William George wrote of his brother,

> 'The awakening of political consciousness in Dafydd was largely the result of the environment in which he was brought up. The village of Llanystumdwy was owned and surrounded by a ring-fence of landlords, who formed a class by themselves. They were rarely seen by us in the village, and none of them seemed to take any interest in the welfare of the villagers, except on rent day, and that generally through their agents.'[3]

However, more recent biographers of Lloyd George, like John Grigg and Martin Pugh,[4] have moved away from viewing Lloyd George as someone committed to working out the themes of traditional radicalism in his career, even in its pre-World War One phase. Though Lloyd George led the Welsh campaign against the 1902 Education Act, he seems to have had no personal hostility to the measure, or, indeed, any enthusiasm for sectarian causes in education.[5] Temperance played only an intermittent role in his career. His reaction to the Boer War was much more equivocal than has usually been accepted - in fact he was something of a Roseberyite in his attitude to the British Empire.[6] Even on the greatest radical shibboleths, Lloyd George had a remarkably elastic attitude. He said of Free Trade to Charles Masterman, 'I don't regard it as sacred. Some of you chaps have got Free Trade consciences. Now I haven't'.[7] In his proposals for a Coalition Government in August 1910, Lloyd George even flirted with the idea of conscription.[8]

---

1   Ld. Winterton, *Pre-War* (1932), p. 27, describing Nonconformist attitudes to landowners.
2   H. F. Owen, *Tempestuous Journey* (1955), p. 224.
3   W. George, *My brother and I* (1958), p. 126.
4   J. Grigg, *The Young Lloyd George* (1973), *Lloyd George: the People's Champion* (1978), *Lloyd George: from Peace to War* (1985); and M. Pugh, *Lloyd George* (1988).
5   D. to M. Lloyd George, 24 March. 1902, quoted in *Lloyd George: Family Letters 1885-1936*, ed. K. Morgan (1973), pp. 121-2.
6   Pugh, *Lloyd George*, pp. 20-7 provides the best recent summary of Lloyd George's attitudes to Empire.
7   Owen, *Temp. Journey*, p. 192.
8   Lloyd George's proposals are published in the Appendix to Grigg, *Lloyd George*, ii. pp. 362-8.

Far from being driven by the political nostrums he learnt in Llanystumdwy, Lloyd George felt constrained, rather than defined by, his background. He left his village, 'without a feeling of regret, remorse or longing' he wrote in his diary.[9] Its influence on his later career has not been emphasised by recent biographers. John Grigg has called Richard Lloyd's effect on his nephew's political career once it was launched, 'negligible'.[10] There has been a return to the view of Lloyd George held by some of his contemporaries, that he was a man untrammelled by conventional party views, who approached problems purely with the object of finding solutions, whatever new and dangerous course this might require. As A. G. Gardiner wrote of the new Chancellor in 1908, 'No anchor of theory holds him. He approaches life as if it were a new problem ... There is no past: only the living present; no teachers: only the living facts'.[11] It is, therefore, difficult to see why, as, for instance, Bentley Gilbert has asserted, hostility to landlords alone should remain from Lloyd George's background as a theme to which he had 'a real and genuine personal commitment' that would 'remain the constant in a varied and hectic political life'.[12]

Rather, it is more plausible to suggest that when Lloyd George had achieved sufficient authority to help direct events in British politics, he selected the land issue to arouse Liberal enthusiasm and assault the Unionists because he saw it as the most effective means to these ends. The success of this approach in 1909 and, I will argue in 1912-14, reveals the land issue was not an arcadian fantasy of Lloyd George's own that he irrelevantly projected into the centre of British politics, but a crucial theme of the Edwardian era. Its treatment by Lloyd George is ample evidence, first of the continued vitality of Liberalism over 1910-14; and second of Lloyd George's energy and sureness of touch in pressing on from the social programme he had done so much to outline in 1908-11. Far from being exhausted in 1914, both the chancellor and his party were pushing on to new achievements when war intervened.

The choice made by Lloyd George in 1912 to use the land issue to lead the Liberals into the next General Election was conditioned by both the success, and the limitations, of the land taxes he had introduced into the 1909 Budget, and the previous Liberal involvement with the land issue. Lloyd George himself had a long history, going back into the 1880s, of advocating in very general terms some form of land taxation.[13] This was not an idiosyncratic policy amongst Liberals. Henry George's widely publicised campaigns had pushed land taxation into the Newcastle programme of 1891 as one of a number of Liberal plans to attack landlords. This had become possible because the breakaway of the Liberal Unionists in 1886 had removed a large part of the Liberal party's landed wing. Instead of being a loose coalition under Whiggish leadership that wished to dismantle some of the features of landed privilege, like agricultural protection, or the special position of the Church of England, the Liberal party

---

9   Cited in Pugh, *Lloyd George*, p. 5.
10   Grigg, *Lloyd George*, i. p. 29.
11   A. G. Gardiner, *Prophets, Priests and Kings* (1908), p. 157. Gardiner believed, 'The Parnell of Wales
         has become the Chamberlain of England', *ibid.*, p. 159.
12   B. Gilbert, *David Lloyd George: a Political Life* (1987), p. 371.
13   *Ibid.*, pp. 93-5 for Lloyd George's speech at Bangor 21 May 1891.

was able to become a radical party of working and middle class elements that could challenge the fundamentals of landed power.[14]

Land taxation gradually assumed a more important role in Liberal plans up to 1908. Its advocates were able to argue it would provide an attractive alternative or supplement to the rating system. They hoped it would provide an extra source of revenue for local government and stimulate housebuilding by forcing more land onto the market.[15] This kind of argument gave land taxation overwhelming support in the Liberal Party. Campbell-Bannerman received a deputation of over 400 M.P.s demanding action on the subject in November 1906 and a Bill to reform the method of valuing land and buildings was in preparation at the Local Government Board throughout 1906-08, under John Burns' rather lethargic guidance.[16] It was Lloyd George's stroke of genius to pick land taxation out from among a number of Liberal commitments and place it at the forefront of his 1909 Budget. This strategy succeeded in both arousing the enthusiasm of committed Liberals and of delivering a blow to the Unionist opposition. The land taxes were obstructed for 22 days in the House of Commons and the Unionist leadership decided to support the Lords in their rejection of the Budget.

In the ensuing General Election the ingenuity of the Budget became apparent. Previously, the Unionists had gained, if anything, from their umbilical link with landlordism.[17] They could rely on assaults on the landlords alienating other property holders while failing to arouse mass enthusiasm. But the land taxes and the rejection of the Budget by the House of Lords associated landownership with hostility to constitutional government and to the social reforms-especially old age pensions - which the Budget was to pay for. This allowed the Liberals to retain some significant middle class support, especially in the towns of the North East, Yorkshire, the East Midlands, Scotland and Wales, and to keep the allegiance of much of the working class support they had won in 1906.[18] In other words, traditional radicalism and social reform had been joined under the aegis of hostility to landlords, thus allowing the cross-class coalition of Liberalism to continue to govern after 1910, in alliance with Labour and the Irish Nationalists.

---

14   The Home Rule split was, of course, the culmination of a long term drift out of the Liberal Party by its landed element, but the exodus in 1886 meant the remaining landowners were too small a group to block Liberal espousal of land reform. After 1886 only 45 of the 189 Gladstonian M.P.s were landed while 34 of the 77 Liberal Unionists belonged to this category. The 1893 Home Rule Bill revealed only 41 Liberal Peers in the House of Lords - see T. A. Jenkins, *Gladstone, Whiggery and the Liberal Party* (Oxford, 1988), p. 286, n. 43. Also, T. W. Heyck, *The Dimensions of British Radicalism* (Illinois, 1974), especially pp. 5-15, 144-56 for the subsequent convergence of Liberal and Radical ideas on land and other matters.

15   These arguments were given official Liberal sanction in Lib. Pub. Dept. leaflets nos 1847 *Rates and Rents*, and 1848 *Reasons for Taxing Land Values*, Aug. 1900.

16   P. W. Raffan, *The Policy of the Land Values Group in the House of Commons* (address delivered at the National Liberal Club Political and Economic Circle, 25 Nov. 1912), p. 9. B. Murray, *The People's Budget* (Oxford, 1980), pp. 48, 101-02.

17   F. M. L. Thompson, 'Land and Politics in England in the late Nineteenth Century', *Transactions of the Royal Historical Society*, xv (1965), pp. 23-44.

18   N. Blewett, *The Peers, the Parties and the People: the General Elections of 1910* (1972), pp. 400-08.

While the Budget and the House of Lords remained at the forefront of politics during 1909-11, the Liberals were able to maintain this level of support. By late 1911, though, the government began to sustain losses at by-elections and it became clear Lloyd George's National Insurance programme was an electoral handicap, rather than a boon.[19] Nobody believed that two years devoted to Home Rule and Welsh Church disestablishment would revive support. It is, therefore, not surprising that Lloyd George returned to the land in an attempt to recreate his success of 1910. He did not, however, return to land taxation. Even by 1912, it was obvious this policy had not been the hoped for success in practice. It had failed to provide any significant revenue and, far from stimulating housebuilding, the 1909 land taxes had coincided with a slump in housing.[20] Nor could it be concealed that while the land taxes may have been popular in the towns in 1910, they had not saved the Liberals from severe losses in the agricultural seats.[21] The traditional Liberal policy of appealing to agricultural labourers by offering them the chance to become tenants of County Council smallholdings seemed to have had no more success in winning rural support. Though the Liberals had passed a comprehensive Smallholdings Act in 1907, only 2% of agricultural labourers even applied for land during 1908-14.[22]

Instead, Lloyd George hit on a plan which, he hoped, would rally Liberal support in the towns for an attack on the landlords and boost Liberal support in the countryside. In an interview with the *Daily News* of 13 May 1912 he declared all agricultural labourers should be guaranteed a minimum wage by the State. The Government's settlement of the March 1912 coal strike seems to have been instrumental in convincing the Chancellor that a minimum wage policy could be practical in a major industry.[23] But the new initiative was meant to do more than raise agricultural wages. Through rent tribunals Lloyd George said he hoped to deduct the necessary wage rises from the landlord's rent.[24] This was meant to focus hostility, both urban and rural, on the landlord as the person responsible for the appalling conditions of low pay in the countryside. Lloyd George also expressed in the *Daily News* the common radical opinion that if agricultural wages rose, this would increase urban wages, by stemming rural migration to the towns and raising the level against which many urban wage rates were set. In other words, the new initiative was planned to recreate the programme of 1910 by combining traditional radical hostility to landlords with practical benefits for urban workers.

However, as an election was not due until 1915, the Chancellor could plan carefully. In May 1912, he had only thrown out a few ideas. He decided to appoint a committee, the Land Enquiry, to provide facts and arguments to flesh out the policy he had advocated and

19   P. Clarke, 'The Electoral Position of the Liberal and Labour Parties 1910-14', *English Historical Review*, xc (1975), pp. 828-36.
20   Murray, *Budget*, pp. 296-9.
21   Blewett, *Peers*, p. 400, Table 18.11.
22   This policy and its failure have recently been surveyed in A. Adonis, 'Aristocracy, Agriculture and Liberalism: the Politics, Finances and Estates of the third Lord Carrington', *Historical Journal*, xxxi (1988), pp. 871-97.
23   Compare Ld Riddell, *More Pages from my Diary 1908-14* (1934), p. 38, entry for 15 Feb. 1912 with pp. 47-9, entries for 24-7 Mar. 1912, for Lloyd George's change of mind on the minimum wage.
24   *Ibid.*, pp. 63-4, entry for 27 May 1912.

extend it where necessary.[25] It would publish a definitive report on the land question to back up Lloyd George's plans to win over the Cabinet and the party to his new policy. The Enquiry was to be entirely under Lloyd George's control. It was appointed by, and reported to, only him and it was financed by a few of his wealthy friends.[26] But Lloyd George was careful to gain Asquith's approval before setting up the committee. This was a mutually convenient arrangement that allowed the Enquiry general Government approval without committing the Cabinet to any of its findings.[27]

The dominant figure on the Enquiry was Seebohm Rowntree - the only man among those recruited by Lloyd George with both the experience and time to conduct such a large-scale operation.[28] Rowntree arranged separate enquiries and reports for Scotland and Wales to reflect different conditions there. He also decided to divide the main Enquiry into two and publish separate rural and urban reports.[29] Many urban land issues, particularly land taxation and housing, could not be ignored in a comprehensive enquiry and their complexity demanded a separate investigation. This decision opened up the possibility of creating an urban land programme which would provide direct benefits to towndwellers, rather than relying on the indirect effects of an increase in rural wages. This was an idea that Lloyd George and Rowntree were to develop extensively over 1912-13 - thus demonstrating the value of Lloyd George's decision to commission a detailed study of the land question before taking action.

The Enquiry was organised very simply. Rowntree recruited a head office staff of sympathetic economists and social commentators to study the existing evidence.[30] To gather new information, he prepared questionnaires (or schedules as he called them) for local people to fill in describing conditions in their own areas.[31] As most of these informants were necessarily Liberals and their evidence was quoted only selectively and anonymously in the final reports (to prevent 'intimidation' of witnesses it was claimed)[32] it was little wonder that Unionists complained bitterly about the trustworthiness of the report's findings.

Certainly, the Enquiry was intended to confirm rather than contradict Lloyd George's initial instincts on the land question. But it also had a good deal of scope, particularly on urban matters, to suggest policies where Lloyd George had no definite ideas. It was no surprise, though, when the Rural Report was finally published on 15 October 1913, to find it retained Lloyd George's plan of an agricultural minimum wage as the centrepiece of the Liberal strategy in rural areas. The Enquiry produced a wealth of evidence to demonstrate how low wages were and suggested local statutory wages boards should be used to raise them,

---

25   See Joseph Rowntree Social Service Trust, York, Joseph Rowntree MSS. 1 vi a: B. S. Rowntree to O. F. Rowntree, 26 June 1912 for the breakfast meeting at which Lloyd George set up the Enquiry.

26   These friends included Sir W. Lever, Baron de Forest and Joseph Rowntree. See H. of L. R. O., Lloyd George MSS. C/2/2/5: Heath to Lloyd George, 18 Mar. 1913. Lloyd George MSS. C/2/2/23: Rowntree to Lloyd George, 26 June 1913. Joseph Rowntree Social Service Trust, exec. mins., 22 Dec. 1913.

27   Riddell, Diary, p. 70, entry for 19 June 1912.

28   A. Briggs, Social Thought and Social Action: a Study of the Work of Seebohm Rowntree (1961), pp. 65-7.

29   Lloyd George MSS. C/2/1/9: Heath to Buxton, 17 Aug. 1912.

30   Lloyd George MSS. C/2/1/5: Rowntree to Lloyd George, 10 Aug. 1912.

31   Reprinted in Report of the Land Enquiry, The Land, i. pp. 471-8.

32   The Land, i. p. xvii.

without fixing a national minimum figure.[33]   But the Report also extended this idea by recommending that the wage award should include a sufficient sum to allow the labourers to pay an 'economic' rent on a cottage. This would allow the State to build housing for them without incurring any loss.[34] The only group to lose would be landowners, whose rent would be reduced by rent courts to compensate farmers for higher wages.   The Report also recommended that rent courts should have a general review of farmers' rents and provide security of tenure in normal circumstances, thus producing a comprehensive scheme to attract farmers.[35]

In contrast to the Rural Report, the Urban Report did not appear until 2 April 1914. This was not because it was accorded a lower priority but because its composition presented more difficulties. The Urban Enquiry was initially in the hands of E. R. Cross, Rowntree's friend and Chairman of Directors of the *Nation*.[36] He was far less sure what policies he was supposed to be finding evidence to support as most of the urban programme had not been predetermined by Lloyd George. The issues were vastly complicated and it was difficult to find urban Liberals with sufficient expertise to delineate, for instance, the incidence of rates in their towns or the rate of housebuilding. It proved beyond Cross to deduce a comprehensive urban land policy from the mass of data he eventually received, and the task had to be taken over by Rowntree in the summer of 1913.[37]

When the Urban Report did finally appear, though, it was clear the Enquiry had been successful in producing a series of policies that would ally hostility to landowners with practical benefits to urban voters. The Enquiry chose the promise of more and better housing to appeal to the urban working class. It proposed each local authority should have a duty to ensure there was a decent amount and standard of accommodation for its population. To fulfil this duty, they would be empowered to compulsorily purchase land on their outskirts at its use value and lease it for development. Town planning would ensure the new building was of a high quality, while the cheap price of the land would prevent it being too expensive. For the estimated 5-10% of the urban population who could not afford an economic rent, the Enquiry recommended a minimum wage to bring them up to this standard.[38] These policies again repeated the strategy of 1909-10. Social reform was offered with the landlord identified as the enemy - this time because the high prices he charged for land created housing shortages and increased prices.

The urban middle class were not forgotten, either. If they could not be rallied by the threat to constitutional government, as in 1909-10, they could be offered material benefits. For those who leased their homes from landlords on long leases, or shopkeepers who leased

33   *The Land*, i. p. 47.
34   For Lloyd George's intervention in this matter, see Lloyd George MSS. C/2/2/31: Buxton to Lloyd George, 17 July 1913.
35   *The Land*, i. pp. 323, 382-3.
36   Lloyd George MSS. C/2/1/9: Heath to Lloyd George, 17 Aug. 1912. For Cross, see M. Wilkinson, *E. Richard Cross: a biographical sketch* (1917), pp. 3-12.
37   Lloyd George MSS. C/2/1/7: de Forest to Lloyd George, 15 Aug. 1912. Lloyd George MSS. C/2/2/48: Rowntree to Lloyd George, 25 Aug. 1913.
38   Report of the Land Enquiry, *The Land*, ii. pp. 115-22, 148-61.

their premises for shorter periods, this was relatively easy. They were offered security of tenure and fair rents from rent courts, much like the farmers. But this policy would effect only about 30% of urban England - in the rest of the country freehold tenure predominated.[39] To appeal to the rest of the urban middle class the Report offered State grants to relieve the rates. There would also be a gradual introduction of site value rating to make sure landlords could not benefit from lower rates by raising rents, and to reflect the enthusiasm for this measure in the Liberal Party.[40] In effect, the Report displaced land taxation from the centre of the Liberals' urban strategy in favour of a cohesive package of housing and rating reforms, designed to hold together the radical coalition that had allowed the Liberals to retain power in 1910.

Lloyd George decided in mid-1913 that he would have to launch his Land Campaign that autumn.[41] Time would be required to build up the necessary momentum and counteract the Government's unpopularity. Moreover, the Irish crisis would reach its climax in 1913-14 and might precipitate a General Election at a moment's notice. Lloyd George displayed his usual tactical skills in winning over the Cabinet to the idea of a Land Campaign over July-October 1913 - first making sure that he secured the co-operation of key figures like the Prime Minister, Haldane and Grey, so that the Cabinet was presented with a virtual *fait accompli* when it considered the matter on 14-16 October 1913.[42] Actually, in contrast to 1909, there was little opposition in the Government to Lloyd George's initiative.[43] There were no other effective plans to revive the Liberals' popularity and his colleagues had little option but to trust Lloyd George to repeat his feat of 1909. But the Cabinet's acquiescence was also a tribute to the diligence of the Enquiry's research and the convincing nature of the programme they had produced.

Lloyd George was able to launch his Land Campaign in a blaze of publicity with two great speeches at Bedford on 11 October and Swindon on 22 October. But the programme he outlined was almost entirely rural. Since July 1913, Rowntree had desperately been working to produce at least an outline urban programme for Lloyd George to put to the Cabinet. But when it met to consider the Land Enquiry on 14-16 October, the Chancellor still had only a few fragments of his urban policy to present. The Campaign that the Cabinet approved was, therefore, almost entirely rural in nature.[44] Rowntree was able to produce a sketch of the

39   *The Land*, ii. pp. 349, 398-401.

40   *The Land*, ii. pp. 629-31.

41   Riddell, *Diary*, p. 171, entry for 19 July 1913 for Lloyd George's initial approaches to some of his Cabinet colleagues.

42   *Ibid.*, when Grey and Churchill were generally favourable, while Asquith was as yet undecided. Haldane's idea for a campaign centred on educational reform received little support, Vt. Haldane, *An Autobiography* (1929), pp. 218-19.

43   Accounts of the October Cabinet meeting can be found in Nuffield Coll. Lib., Oxford, Gainford MSS. 39: J. Pease Diary 14 Oct. 1913. *Inside Asquith's Cabinet: From the diaries of Charles Hobhouse*, ed. E. David (1977), pp. 147-8, entry for 17 Oct. 1913. Gainford MSS. 90: Hobhouse to Pease, 22 Oct. 1913. B. L., Add. MSS. 62973 (Riddell MSS.), f. 56: Riddell Diary 17 Oct. 1913 (manuscript containing unpublished parts of the Diary). All agree on the lack of serious dissent in the Cabinet.

44   The Cabinet's decisions were summarised in a memorandum. This is preserved in Bodleian Lib., Oxford, Harcourt MSS. 443, ff. 201-05: Cabinet Note on Ministry of Land, 18 Oct. 1913.

urban programme for two speeches by Lloyd George in November 1913, but it was thin stuff.[45] The urban minimum wage, for instance, was mentioned in one sentence. As they had not been approved by the Cabinet, most of the urban proposals did not appear in the speeches of any of Lloyd George's colleagues. Even the Chancellor had nothing to say on the rating system until 4 February 1914 at Glasgow.

The campaign that the Liberals launched, though almost entirely rural, was impressively organized. It did not just rely on speeches from Ministers. The Chief Whip, Percy Illingworth, set up a Central Land and Housing Council, with regional branches, to conduct a continuous barrage of propaganda.[46] It recruited 150 voluntary and 80 full-time, paid speakers to work under its control. They were launched on the country in January 1914 and the Campaign was stepped up in May-June 1914. There was a truly staggering distribution of literature - 1.5 million leaflets by May 1914.[47] Although a campaign of this nature, which relied on small scale meetings and the local distribution of literature, could not distract national political debate from the Irish crisis while civil war seemed a real possibility, it proved remarkably successful on its own terms.

It united the Liberals at a time when a whole host of issues, from industrial unrest to women's suffrage, divided them. Social reformers, like the 'New Liberal' writers and journalists grouped around the *Nation* weekly paper, could see it as a step towards the 'minimum standard of life' they advocated. L. T. Hobhouse and J. A. Hobson wrote articles of enthusiastic praise for the Chancellor's new initiative.[48] More traditional radicals saw the campaign as yet another assault on the citadel of privilege, much on the lines of 1909-10. Some of the party's wealthiest and most socially conservative figures, like Sir Walter Runciman and Sir Courtenay Warner, agreed to take a prominent part in the Campaign.[49] In the rural areas, the Campaign provided a welcome boost for often moribund Liberal associations, supplying a programme of speakers to cover the whole countryside. Without resident wealthy Liberals many of these associations were at a permanent disadvantage against Unionist opponents. But intervention from above with funds and encouragement could put them on more level terms.

Moreover, it can be argued that the Campaign had the effect of counteracting the disillusion felt with the Liberals in English rural seats - a feeling that largely stemmed from the unpopularity of National Insurance, whose flat rate contributions hit poorly paid workers like agricultural labourers very hard. This was the reason universally attributed by commentators for the loss of the rural Liberal seat of Newmarket on a 6.6% swing in May 1913.[50] In contrast, the only by-election in an English rural seat after the Land Campaign's

---

45   *The Times*, 10 Nov., 1 Dec. 1913.
46   *Liberal Magazine*, xxi (1913), pp. 770-2.
47   Bodleian Lib., Oxford, Asquith MSS. 25, ff. 63-6: Lloyd George to Asquith, 5 Dec. 1913. Lloyd George MSS. C/2/4/20: Carter to Lloyd George, 28 May 1914.
48   *Manchester Guardian*, 2-10 Oct. 1913. B. L. P. E. S., Coll. Misc. 575 (Rainbow Circle MSS.) J. A. Hobson, 'Rural Wages', 12 Nov. 1913.
49   Both were on the executive committee of the Central Land and Housing Council, *Liberal Magazine* xxi (1913), pp. 770-2.
50   See *e.g.* the *Daily Herald, Daily News* and *The Times* for 19 May 1913.

launch was at Wycombe in February 1914. The Liberals faced a multitude of difficulties in this contest - an increase in the, largely Unionist, commuter vote, a strike amongst the chairmakers of High Wycombe, usually the Liberal's strongest supporters, and the general anti-Government swing.[51] But a vigorous Land Campaign in the seat's rural areas produced a swing of 1.2% to the Liberals.[52] This suggests that in a General Election the Liberals could hold the English rural seats they had won in December 1910. A repeat of the 1.2% swing at Wycombe would give them further seats like Mid Norfolk, Stowmarket and Chippenham. In addition, if the election was held after March 1915, the abolition of plural voting would help the Liberals to gain a number of rural seats as long as the Land Campaign could cancel out any pro-Unionist swing.[53] In rural areas, therefore, the Land Campaign offered the Liberals advantages that might be crucial in a closely fought election.

On the other hand, the urban campaign did not so much fail as fail to happen. As most of the urban programme had not been endorsed by the Cabinet, the speakers sent out by the Land and Housing Councils had very little to say on urban issues. Rowntree could not even prepare any propaganda to distribute in the towns.[54] Many urban Liberal associations would have nothing to do with the Land Campaign until its programme for the towns was more definite, and some areas, like Manchester, saw nothing of the Land Campaign until June or July 1914.[55] By then, the Government had approved most of the contents of the Urban Report, in piecemeal fashion, in the time they could spare from the crises surrounding the Cabinet. Asquith only approved the urban minimum wage on 11 June 1914.[56] This was too late to be of any help before war intervened. But it did clear the way for a proper launch of the urban campaign in the autumn of 1914. Then, its combination of social reform and traditional hostility to landlords would have made it a formidable attempt to repeat the success of a similar programme in the towns in 1910, especially if the Irish crisis could have been resolved.

Even if the urban half of the Land Campaign was barely underway before war broke out in August 1914, its rural aspect had been sufficiently alarming to provoke some confusion in the Unionist ranks. Indeed, the Unionists seemed at a loss to produce any convincing response. They initially considered extending and promoting their traditional policy of offering the labourers State loans to purchase smallholdings. But a close examination of this option by several party committees revealed the Unionist leaders had little faith in it. It was too expensive, it might alienate the farmers and there was no guarantee it would be viable or

---

51   *The Times*, 16 Feb. 1914.
52   The best account of the campaign is in *South Bucks Free Press*, 6 Feb. 1914.
53   Scottish Record Office, Steel-Maitland MSS., G. D. 193/202/62: Memorandum by W. Gales, n.d., where
        the Unionists calculated they had won 29 seats in December 1910 because of plural voting. Many of these
        seats had a substantial agricultural population.
54   Lloyd George MSS. C/2/4/6: Reiss to Rowntree 4 Feb. 1914.
55   Manchester Central Ref. Lib., M 283/1/3/3: exec. ctte., Manchester Liberal Federation, 14 May 1914.
56   Lloyd George MSS. C/1/1/18: Montagu to Lloyd George, 12 June 1914.

popular with the labourers.[57] It was persisted with for lack of any alternative and in the hope of marginal benefits. When the Land Campaign was launched in October 1913, the Unionists revealed how little confidence they had in their policy by instructing M.P.s and speakers to ignore the land altogether for Ulster.[58]

In fact the Unionist leaders were faced with an impossible dilemma. They feared to alienate the farmers and the more reactionary element of their landlord following by making concessions in their rural policy towards the labourers. But Central Office was bombarded by reports that the Land Campaign was winning votes among the labourers and that the land issue could not be ignored in rural areas.[59] Meanwhile, the party was openly divided between some of the M.P.s in the Unionist Social Reform Committee who wished to neutralise Lloyd George's appeal by adopting a minimum wage policy, and the party's reactionaries who wished to die in the last ditch.[60] The result was a half-hearted compromise in April 1914. The Unionists agreed to support wages boards which would recommend a minimum wage for labourers in low pay areas. But they insisted these boards should not have any compulsory powers - merely relying on 'public opinion' to enforce their recommendations.[61] This pleased nobody and by mid-1914 the Unionists were at a loss to see how they were going to prevent Liberal gains in rural seats at the next election.[62]

In conclusion, then, it is clear that Lloyd George's concentration on the land issue in Edwardian politics does not need to be explained by reference to his village background in North Wales. Rather, it is an example of his consummate adaption to the demands of *British* politics that he was able to identify this question as a key to success for the Liberals. Lloyd George did not merely express the traditional radical hostility to landlords, he reinvigorated the whole idea by combining it with the politics of social reform, both urban and rural. This allowed the Liberals, a party with both middle and working class elements, to retain their fragile unity and to launch attacks on the Unionists with some success. In 1912-14 with his Land Campaign, Lloyd George was following up his great triumph of 1909-10, extending the Liberal's commitment to radical social reform, while retaining the form of a crusade against landed privilege. Only the intervention of the First World War prevented Lloyd George from bringing his plans to fruition.

---

57   See the reactions to Milner's land reform schemes in, *e.g.* Steel-Maitland MSS., G. D. 193/5/163-94: Ld.
       Lansdowne, 'Observations on Ld. Milner's Memorandum', 8 Apr. 1913. Bodleian Lib., Oxford, Milner
       MSS. 159, ff. 75-82: 'Land Scheme: Mr. Steel-Maitland's criticisms', n. d.
58   Steel-Maitland MSS., G. D. 193/119/99: Ld. Lansdowne to Steel-Maitland, 31 Oct. 1913.
59   *E. g.*, Steel Maitland MSS., G. D. 193/119/5/59: C. H. Simpson to J. Boraston, 21 Jan. 1914.
60   The Unionist Social Reformers published draft Bills advocating wages boards with compulsory powers in
       May 1913 and April 1914. The reactionaries were marshalled by E. G. Pretyman's Land Union, which
       was still strenuously campaigning against the 1909 land taxes.
61   *Hansard*, 5th Series, 1914, xv. 942-55, 976-89.
62   H. of L. R. O., Bonar Law MSS., 39/4/40: Steel-Maitland to Bonar Law, 23 June 1914.

LLOYD GEORGE,
THE BISHOP OF ST. ASAPH
AND THE DISESTABLISHMENT CONTROVERSY

NEIL PURVEY-TYRER

On 15 December 1901 at Chesterfield the Liberal party leader Lord Rosebery appealed for the total revision of his party's policies. Instead of the "fly-blown phylacteries" of the Gladstonian Liberal creed the Party must build a new programme from a "clean slate" and bring to an end the old party antagonisms.[1] The dramatic 1906 Election gave the Liberals an absolute majority in the Commons and an almost free rein to introduce new and radical reform.[2] Old Liberalism, however, died hard. Cobdenite Free Trade, laissez-faire principles and the Nonconformist Conscience, the politics of Victorian radicalism, dominated. Irish Home Rule and Welsh Disestablishment persisted even though theoretically Liberalism was freed from the 'the celtic fringe'. Gladstone's legacy was such that not even the talented forces of a David Lloyd George or a Winston Churchill could steer the Party into new waters of social reform and working class politics.

After the election successes of 1906 pressure for Welsh Church Disestablishment and Disendowment began to be re-applied. This time it came not from Lloyd George as in the 1890s but from his arch-rival D. A. Thomas.[3] For Lloyd George it was a secondary and slightly false, but potentially an explosive, problem for the new Liberal Government already engaged in finding a solution to the continuing education dispute. As he realised there was generally little enthusiasm for a renewed assault on Anglican privileges. Establishment meant very little to the industrial generation. The King's Speech dealt with the issues of unemployment, education and the status of trades unions and failed to make any mention of Welsh Disestablishment. At both ends of the political spectrum disestablishment was a divisive issue in the Twentieth Century and one which according to the Bishop of Bangor the British people "are not troubling their heads about ... and they do not want to hear anything about it".[4] But it had become an inextricable part of the Welsh political scene, a remaining vestige of past endeavours and the symbol of Welsh oppression. It could not so easily be overlooked.[5]

---

1   Chris Cook *A Short History of the Liberal Party 1900-1984* (1976) p34.

2   Election results;

	seats	Total votes	% of total
Unionists	157	2,463,606	43.7
Liberal	375	2,583,132	45.9
Labour	54	528,797	9.4
Nationalist	83	35,109	0.6
Others	-	21,557	0.4

Figures from Cook (1976) p 40. See also Arnold J. James and John E. Thomas *Wales at Westminster. A History of the Parliamentary Representation of Wales 1800-1979* (1981) p82.

3   D. A. Thomas and Lloyd George had become alienated over the financial arrangements of the 1895 Welsh Disestablishment Bill. B. B. Gilbert *David Lloyd George a Political Life. The Architect of Change 1863-1912* (1987) p126-127. N. Tyrer *Church and State Relations in Britain 1868-1920 With Reference to Welsh Disestablishment* (Unpublished M.A. Thesis University of Leeds 1988) p78f.

4   Bishop Watkin Herbert Williams. E. E. Owen *The Later Life of Bishop Owen* (1961) p135.

5   P. M. H. Bell *Disestablishment in Ireland and Wales* (1969) p228-229 & 271ff.

At the start of the new Parliament of 1906 Lloyd George had a meeting with the Bishop of St. Asaph, Alfred George Edwards, the leading Welsh Church defender. He asked whether the Church would accept a compromise solution to the disestablishment issue. Would the Church accept disestablishment if left with all its property except tithe? Disestablishment without the excesses of disendowment? One should not underestimate the horror and amazement that such a meeting would have created at that time if Welsh Liberationists and/or Church Defenders had known the details.[6] Edwards and Lloyd George had recently explored the idea of a concordat over the education crisis created by the Balfour Act of 1902, much to the derision of Bishop Owen of St. David's. The relationship between Edwards and Lloyd George had seemingly transformed from one of hostility during the 1890s into an amiable, if not warm, friendship in the 1900s (in private more than in public).[7] Were moves afoot to settle the long standing Welsh Church issue based on this friendship? It appeared that Lloyd George in 1906 was attempting to renew the Bangor Scheme of 1895.[8]

Lloyd George may well have moved beyond Welsh Party politics, now as President of the Board of Trade in the new Liberal administration, and have hoped to settle the sectarian issue which had aided his political rise. Bishop Edwards' motives for compromise, however, are far from clear. He was certainly not beyond suspicion by Welsh Churchmen. Churchmen who felt that the Bishop had betrayed their confidences over the attempted education concordat. It is interesting that as the relationship between the Bishop and the politician grew that between St. Asaph and the Bishop of St. David's soured. Owen was the leading Welsh bishop in the south and had been a contemporary of Edwards at Jesus College, Oxford, Edwards' successor at Llandovery College, made Dean of St. Asaph in 1889 at Edwards' request and was until 1902 a valued friend. The relationship however was far from harmonious over the education dispute.[9]

---

6   K. O. Morgan *Wales in British Politics 1868-1922* (1980) p233.
7   W. R. P. George *Lloyd George* (1983) p373 letter from Lloyd George 7 February 1903; "Who do you think travelled with me from Chester up to London Wednesday evening? You will never guess - the Bishop of St. Asaph. Most friendly. He says the Voluntary Schools will be things of the past in ten years time. He is most anxious for a settlement and is inclined to accept my manifesto. He is going to consult Morant (Chief of the Education Dept.) about it. The Church laity, he tells me are anxious for settlement on those lines!"
8   A repeat of 1894/95? In January 1895 a disestablishment compromise had been put together by a number of churchmen associated with the Cathedral School at Bangor. It seemed independent of Lloyd George's direction. Revd. R. E. Jones, Warden of Bangor Divinity School, wrote in *The Times* on 30 March 1895; "The main features of the scheme are disestablishment without disendowment, the better and more equitable distribution of our existing endowments; the abolition of the evils which accompany lay patronage; a greater share in church management to the laity; a thorough reform ... of the present antiquated Cathedral system; the constitution of the ancient British church into a separate province under its own Archbishop, and the consequent restoration to our beloved Church of her ancient national character". There is little evidence that the Bangor Scheme was to be the basis of a Lloyd George compromise. But for K. O. Morgan, "There is a suggestion that the ubiquitous hand of Lloyd George was even here, as ready in conciliation as in extremism, in unexpected and temporary collusion with the Bishop of Bangor". *Wales in British Politics 1868-1922* (1980) p148.
9   E. E. Owen *The Later Life of Bishop Owen* (1961) p37 and N. Tyrer (1988) p91.

Bishop Edwards reported the Lloyd George proposals to the Archbishop of Canterbury and in a memorandum of the conversation Randall Davidson wrote:

> Mr Lloyd George has been in private communication with the Bishop (of St. Asaph), and has asked him whether the government were to introduce a very mild and kindly Welsh Disestablishment Bill the Welsh Church would modify its opposition and practically allow the matter to go forward even if outwardly opposing ... the Bishop believes that Lloyd George would rather like to get disestablishment carried with a minimum of friction.[10]

Archbishop Davidson was sceptical of Lloyd George's proposals but not unfriendly. He was perhaps wary of motives of his Bishop of St. Asaph as much as of the Welsh politician. On 22 February Davidson, Lloyd George and Edwards met in the Bishops' Robing Room in the House of Lords and Lloyd George asked what the Archbishop would think of a Royal Commission on the state of religion in Wales.[11] Davidson was cautious and warned Edwards not to be seen to negotiate with Lloyd George; "I warned the Bishop against leaving Lloyd George in a position which could enable him to say that the bishop had been negotiating with him the subject." Certainly in public the Bishop continued to rail against the liberationists and at a meeting at Wrexham he warned that never during the seventeen years he had been bishop had the outlook for the Church been more serious. "As a citizen, patriot and Churchman" he was determined to resist the threat of disestablishment and disendowment of the Church.[12] Edwards, like Lloyd George, was a pragmatist, an opportunist, and worked on various levels.[13]

In May 1906 the royal Commission "To enquire into the nature, origin, amount and application of the temporalities, endowments, and other properties of the church of England in Wales and Monmouthshire; and into the provision made and work done by the churches of all denominations"[14] was announced. It began its work in October. The Commission was to drag on until December 1910 and was characterised by disputes, intrigues and resignations. The nine commissioners initially appointed included four churchmen and four free churchmen, chaired by Rt. Hon. Sir Roland Vaughan Williams, a Lord Justice of the Court of Appeal.

---

10   G. K. A. Bell *Randall Davidson I* (1952) p504f.

11   In March 1906 Sam Evans gave notice of a Welsh Suspensory Bill, although the Liberal whips persuaded him to withdraw the measure. G. I. T. Machin *Politics and the Churches in Great Britain 1869 to 1921* (1987) p299.

12   *The Times* 2 April 1906.

13   A detailed examination of A. G. Edwards is certainly called for. See T. I. Ellis' review of K. O. Morgan 'Freedom or Sacrilege?' in *Journal of the Historical Society of the Church in Wales* XVII (1967) p64; "We still lack a full-length study of A. G. Edwards ... One wonders what has happened to all his papers. We have his *Memories*, and Mr. George Lerry's little book published in 1940: but if we are to see the whole disestablishment controversy in its true light, we must be able to examine in detail the work of the man whom W. J. Gruffyd once described as 'y gwr mwyaf trychinebus a welodd Cymru erioed' ('the most disastrous man that Wales has ever seen'".

14   *The Daily News Year Book* 1910-1913 (1972) Section B.

The Commission was unpopular in Wales. For D. A. Thomas the Commission was to take evidence after the verdict had been given.[15] The Welsh Party was not consulted over its appointment and in April 1907 the Welsh Liberal Press denied that the idea had originated from Lloyd George.[16] In any compromise talks both sides needed to be seen to outwardly oppose if inwardly allowing "the matter to go forward".

The Bishop of St. Asaph welcomed the Commission and it came for him, at least, "as a great deliverance".[17] The case for Welsh Disestablishment he believed was built on "facts and figures" which proved inaccurate; the commission would establish the true state of affairs. Bishop John Owen did not share this enthusiasm and when he first heard of the Commission on 23 March, "it filled him with dismay".[18] The following day he wrote to Davidson, "I am certain the Commission would introduce fresh bitterness over the Disestablishment controversy, into every part of Wales".[19] It would change the social relations of Churchmen and Nonconformists and would play into the hands of those who desired disestablishment for political advantage. The Commission, designed to forestall calls for disestablishment, after only a year did indeed create an increase in tension in the Principality. Owen's fears were partly realised. In April 1907 three Nonconformist Commissioners resigned in protest of the behaviour of the chairman. Bishop Edwards, with the advantage of hindsight, later stated, "It would have been better if the Commission had died in May 1907".

In 1907 with the Commission in near deadlock and Church and Chapel leaders absorbed in presenting evidence to the inquiry, much political unrest became evident in the Principality. On 17 January in the so called 'Guard Room' speech in Caernarvon Lloyd George implied that Welsh Disestablishment would be withheld until something was done with the House of Lords; "The fact was that Wales would not get a dog's chance of fair play from the Lords". "The Welshmen", he claimed, "who worry the Government into attending to anything else until the citadel has been stormed ought to be put in the guard room".[20] In December 1906 the Upper chamber had rejected the Education Bill, the Plural Voting Bill and the Land Bill of the Liberal administration. In many respects the reform of the Lords was an important preliminary for Welsh Disestablishment, but for many Welsh radicals it seemed that the Government was betraying their trust. The Commission had undermined their moves for a Welsh Bill and Lloyd George, himself a rebel twelve years before over the disestablishment issue, found himself having to restrain the Welsh radicals on the same debate.

On the 30 May 1907 a summary of Nonconformist denunciations of the Liberal Government appeared in the *British Weekly*. Although English Free Churches had little sympathy for Welsh Disestablishment they were angered that their own interests in education, temperance and social reform were being blocked by the Lords and treated with indifference by the Government. The *British Weekly* called for a revolt of Nonconformist M.P.s. On

---

15   Morgan (1980) p233.
16   Morgan (1980) p233-234. Machin (1987) p299.
17   A. G. Edwards *Memories* (1927) XI p222.
18   Owen (1961) p82.
19   Ibid.
20   Machin (1987) p299.

4 June the Congregational Association of North Caernarvonshire, in Lloyd George's heartland, demanded that the Welsh members should refuse their support to the Government unless a Welsh Church Bill was introduced in the 1908 session.

On 11 June Campbell Bannerman replied to a question from Ellis Griffith in the House of Commons that he could not "hold out any expectation" of a disestablishment measure in 1908. Six days later he reiterated to a Welsh deputation that as long as the Lords question remained there could be no pledge of Welsh Disestablishment. For Lloyd George the Lords blocked the way and anyway education was the prime Welsh demand not disestablishment. The Welsh Free Churches were stung and local associations carried motions strongly critical of the Governments attitude. Lloyd George was singled out for much abuse,[21] although according to K. O. Morgan, the Welsh press was on the whole favourable to him;

> The picture of nation-wide opposition painted by some of Lloyd George's biographers, while artistically effective, is historically much exaggerated. Perhaps the most perceptive attitude was that adopted by the Caernarvon journal, *Y Genedl*. It showed that, while the position of the establishment was an injustice, it was scarcely the most serious evil from which Wales suffered.[22]

Nevertheless there existed an undercurrent of protest which swelled radical agitation in Wales. And this agitation was symbolised in Disestablishment claims. It reached a climax in the organisation of a Welsh National Convention at Cardiff on 10 October 1907. Arranged by the Calvinistic Methodists it was intended to be a protest against the Governments failure to disestablish the Church and to attack the reluctance of some Welsh M.P.s to promote the Welsh cause. Lloyd George attended the conference and attempted to placate its committee with an implicit reference to the introduction of a Welsh Church Bill in 1909. The delegates were won over by his emotional oratory and vague promises and the convention turned into a personal triumph. According to B. B. Gilbert, "Lloyd George moved to his peroration, perhaps the most famous he ever delivered in Wales". The main interest of Wales, Lloyd George claimed, was the settlement of the position of the Lords and then, once that question was settled he seemed to imply that a Welsh Disestablishment Bill would be introduced and successfully passed; "Am I going to sell the land I love? (A breathless silence, then in Welsh) God knows how dear Wales is to me!"[23] The Welsh free Churches were satisfied, although they had received no specific pledge. On 17 October Lloyd George wrote to Campbell Bannerman that Cardiff "went very well ... You will not be troubled by Welsh Disestablishment any more this session".

Lloyd George does not, however, seem to have given up plans for a compromise solution being reached. Relations between the politician and the Bishop of St. Asaph remained

---

21   It seems that Lloyd George attempted to minimise the damage by courting the friendship of Robertson Nicoll the editor of the *British Weekly*. See Gilbert (1987) p308-310.
22   Morgan (1980) p236-238.
23   Gilbert (1987) p312.

strong and were strengthened by personal tragedy. In the winter of 1907 both men suffered the loss of a daughter; Lloyd George lost his favourite Mair Eluned, and Edwards, Katharine Louisa. On 12 December Edwards wrote to "My Dear George", suggesting that he take his family on holiday; "I wish I could be of any comfort or help personally. I would gladly do so, if I could".[24] Lloyd George replied asking Edwards to accompany him to France, although the bishop could not accept the offer. These letters are the only existing records of this period exchanged between the two men which allude to a warm understanding. The friendship was nevertheless well known by the popular press and it had apparently lost its ability to shock. In 1904 the *Saturday Review* had written, "Public men, of course, rarely carry political feuds into private life"[25] and in the October edition of the *Review of Reviews* Lloyd George, it was claimed, while attending the Eisteddfod at Rhyl, had arrived at St. Asaph Palace where he was staying without golfing costume:

> To golf in a long tail coat is to court destruction. What was Lloyd George
> to do? The difficulty was surmounted by the intervention of the Bishop,
> who lent the redoubtable Dissenter an episcopal suit which was eminently
> suited for the golf links.

It was perhaps while at St. Asaph in 1904 that Lloyd George had accepted communion from Edwards, a daring gesture indeed.[26]

In August 1908 Lloyd George, this time with Winston Churchill, stayed at the Bishop's palace. Lloyd George was attending the National Eisteddfod at Llangollen. The three men were on 12 September to meet once again. This time in London at Churchill's wedding to Clementine Hozier. Bishop Edwards was asked to officiate at the ceremony although according to Gilbert;

> Randolph Churchill in the biography of his father states that he does not
> know why (the Bishop of) St. Asaph was asked to perform the ceremony.[27]

One should not forget that these friends had been arch enemies back in the 1890s and as late as 1898 Lloyd George had claimed Edwards "a third-rate scholar, a no-rate theologian and an

---

24   Lloyd George Papers Series I 1905-1908 .
25   *Saturday Review* 10 September 1904.
26   W. George *My Brother and I* (1958) p169 and Gilbert (1987) p245, footnote 96.
27   Gilbert Ibid p354.

irate priest".[28] They had been furthermore the figureheads of the Welsh Church-Chapel conflict in the Nineteenth Century and had risen as defenders of their respective positions.[29]

Bishop Owen of St. David's remarked, however, that Concordat could not be achieved by friendship alone. For the *Saturday Review* of October 1904;

> It is necessary to remember that there are three Bishops in Wales besides his
> Lordship of St. Asaph, and that these three prelates have in the past shown
> themselves a little shy of the Concordats of these two original thinkers.[30]

Bishop Owen of St. David's remained concerned by the company his fellow prelate in the north was keeping. He was troubled that the Defence Campaign should be so seriously weakened. Owen had not been consulted over the 1906 compromise talks and was anxious to fix Edwards firmly in the Defence Party. For Owen, "If (Lloyd) George had his way, the church will be hampered in her work in every possible respect"[31] and according to Owen's biographer; "It is clear that Bishop Owen whenever he saw a chance, set himself to the task of steadying his friend and getting him to come out openly as the Welsh Church leader in the threatened attack".[32] Publicly the Bishop of St. Asaph had never swerved from church defence. At the Central Church Committee in October 1908 Edwards openly aligned himself with Owen. Any hopes of educational peace in Wales or of Welsh Disestablishment by consent had by this time evaporated anyway.[33] But, as with Lloyd George, for Edwards a behind the scenes agreement to solve a seemingly intractable problem was a normal tactic and was one not so easily given up; "Concordat was a strange but appealing watchword: once invented it was never lost".[34]

In April 1908 Campbell Bannerman resigned the premiership. The new prime minister was H. H. Asquith who had introduced the first Disestablishment Bills in 1894 and 1895. Welsh radical hopes were high and given further encouragement by the inclusion in the Cabinet of Lloyd George and Sam Evans, Chancellor of the Exchequer and Solicitor General respectively. On 21 April 1909 Asquith moved the second Welsh Church Bill. The Lords

---

28   *North Wales Observer* 25 November 1898.

29   See John Grigg *Lloyd George; From Peace to War 1912-1916* (1985) Grigg wrongly assumes that "These two men (Lloyd George and Edwards) might have settled the Welsh Church question between them as far back as 1895, and again in 1903, if left to their own devices". See Gilbert (1987) p127. Although Grigg may have been nearer the truth, if a shade melodramatic, when he continues, "Eventually, after much further controversy - and after a World war - they did settle it between them. Meanwhile the tedious ritual of another Disestablishment Bill had to be gone through in successive sessions, and Lloyd George had to try and think of new ways to make an old act entertaining". p27.

30   *Saturday Review* 10 September 1904.

31   Owen (1961) p89. Owen had been furious with Edwards over the 1902 Education dispute for attempting a compromise and particularly for Edwards conversations with Lloyd George of whom he wrote, "My temptation is unalterable disdain of George and all his words and deeds. He is a very little man, in my opinion, with all his cleverness and audacity, very little in the heart and soul of him ..." p68.

32   Ibid p135.

33   *The Times* 1 February 1907, 6 November 1907.

34   Edwards *Memories* (1927) p192.

were in full possession of their powers and were unlikely to pass such a Bill. It was almost inevitable that such a measure would fail. Even Welsh Nonconformists were sceptical. The Bill was seen for what it was, a piece to pacify the Welsh radicals, although, unlike in 1894, they no longer held the balance of power in Parliament. The measure was merely "a parade ... to satisfy the inconvenient protests of a section of the Government supporters".[35] It was furthermore an ironic commentary on the Royal Commission that the Government should introduce a Welsh Disestablishment Bill before its report had been issued.

The first reading debate was brief and uneventful. The proposals resembled those of 1895. The four dioceses of Bangor, St. Asaph, Llandaff and St. David's would be disestablished on 1 January 1911 and ecclesiastical corporations would be dissolved. The disendowment provisions were more moderate than the earlier bills'; a Church Representative Body would receive the four cathedrals, Church buildings and residences, closed burial grounds and benefactions obtained since 1662; the Ecclesiastical Commissioners would be only temporary, the secularised endowments being given to the county councils for social purposes, health and education. Asquith justified his bill on the grounds of Free church predominance in Wales and that it was the expressed opinion of the Welsh people as shown repeatedly in elections since 1880. These were well worn arguments and ones which Bishop Edwards had combatted in 1892 and in a letter to *The Times* on the 6 May he was to belabour again.[36] Certainly for Edwards the Prime Minister's arguments did not stand. The alien character of the Church he claimed was little more than a myth; Nonconformity was not the 'true national body' because it was not united in itself; Edwards ridiculed the idea that disestablishment and disendowment would benefit the Church and make cooperation possible among the sects and he dispelled the parallel with Ireland.

There was little excitement in the country over the Welsh Church Bill. There was an air of unreality about the whole proceeding. The arguments on both sides had already been heard and in an age of industrial unrest, unions and labour movements, few were interested in the disestablishment and disendowment of four ancient dioceses of the Province of Canterbury. Lloyd George recognised that "fifteen years have now gone by and a new nation and new questions have come to the surface. The nation does not look at disestablishment now as it did then. All is now social questions".[37] At least for the 'Welsh Wizard' all was now social questions for this was politically expedient. A few days later Lloyd George introduced his "People's Budget" and Welsh Disestablishment was once again pushed into the background. Those who had seen the 1909 Church Bill a sop to the Welsh M.P.s were manifestly correct.

For Welsh Church Defenders in 1909 there was the danger of complacency. They were caught on the horns of a dilemma; if too strenuous in defence of the Church Establishment they would stir up opposition but if they refused to say anything the danger of disestablishment would increase. Compromise Edwards believed was better than confrontation

---

35   Machin (1987) p302 quote, Lord Robert Cecil.
36   Edwards at the St. Asaph Diocesan Conference September 1909 and at Liverpool, November and
      December, and Wrexham, January 1910. Reports in *The Times*.
37   Gilbert (1987) p313.

but the 1909 Church Bill was not the settlement Lloyd George had promised in 1906. For Bishop Edwards while he privately believed in the need to seek a settlement he realised there was little to be gained in offering the Establishment to the Liberationists. Disestablishment was unlikely to become a reality with the Lords in full possession of their powers and compromise for a solution beneficial, or at the very least less injurious, to the Church but which would satisfy the Free Church radicals was, for the moment, unrealistic. Was Edwards waiting for an opportunity to bargain the Establishment away? He was certainly looking for the "mild and kindly" Bill promised by Lloyd George in 1906. The 1909 Welsh Church Bill however proposed to destroy the Church and it was therefore to be opposed;

> If the proposals of the Government become law the church would be stripped bare. All the Church property despoiled was to be transferred to five Welsh commissioners ... They were then to be succeeded by a central authority called the Council of Wales ... a new idea, and naturally a step to a Parliament for Wales. Disendowment took funds which were now used, and nobly used, for work which was purely religious, and applied them to objects which were purely secular. The proposals were unjust. (We) must make their passage into law impossible, and it (is our) duty, not only as churchmen, but as citizens, to make the justice of (our) cause known.[38]

On 30 November 1909 the House of Lords rejected the Liberal Budget by 350 to seventy-five votes, a move unprecedented in that chambers history. They had thwarted Gladstone's second Irish Home Rule Bill in 1893 and rejected many of the Liberal Administrations reforms from 1906. The Government now seemed determined to curtail their lordships powers. Lloyd George wrote, "Well the Lords have made up their minds. The Lord hath delivered them unto our hands".[39] It is unlikely that the Lloyd George Budget was designed to ensnare the Lords in a constitutional crisis, although senior Liberal M.P.s were tired of such obstruction. It was perhaps rather a piece of Lloyd George opportunism, a crisis cultivated rather than calculated. With the subsequent passage of the Parliament Act of 1911 such measures as Irish Home Rule and Welsh Disestablishment, the issues of the 'celtic fringe', were made for the first time politically possible. Those Welsh radicals locked in Lloyd George's "guard room" in 1907 now waited impatiently for their release. For Edwards "the day for Royal Commissions and Parliamentary Inquiries" was now over. The first duty of Churchmen is to take up arms against Welsh Liberationist misrepresentation.[40]

38   *The Times* 4 January 1910.
39   Letter 16 November 1909 K. O. Morgan *Lloyd George. Family Letters 1885-1936* (1973) p151.
40   Edwards (1927) p237.

History
miller f